Managing the Infosphere

Managing the Infosphere

*Governance, Technology, and
Cultural Practice in Motion*

Stephen D. McDowell
Philip E. Steinberg
Tami K. Tomasello

TEMPLE UNIVERSITY PRESS
Philadelphia

Stephen D. McDowell is John H. Phipps Professor of Communication and Chair of the Department of Communication at Florida State University. He is author of *Globalization, Liberalization, and Policy Change: A Political Economy of India's Communications Sector.*

Philip E. Steinberg is an Associate Professor of Geography at Florida State University. He is author of *The Social Construction of the Ocean* and co-editor (with Rob Shields) of *What Is a City? Rethinking the Urban after Hurricane Katrina.*

Tami K. Tomasello is an Assistant Professor in the School of Communication at East Carolina University.

TEMPLE UNIVERSITY PRESS
1601 North Broad Street
Philadelphia PA 19122
www.temple.edu/tempress

⊗ The paper used in this publication meets the requirements of the American National Standard for Information Sciences—Permanence of Paper for Printed Library Materials, ANSI Z39.48-1992

Library of Congress Cataloging-in-Publication Data

McDowell, Stephen D., 1958–
   Managing the infosphere : governance, technology, and cultural
practice in motion / Stephen D. McDowell, Philip E. Steinberg, Tami K.
Tomasello.
      p. cm.
   Includes bibliographical references and index.
   ISBN 13: 978-1-59213-279-9   ISBN 10: 1-59213-279-0 (cloth : alk. paper)
   ISBN 13: 978-1-59213-280-5   ISBN 10: 1-59213-280-4 (pbk. : alk. paper)
   1. Telecommunication policy.   2. Internet–Management.   3. Information
technology–Social aspects.   I. Steinberg, Philip E.   II. Tomasello, Tami K.
III. Title.
   HE7645.M393 2008
   303.48′33–dc22

                                                          2007021525

2 4 6 8 9 7 5 3 1

Contents

 Acknowledgments

T his is a collective work whose production has crossed disciplines, writing and work styles, and, at times, continents. Steve McDowell is trained as a political scientist with expertise in telecommunication policy. He has undertaken research on communications policies in India, Canada, the United States, and international organizations as well as research on the governance and uses of new communication technologies. Phil Steinberg is a geographer with a broad interest in sociospatial theory, particularly as it applies to problems of governance in spaces of mobility that exist beyond the control of territorial states. Although he has published previously with McDowell on issues of Internet governance, most of his work to date has been on historic and contemporary uses, regulations, and representations of the world-ocean. Tami Tomasello is a communication scholar whose research and publications focus on the historical and social implications of new communication technologies, particularly as these relate to the ideal of free access to networked communication and information resources.

Although we each took primary responsibility for specific chapters, the end result in each chapter, as in the book as a whole, is a collaboration. Specifically, the collaboration behind this book applies Steinberg's insights on governing mobility, gathered primarily from his ocean research, to telecommunication policy, the area of McDowell's expertise, and to Tomasello's understanding of new communication technology access issues. The result, if we have achieved our goal, blends theoretical depth with empirical detail, drawing in near-equal parts on literature emanating from geography, political science, international relations, and communication studies.

Portions of this book are derived from articles and presentations, written individually and together, some of which have appeared in a number of journals and books. We are grateful to each of the original publishing venues for allowing revised versions of these articles and chapters to appear in this book. In particular, we would like to note the origins of the following chapters:

> Parts of chapter 1 are derived from "Global Communications and the Post-Statism of Cyberspace: A Spatial Constructivist View" (by Steinberg and McDowell), which appeared in Volume 10 of *Review of International Political Economy* (2003).
>
> Chapter 3 is derived from "Globalization, Local Governance, and the United States Telecommunications Act of 1996" (by McDowell), which appeared in *Cities in the Telecommunications Age: The Fracturing of Geographies*, edited by J. Wheeler, B. Warf, and Y. Aoyama (Routledge, 2000).
>
> Chapter 5 is derived from "Mutiny on the Bandwidth: The Semiotics of Statehood in the Internet Domain Name Registries of Pitcairn Island and Niue" (by Steinberg and McDowell), which appeared in Volume 5 of *New Media & Society* (2003).
>
> Chapter 6 is derived from "Non-State Governance and the Internet: Civil Society and the ICANN" (by McDowell and Steinberg), which appeared in Volume 3 of *Info: The Journal of Policy, Regulation and Strategy for Telecommunications Information and Media* (2001).

The comments and contributions of editors and peer reviewers for each of these articles and chapters have been so thoroughly assimilated into these chapters that we would be hard pressed to identify them. Nonetheless, we know that this book reflects the collective wisdom of these (in most cases unknown) individuals, and we are grateful for their input. We also are grateful to our editors at Temple University Press for encouraging us to write this book and for leading us through the production process.

On a more personal note, **Stephen McDowell** would like to thank Phil Steinberg and Tami Tomasello for their insights, good humor, and energy in collaborating on this project. Our discussions and work together have been stimulating, and I have appreciated greatly the commitment that each brings to our work. Reviewers of conference papers and articles upon which some of these chapters are based provided valuable comments and suggestions.

I also benefited from the conversations and work with doctoral students in the Department of Communication at Florida State University on new technology issues, especially Jenghoon Lee, Hua-lin Sun, and Chuan-yang Hsu. I am especially grateful for the collegial support of John Mayo, Gary Heald, Donna Nudd, Art Raney, and Andy Opel, and that of friends Dennis Hardin, Norma Ressor, Peter Smith, and Jeannie Green. Conversations and work with others, including Michele Jackson, Sharon Strover, Mark Neufeld, and Harmeet Sawhney, on new technology research has helped in developing these ideas.

Phil Steinberg owes a debt of gratitude to those who encouraged him to extend his interest in ocean governance to the infosphere. In that spirit, his first acknowledgment must go to his Ph.D. dissertation committee which, during his defense in 1996, asked him to what other spaces this analytical framework that he was using to analyze the ocean might be applied, leading him to blurt out (since he had to say *something*), "Cyberspace!" A second debt goes to Barney Warf, who has provided encouragement and inspiration throughout, not only as a friend, colleague, and boss, but also as one of the few other geographers who has moved from maritime issues (port modeling, in his case) to communication studies. Third and fourth debts go to Steve McDowell and Tami Tomasello, who welcomed him as a collaborator despite his ignorance of the field's technicalities.

He also thanks Donna Jo Hall, for sequestering him in the cellphone-free "dead zone" of East Tennessee during the summer of 2003 so that he could draft portions of this book. Thanks also go to his brother, Jeff Steinberg, Deputy Chief of the Federal Communications Commission's Wireless Bureau's Spectrum and Competition Policy Division, for permitting a second family member to enter the communication field while steering clear of sibling rivalry (and also for providing some excellent comments on a draft of Chapter 3), and to the community of communications specialists encountered at meetings of the National Communication Association and the International Studies Association who welcomed him into this world where words like "surf" and "waves" have rather different meanings than those to which he was accustomed. Finally, he thanks his colleagues and students in Florida State University's Department of Geography and in the community of ocean scholars who haven't quite figured out how he got from the ocean to the Internet but who have wished him well nonetheless, and various members of the extended McDowell clan who made their cabins in the woods of Ontario available to the authors for an intense writing retreat in July 2006.

Additionally, he acknowledges that portions of this book were conceived and written while he was being supported by a number of institutions, including the American Geographical Society Collection at the University of Wisconsin-Milwaukee, the Newberry Library in Chicago, the Dorothy and Lewis B. Cullman Center for Scholars and Writers at the New York Public Library, the History of Cartography Project at the University of Wisconsin-Madison, and the Rockefeller Foundation-funded "Other Globalizations" program at the University of California, Santa Cruz, Center for Cultural Studies. Although none of these fellowships was directly connected with his work on this book, they focused his interest on constructions of mobility, and these thoughts, in turn, influenced many of the thoughts on spaces of movement that are applied herein.

Tami Tomasello wishes to acknowledge the unwavering support of her immediate family, which includes her parents, Tom Tomasello and Jan Ferguson; her two younger sisters, Jessica and Summer; and her stepfather, Doug Ferguson. Although cyberspace is a place they are comfortable visiting but, unlike her, do not wish to investigate closely, they have always proudly encouraged her academic endeavors. The list would not be complete without also recognizing the genuine support offered by close friends Bill Dulaney, Missy James, and Helena Angel. Bill, in particular, witnessed firsthand the challenges and triumphs involved in the publication process and always knew when to head out on his Harley to give her the space and quiet that this project sometimes required. Missy, having co-authored texts herself, offered that unspoken understanding that goes with the territory of writing, and Helena is one of those rare and special friends who cheers loud and long at each accomplishment.

She also wishes to acknowledge the institutional support of the Department of Communication at Florida State University and the School of Communication at East Carolina University, where work on this book took place. Finally, Tami thanks Steve McDowell and Phil Steinberg for offering her the invaluable opportunity to collaborate on this text; it has been a wonderful learning experience.

 Managing the Infosphere

Where and What Is the Infosphere?

Locating the Infosphere: The View
from Appalachia

Managing the Infosphere was conceived in the summer of 2003, when
one of us (Steinberg) was located in Mountain City, Tennessee, a town
of 2,443 residents nestled in a valley in the Appalachian Mountains,
about 12 miles from the borders of both Virginia and North Carolina.
By any measure, Mountain City is one of the more isolated points in
the eastern United States. It is the only incorporated town in Johnson
County (pop. 17,499), and much of the 298-square-mile county consists of uninhabited National Forest land. Fewer than 60 percent of
adults in the county have a high school degree, and fewer than 7 percent are college graduates (figures for the United States as a whole, by
comparison, are 80 percent with a high school degree and 25 percent
with a college degree). The nearest access to the Interstate highway
system is in Abingdon, Virginia, a 40-minute drive away, across wind-
ing mountain roads that become treacherous in winter, and, as the
ultimate indicator of isolation in rural, twenty-first-century America,
Mountain City is probably one of the very few points in the eastern

United States where one must drive more than 30 minutes to get to a Wal-Mart.

Technological innovations do get implemented in Mountain City (albeit, a bit later than in the rest of the country), but adoption is selective and uneven. To some extent, selective adoption of new technologies is likely the result of corporate calculations regarding the small market in this sparsely populated, low-income county. However, selective technology adoption also appears to reflect residents' desires to maintain small-town social norms. For instance, although one of the three banks on Main Street has an Automated Teller Machine (ATM), as late as 2003 most residents used it only when the bank was closed. When the bank was open, the ATM sat unused while customers idled in their trucks as they waited their turn in the drive-through lane, where they could communicate with a teller via intercom and pneumatic tube. It is difficult to know exactly why local residents avoided the ATM. Perhaps the explanation lies in the rural population's conservative resistance to change. Perhaps local residents were semiconsciously affirming their small-town lifestyle, as speed and efficiency were sacrificed for the familiar and the personal. Residents' reluctance to use the ATM during banking hours may even have been an indirect but purposeful act of resistance against outside forces, as local farmers and factory workers recognized that the job of their former high school classmate working at the bank depended on their willingness to wait in line for fifteen minutes to withdraw money.[1]

Even if local residents' refusal to use the ATM was primarily rooted in small-town conservatism and resistance to change, one should not use the ATM example to reach the conclusion that Mountain City folkways lead to a blanket rejection of technological innovations. Mountain City residents have had few qualms about adopting technologies that are seen as compatible with and supportive of local social institutions and cultural norms. For instance, the reluctance of Mountain City residents to use their local ATM can be contrasted with the enthusiasm with which they have taken to installing caller-identification options on their landline telephones. Presumably, residents have chosen Caller ID as a convenient tool for managing communications (and maintaining the sanctity of the home) in a community where everybody knows everybody and where telephone calls from unidentifiable parties are assumed to be from unknown (and hence unwelcome) outsiders.

Although Mountain City certainly is far from the cutting edge of emerging communication technologies, it is clearly "on the grid." During my stay in Mountain City, my Sprint PCS phone had clearer, more consistent reception than it did in the other places where I had lived over the previous year (in New York City and Tallahassee, Florida's state capital). At least three Internet service providers competed for the opportunity to connect Mountain City residents with high-speed DSL access. The town's public library boasted four public-access Internet terminals, and two even smaller communities just outside the county (Hampton, Tennessee and Damascus, Virginia) had tiny, privately operated "cyber-cafés."

These connections notwithstanding, the expansion of electronic communication systems to rural areas like Mountain City was complex and uneven. Despite the town's surprisingly well-developed communication infrastructure, in the end, Mountain City's physical isolation trumped its electronic connectivity. As soon as I would venture a mile or two outside the town center, the display on my PCS phone would change to "Service Not Available." Mountain City's electronic connectivity thus was recast as electronic insularity.

The electronic insularity of communities in the region was further elucidated on frequent trips to Boone, a much larger town with a population of 13,472 including several thousand university students, just across the state border in North Carolina. As one might expect, wireless telephone service resumed as one entered Boone. However, in Boone, electronic connectivity was trumped by a bureaucratic–administrative divide. Historically, rural areas of northeast Tennessee were served by United Telephone, which merged to form Sprint. Thus the wireless telephone standard in Johnson County was Sprint's PCS protocol. In adjacent North Carolina, however, AT&T historically was the dominant telephony provider, with very small independent cooperatives servicing rural areas. Wireless service in the region thus was dominated by AT&T's "Baby-Bell" offspring, Verizon and Cingular. My Sprint PCS phone functioned in Boone, but because the town was not large enough to support a Sprint outpost, I was forced to cope with poor analog sound quality and large roaming charges as my conversations were channeled via the Verizon network.

This complex texture of connectivity (and disconnectivity) received a further twist when I visited my in-laws' farm in a slightly less remote area of Tennessee, six miles from a small village (Fall Branch, pop. 1,313) and four miles from the nearest Interstate exit. The farm was beyond the range of any mobile phone tower, so to check voice-mail messages when there, I drove to the Interstate highway. The "mobile" in "mobile phone," I discovered, referred not simply to the phone being physically mobile but to the fact that it was designed to function in spaces of mobility. The farm, just off a sparsely trafficked state highway, was located between the threads that connect both moving vehicles and moving bits of information. The Interstate highway, by contrast, was a space of mobility *par excellence*. When on the Interstate, I was in a continuously connected swath of electronic (and asphalt) space that stretched, linearly, for thousands of miles. In effect, I was forced to go from a very real place with distinct social relations (the farm) to the ultimate isolated "nowhere" (the hermetically sealed world of my car) to be connected to "everywhere." Thus I transformed the road, formerly an "in-between" space that was to serve as an ideally friction-free (or "empty") surface as one traversed its length to get from point A to point B, into a destination in its own right. The road, formerly a vector of direction, was now an arena of connection.

Of course, all of the aforementioned technologies are dynamic. Indeed, in the years since 2003 mobile phone access has improved considerably in Fall Branch and Boone (although not in the area around Mountain City). The point of this story is not to document the degree to which the technologies of the infosphere have penetrated an area in rural America. Nor is our aim to document elements of the "digital divide," which remains significant in parts of the world that are not served (or are underserved) by electronic communication networks. Rather, this story illustrates how, when viewed from Appalachia, the infosphere appears as a space of distinct places, where external institutions selectively introduce technologies and where individuals located within these places selectively adopt and adapt these technologies if they have the resources to do so. The Federal regulators who provide funding for the Interstate system while allowing farms within earshot of truckers' horns to fall out of the network, the corporations that develop incompatible communication protocols in Tennessee and North Carolina, the Mountain City residents who eschew ATMs while embracing Caller ID, and the itinerant academic who copes with the problems of uneven telephone coverage by transforming the highway from an empty route that one travels *through* to an arena of communication that one travels *to* are all managing the lived-in and lived-through places of the infosphere.

Locating the Infosphere: The View from Hong Kong

While Steinberg was living in Mountain City, another one of this book's authors (McDowell) was engaged in a series of projects in Asia that involved trips to and through Hong Kong. Like the view from Appalachia, the view from Hong Kong provides a perspective for understanding and identifying the "location" of the infosphere.

Hong Kong was already an entry point to China prior to its seizure by the British in 1841. This function, however, intensified during the British era and has continued since 1997, when it was reincorporated into China as a special administrative region. As a commercial city, Hong Kong is a financial, travel, communication, and production center. Along with providing entry into China, it serves as a focal point for movement within the surrounding region and for connections to other parts of the world. Although assembly and production of goods takes place there, the main economic value added by the city is in commercial and service activities. Facilitating exchange quickly and at low costs, or reducing transaction costs, is the comparative advantage over other locations offered by Hong Kong businesses and governing institutions. Thus, the government of Hong Kong, like local governments throughout the world, devotes resources to developing the infosphere, both to facilitate mobility and to encourage production and consumption in place, a dual mission that we elaborate on further in Chapter 3.

Although unique both in its history and geographic position, the city's role and function today is also explained by the choices of civic and business leaders made in the last decades. Fixed investments in airports, shipping ports, roads, railways, and communication promote connectivity, mobility, and throughput and serve to enhance the city's locational attributes in regional and global political economies. Hong Kong's Internet backbone bandwidth, for instance, is second only to Tokyo's in Asia, with direct connections to San Francisco and Los Angeles, as well as regional links to Singapore, Taipei, Seoul, and Tokyo. Hong Kong's status as a site of global interchange, constructed out of a series of mountainous islands, is evidence of the importance of human action and choice in dealing with the limitations of geographic conditions.

In the area of sovereignty and territorial control, the tensions of Hong Kong's role become apparent. The British were able to treat it as an outpost of capitalism unfettered by democratic accountability. It was both remote from Great Britain and located for almost fifty years next to the largest population and the largest communist country in the world.

Since 1997, China has addressed the challenges faced by the control of this territory in a unique way. For a period of time the Hong Kong Special Administrative Region will be exempted from the laws and policies that govern the rest of Chinese territory. This suspension of full Chinese sovereignty and the lack of extension of full territorial control into Hong Kong arise from a political accommodation. Hong Kong's semi-extraterritorial status also serves to prevent its economy from losing its distinct set of economic advantages in trade in goods and services, and in the mobility of people, that contribute to its unique role in the region. Asserting direct political authority has not been the only goal of China in this ambiguous and contested situation—even for the centralized political leadership and institutions that characterize this state. The identity of Hong Kong citizens remains somewhat blurred as well. They share identity with people of Chinese ethnicity on the mainland, in Taiwan, and in other countries of the region such as Singapore and Malaysia. At the same time, the dominance of mainland China poses the possibility of state power being exercised in more coercive forms if certain boundaries in political behavior are crossed.

Hong Kong thus provides an example, or a complex metaphor of sorts, to assist in thinking about governance, technology, and culture in the infosphere. Rather than juxtaposing state control against noncontrol or statelessness, the Hong Kong model of a special administrative region provides an image with which one can explore these relations in more productive ways, much as Palan (2003) has used Hong Kong's status to investigate the liminal position of the world's offshore financial centers. The lack of formal sovereignty combined with the ever-present exercise of China's power, the contested identity and rights of Hong Kong citizens, the fixed infrastructure and institutions providing for maximum mobility of capital, goods, services, and people, and the importance of specific historical and cultural dimensions provide a basis for the analogy of the infosphere, like Hong Kong, being a special administrative region.

When viewed from the perspective of Hong Kong, the infosphere emerges as a kind of heterotopia, a space of alternate ordering.[2] On the one hand, the infosphere—like Hong Kong—is clearly a creation of the global political–economic system; it would be absurd to label either space as lying fundamentally outside capitalism. On the other hand, because both spaces are organized in ways that push the limits of the standard ways of organizing space and society, each serves as a potential model and resource for systemic change. From the perspective of Hong Kong, the infosphere is a dynamic space of partial incorporation, a continually contested space that is clearly within the system and functional to the system but that lies partly outside its constitutive spatial configurations.

Locating the Infosphere: The View from the Ocean

Although our (temporary) locations in Mountain City and Hong Kong have informed the perspective from which we view the infosphere, our perspective is also informed by the attention that we elsewhere have directed to a much older special administrative region, the ocean.[3] Just as the intersection between the infosphere and Appalachia suggests the construction of the infosphere as a space consisting of places wherein individuals and institutions (from within and outside the region) selectively imbed and adopt technologies, and just as the example of Hong Kong suggests the construction of the infosphere as a space that is within the general workings of society and state power but outside its paradigmatic spatial construction (the sovereign, territorial state), when we view the infosphere from the perspective of the ocean our attention is drawn to the problems and complexities involved in constructing the infosphere as a space of movement.

The historic significance of the world-ocean as a space of movement is well known, from its key role in the early mercantilist empires of Spain, Portugal, and the United Provinces (the Netherlands), to its later role in the British Empire, to its continuing significance today as the space through which, by some counts, 95 percent of goods traded internationally are transported. To facilitate the construction of the ocean as a space of movement, its regulation has centered on limiting formal state involvement to the minimum required to ensure navigational freedoms. States have been empowered only to remove any obstacles that might interfere with the construction of the ocean as an ideally friction-free transportation surface.[4] Additional regulatory measures that might further empower states or imply state territorial rights generally have been eschewed for fear that these would have the undesirable effect of "politicizing" the sea and erecting barriers to free movement across its waters.

Prescribed governance of the sea by modern European states is often dated to the Papal Bulls of 1493. In these documents, which were formalized and amended by the Treaty of Tordesillas (1494), Pope Alexander VI attempted to facilitate missionary and commercial activities by Spain and Portugal in overseas lands. In issuing the Bulls, the Pope was responding to a difficult challenge. On the one hand, he sought to establish a system wherein the two empires could establish the security of title necessary for them to make the spatially fixed investments required for missionary and commercial activities. On the other hand, by establishing a territorial regime for overseas lands, he ran the risk of implying that the sea that provided connection to these lands was similarly claimable territory, a construction that could interfere with its crucial function as a "free" space for the flows that enabled these activities. The Pope made a judicious compromise by allocating the *lands* beyond European waters to the respective European powers so that they could carry out missionary and commercial activities; however, the *seas* in their respective regions were placed in a trust that fell short of territorial control. Spain and Portugal were granted exclusive policing authority in their respective ocean-domains, but this authority fell short of territorial sovereignty; indeed, specific provisions in the documents limited the conditions under which the two states could exclude others from the seas over which they had authority. Already at this early date in the history of the modern world-system, the ocean was being constructed as a unique and dedicated space of flows. Care was taken to establish a governance system that would not impede its mobility functions, even as similar steps were being taken to establish overseas land-space as a series of bounded territories that were suitable for fixed investments. These limitations on the exercise of sovereign rights, designed to preserve the ocean's construction as a dedicated space of movement, foreshadowed a similar set of limitations on sovereignty that were to be applied in a later era to the infosphere.

In the centuries that followed the Treaty of Tordesillas, the international community repeated this pattern of designating the ocean as a special space of movement, in which state intervention was acceptable for the purpose of ensuring its continued construction as a surface for friction-free movement but not to the point at which state activity might generate obstacles to movement. This need for balance became especially evident in the late nineteenth century, when maritime trade (and the use of the ocean as an arena of international competition) intensified and mercantile interests perceived that some form of cooperation and regulation was necessary to ensure preservation of the ocean's friction-free character. In response, nineteenth-century maritime interests, like their fifteenth-century predecessors, developed a set of institutions that met their needs while steering clear of state territoriality. Thus, shippers and insurers, with the blessing of state powers, established the Comité Maritime International (CMI), an association of national maritime law associations that was formed in 1897 and that remains one of the premier bodies responsible for creating international maritime standards. Like the Internet Corporation for Assigned Names and Numbers (ICANN) that governs the Internet (see Chapter 6), the CMI is privately organized but state sanctioned, thus bringing the legitimacy of the state to ocean governance without the "baggage" of state territoriality.

In some instances, CMI standards have required changes in state law, but the CMI has developed an ingenious method of impacting state law while, at the same time, keeping states (and state intervention in the ocean) at a distance. Until 1972, whenever CMI standards required national legislation, the CMI drafted regulations in the form of a treaty that was then proposed by the Belgian government. The Belgian government convened an international intergovernmental conference at which the treaty was adopted, then brought back to the participating states' capitals for ratification. Essentially, participant governments were reduced to bodies that approved or rejected international standards designed and, in large part, implemented by the international shipping community. Since 1972, the Belgian government's function has been replaced by the United Nations, but formal state involvement in global maritime regulation is still kept to a minimum as leading maritime states continue to implement hegemony at sea in a manner that steers clear of direct expressions of territorial power.

The parallels between the ocean and the infosphere are further elucidated when one recalls that capitalism does not survive simply by moving capital about; it also must continually find (or invent) locations for placing fixed investments. Even as the twentieth century saw a dramatic increase in maritime mobility, it also saw the rise of the ocean as a potential venue for placing fixed investments, which has led to a greater demand for state protection. In the infosphere as well, the desire to construct a friction-free space of movement beyond state power (e.g., a space for seamless electronic commerce) has been complemented by the desire to construct the infosphere as an arena of locations wherein one can make fixed investments and wherein the power of state law can guarantee profit recovery (e.g., through intellectual property accords). When viewed from the perspective of the ocean, the infosphere emerges as a space of movement requiring social, but nonterritorial, regulation.

Defining the Infosphere

As the above discussion illustrates, the infosphere is a difficult space to locate. It is also a difficult space to describe or define within circumscribed limits. Although popular discussions (and, indeed, most of this book) focus on applications and uses of web-based technologies, we define the infosphere as encompassing the overall universe of electronic communication and networking. Our definition of the infosphere expands further when we consider that it includes not only the actual connections that join diverse electronic media, but also the idea of a space "out there" that one can enter: a network connected to, but removed from the "real" spaces that one inhabits in everyday life. In offering this broad definition of the infosphere, we envision a field of interaction similar to Shields' (2000) cyberspace, which he defines as "a metaphor that conjures up an image or an idea of the potential of information and telecommunication networks which are formed by computers linked by telecommunications (such as telephone exchanges, fiber-optic cables, or wireless signals)" (p. 66).

In other words, while the infosphere is rooted in an ever-expandable set of electronic connectivity technologies, it also refers to something much larger, a "metaphor [of] an image," an ever-shifting space, constructed and continually reconstructed for and by the movement of information. It is, as the subtitle of this book proclaims, a space of "governance, technology, and cultural practice in *motion*," with the word "motion" referring both to the dynamism of the very concept and to the specific role of the infosphere as a space of movement.

Our discussion of the infosphere thus joins a concern with the rise of material practices of mobility and connection that increasingly characterize the (post-)modern world (e.g., Castells, 1996, 1997, 1998) with the rise of cultural formations that revolve around conditions of betweenness and mobility (e.g., Appadurai, 1996; Bhabha, 1994; Clifford, 1997). All the while, however, our focus remains centered on issues of technology, as individuals and institutions find ways to develop, standardize, regulate, promote, and adopt electronic technologies of connection.

Problems in Conceptualizing Spaces of Movement

The Liberal Perspective on Space

As we attempt to construct a perspective on the infosphere that accounts for the views from Appalachia, Hong Kong, and the ocean, we are confronted with a series of problems in conceptualizing spaces of movement. Classical theories of society (which continue to inform many analyses of political economy and technology) implicitly adopt what Soja (1980) calls a "liberal perspective on space," wherein each place is perceived of as a distinct point on a global grid, with unique natural attributes. Key social activities (production, consumption, social reproduction, etc.) are seen as occurring at these points, which are bounded into stable territories—the state-territories that constitute the fundamental spatial units of society. Over time, increasing investments are located at these points in space, leading to the consequent transformation of nature, which, in turn, brings about the socioeconomic development of state-territories.

When one adopts this liberal perspective on space, movement (whether of capital, commodities, labor, or information) is reduced to a secondary status, and spaces of movement are perceived of as

fundamentally asocial spaces between the territories wherein investment, transformation of nature, and social and state development tran-
spire (Steinberg, 1998). Of course, social scientists who subscribe to this
perspective recognize that trade occurs and that investments move, but
these are seen as derivative activities that may either enhance the exploitation of resources and valorization of places in a state's territory,
leading to further national development (a position that broadly can be
associated with neoliberal economic and political theories) or threaten
the state's power base (a position typically associated with realist and
neorealist theories of international relations). Whether movement is
seen as an opportunity or a threat, when viewed from the liberal perspective on space, movement is not in itself seen as constitutive of state
territory or social power.

   The limits of this perspective in analyzing spaces of movement are
perhaps most evident in the works of individuals who have attempted
to analyze spaces of movement while still subscribing to a liberal perspective on space. Within the discipline of economics, for instance,
scholars who identify with the "new economic geography" (e.g., Fujita,
Krugman, and Venables, 1999; Venables and Boltho, 1998) propose to
spatialize economic thought by focusing on the impacts of trade, relative
location, and spatial agglomeration. They differentiate themselves from
"nongeographic" economists who account for the role of space only by
modeling the impact that transport has on unit price (as expressed by
the difference between c.i.f. [cost, insurance, and freight] and f.o.b.
[free on board] prices). Instead, new economic geographers attempt
to account for the spatial properties of nearness and distance (and the
processes of movement that occur when sites are separated by distance)
by adding an "iceberg" function to economic models. According to this
function, a certain percentage of the value of a good being transported
"melts away" over each unit of distance that it travels.[5] Although this
innovation appears to insert the materiality of space into economic calculations, in fact the space of movement is presented in an abstract way,
removed from the social processes that occur within spaces of movement and that enable movement as a social activity. Indeed, one of the
leading new economic geographers, Paul Krugman, defends use of the
iceberg function not because it accurately portrays the social institutions
and cost frictions encountered, established, and demolished when one
moves across space, but rather because it is a "trick" through which "one

[can] avoid the need to model an additional industry" (Krugman, 1998, p. 11). In short, the new economic geographers fail to recognize that the spaces of movement within which transport occurs are also spaces of *time,* a particularly ironic omission given that, if one engages in a literal reading of the iceberg metaphor, iceberg melt rates are determined not by the area of space over which the iceberg is transported but by the duration of time for which an iceberg is at sea.[6]

One can turn to Manuel Castells for another example of a scholar who seeks to understand movement as a significant social activity but whose lingering adherence to the liberal perspective on space prevents him from fully appreciating the ways in which spaces of movement are socially constructed and contested. Despite conceiving of the world as a networked space of flows, Castells devotes little attention to the actual spaces of movement between the nodes at which people engage in spatially fixed social activities (what Castells calls the "first-level space of flows"). When he does investigate these "first-level" spaces, Castells characterizes them as "hyperspace[s] of pure circulation" (Castells, 1996, p. 475), spaces that are beyond time, beyond society, beyond experience, and beyond politics. Such a perspective is in keeping with a view of the world as a set of points at which social life transpires (Soja's liberal perspective on space), but it provides little ground for understanding the specific imperatives and obstacles that characterize governance, inhabitation, and technological transformation in the world's spaces of mobility.

Recasting Mobility

We take a somewhat different approach as we inquire into the nature of mobility, its spaces, and the ways in which mobility reflects and reproduces power. In contrast to political theories that are informed by the liberal perspective on space, wherein mobility is seen as a secondary activity that is undertaken by states that are fundamentally defined by their bounded insides, we view mobility as an essential aspect of society. Our resurrection of the constitutive role of mobility as a social process is linked with a questioning of "common-sense" assumptions about the nature of territoriality. As Burch (1994) asserts, the discourse of territoriality that underlies the modern state system rests on a manufactured distinction (which had not existed prior to 1700) between a political arena characterized by real, tangible property and an economic arena characterized by mobile, intangible property (see also, Polanyi, 1944). The designation of movement as a secondary activity, outside politics, thus is based on a reified concept of territoriality that, in turn, is based on a relatively recent and manufactured epistemological distinction.

If indeed the modern system of sovereignty—with its binary distinction between "insides" and "outsides"—rests on a discursive construction of fixity as the exclusive domain of the political and mobility as the exclusive domain of the economic, then a good place to begin deconstructing the distinction between "inside" and "outside" may be through an investigation of the (hidden) role of mobility in the construction of the political. Deleuze and Guattari (1988) shift the focus of sovereignty to the process of mobility by defining state practice as the continual processes of deterritorialization and reterritorialization, through which states mark boundaries and their crossings as means toward facilitating and controlling the movements that simultaneously enable and threaten state power. As Albert, expanding on Deleuze and Guattari, notes: "Sovereignty is something that has to be *practised* through 'marking' space by boundaries of various kinds—and by mapping these boundaries in an exact science.... For territory to be meaningful it has to be reproduced by the enactment of challenges to it, by questionings and erasures of boundaries as markers of space, but also through the inscription of new boundaries" (Albert, 1999, p. 61). In other words, through the marking and crossing of boundary lines, one defines not merely the scope of what is inside the territorial unit but also the nature of the system itself, because the system is represented as being the sum of its bounded units. This mode of thinking has led to a series of studies on the signification of national borders (Paasi, 1996); the interactions that take place in the borderlands between cultural worldviews (Dening, 1980); the significance of minority communities that reterritorialize by forming new "borderlands" within bounded territories (Doty, 1999); the role that the fear of a backflow of knowledge from the colony to the core plays in constructing the boundaries that both facilitate and retard these flows (Richards, 1993); and the function of boundaries within the territorial state that, through their crossing, reproduce discourses and structures of both unity and hierarchical differentiation on the "inside" (Rubenstein, 2001).

For this study, Deleuze and Guattari's insights regarding the continuing function of reterritorialization through boundary-drawing and boundary-crossing are important because they suggest that the relationship between movement across space and fixity in place is more complex than simply being a site of contradiction where the fundamental political need to control and develop the "inside" meets the secondary, economic need to maintain flows with the "outside." If, as Deleuze and Guattari assert, movement across borders *constitutes* the state, then positing a diametric relationship between fixity and movement, or between inside and outside, misses the point. Movement and fixity, and inside and outside, are so constitutive of each other that the very reification of these concepts into oppositional categories unwittingly accepts the (manufactured) discourse wherein stable, unitary territorial entities engage in relations with each other across the boundaries that divide an abstract, and otherwise friction-free Euclidean plane.

An alternative perspective, in which movement is recognized as a constitutive force in global society, follows from our critique of the liberal perspective on space. Table 1.1 identifies assumed binary oppositions that emerge when the liberal perspective on space is applied to state-societies, across four attributes: the nature of economic activity, the spatial characteristics or properties of capital, the spatial attributes of economic production and exchange, and the goals that orient states' intervention in national economies. Along each row, the table divides each attribute into those aspects considered essential to states and those considered nonessential or outside the fundamental purview of state

TABLE 1.1. FOUR ATTRIBUTES ASSOCIATED WITH THE LIBERAL PERSPECTIVE ON SPACE

Attributes	Essential State Aspects	Nonessential State Aspects
Economic activity	Production	Trade
Spatial property of capital	Fixity	Mobility
Space of economic activity	Discrete points within state territory	Channels and surfaces of movement across state boundaries; spaces outside any state's territory
Reason why states care about strong national economy	Economy as means for building political power	Economy as end in itself

governance or competence. Again, we stress that even among scholars working from a liberal perspective on space there is considerable difference of opinion regarding the implications of the nonessential state aspects for state practice and state power: Neorealists view nonessential state attributes as insignificant given state competition, whereas neoliberals view these as potential arenas for cooperation that will energize economic activity and override state competition. Our aim, however, is not to come down on one side or the other in this debate. Rather, we wish to propose that the very division between essential and nonessential state aspects rests on a conception of space that is particularly ill-suited for interpreting spaces of movement like the infosphere. To this end, the remainder of this section is devoted to exploring how, for each of these attributes, the division between essential and nonessential state aspects can be reconsidered when one abandons the liberal perspective on space and adopts a more explicitly spatial constructivist perspective.

Production vs. Trade

Turning to the first row in Table 1.1, one sees that the liberal perspective on space supports a conceptual distinction between production and trade. Production is seen as an activity that occurs within state borders and thereby strengthens the nation–state–territory bond that is the root of political power. Trade is seen as a secondary activity that occurs subsequent to this fundamental political, economic, and geographical formation. As we have seen, even new economic geographers who attempt to highlight the significance of moving commodities across space (i.e., trade) in their calculations maintain this privileging of production and the spaces of production and consumption. Of course, with a few exceptions (such as futures markets), production of an object historically occurs prior to its being traded, but the establishment of logical priority implies a conceptual distinction between production and trade—and between their respective spaces—that we find difficult to support.[7]

As Wallerstein (1979) notes, if one accepts that production is organized at the world-systemic scale, then trade—rather than being an external activity among independent producers or states—is an internal aspect of the division of labor. It follows that trade, like production, is constitutive of territorially defined social units (states) and that regulatory measures taken to facilitate international transportation and communication are fundamental acts in the construction of global society, not secondary activities undertaken by state-actors attempting to maximize economic or political power within their state territory. The distinction between production and trade is further challenged when one considers the large percentage of trade that is intrafirm, typically the result of foreign direct investments. Hence, it follows that the spaces wherein trade occurs are integral spaces of global society and not merely "empty" and "asocial" spaces between the state–society units where the seemingly essential social acts of production and consumption occur (Ciccantell and Bunker, 1998).

Fixity vs. Mobility
Our second critique of the liberal perspective on space centers on its conception of the dichotomy between capital fixity and capital mobility. For liberals, space is a pre-existing grid of locations, "something physical and external to the social context and to social action, a part of the 'environment,' a context *for* society—its container—rather than a structure created by society" (Soja, 1980, p. 210, emphasis in original). According to this perspective, the art of the capitalist is to identify the point at which transport and labor-force reproduction costs are lowest and to locate production there. The emphasis is on locating spatially fixed investments, which serve to develop territory and, ultimately, the state that bounds the territory. The liberal spatial perspective does recognize that capital is mobile, but only in that capitalists have a choice regarding where to locate their investments, and in the domain of trade which, as has been noted, is conceived of as an activity subordinate to production and consumption.

This view of the relationship between capital fixity and mobility has been thoroughly critiqued by geographers and institutional economists. As a number of geographers (most notably, David Harvey) have stressed, investment decisions, rather than involving a set of rational choices regarding placement of capital against a static environment of locations, take place within a highly politicized environment wherein space is continually "constructed" and "annihilated." Capital mobility is essential to the workings of capitalism, as it is only through the interplay of tendencies toward mobility and tendencies toward fixity that places are valued and devalued, providing economic rents for speculators and investors (Harvey, 1982; Smith, 1990). As places take on distinct values, further rents are obtained by moving production and consumption activities from one place to another, a process that often takes the form of trade and that leads to new cycles of valuation and devaluation. This is a fundamentally different vision of the spatiality of capital than that held by those who view capital as being inherently "intangible" (to use Burch's term), circulating across space until it is captured and its value is realized through emplacement. Instead, places of fixed investment and the spaces through which capital moves are mutually constitutive, as producers, consumers, speculators, and traders navigate through capital's dialectical tendencies toward both fixity and mobility.

Amid these cycles of investment and disinvestment, there is an ever-intensifying attempt to "shrink" space so as to accelerate the speed and efficiency of movement. This tendency, however, has its own contradictory attributes, as Harvey elaborates in his discussion of the technological improvements and political regulations that facilitate transportation and communication:

> Capitalism . . . is necessarily characterised by a perpetual striving to overcome all spatial barriers and "annihilate space with time." But it transpires that these objectives can be achieved only through the production of fixed and immobile spatial configurations (transport systems, etc.). In the second instance, therefore, we encounter the contradiction: spatial organisation is necessary to overcome space. . . . [There is] a tension within the geography of accumulation between fixity and motion, between the rising power to overcome space and the immobile spatial structures required for such a purpose. (Harvey, 1985, pp. 145, 150).

In other words, fixed investments (and complimentary political regulatory mechanisms) implemented in transportation–communication spaces to facilitate mobility create new opportunities for valorizing space. The attempt to "annihilate space" (through mobility) leads to the creation of places (locations for spatially fixed investments), which leads to a further search for still other means of space annihilation. This dialectic, perhaps most clearly seen in the tendency to locate export processing zones adjacent to airports and shipping terminals, is the foundation of a crucial dynamic within the continual restructuring of space in the modern political–economic system.

A similar questioning of the distinction between fixity and mobility (and the privileging of fixity) has been undertaken by institutional economists, especially those working in the tradition of Harold Innis (1951, 1995). For institutional economists, economic choices are made within highly complex and specific institutional environments, wherein norms and technologies do not so much add variables to the calculations made by *homo economicus* as they shape the very way in which calculations are made (or, put even more strongly, they shape the very concept of what calculation is). For Innis in particular, technologies and infrastructures of mobility play a crucial role in shaping norms and calculative environments, as past investments in infrastructure for moving resources (staples) and ideas (communications) construct the places within which norms are encountered and economic decisions are made. Thus, mobility, far from occurring subsequent to spatially fixed economic activities, is constitutive of their essences.[8]

As with our rejection of the production–trade distinction, our rejection of the liberal perspective's emphasis on capital fixity at the expense of capital mobility suggests a new appreciation for transportation–communication activities and the governance of the spaces within which they are carried out. When one acknowledges that the spaces of capitalist society always have been constructed amid a continual cross-current of factors favoring mobility and factors favoring fixity, then the recent trend of globalization appears, at most, as a quantitative change rather than a qualitative threat to the territorial state and the distinct locality (Cox, 1997). It follows that, even as the world becomes a web, whose channels of interaction constitute a postmodern equivalent of "place," this transformation in global spatiality is merely the latest episode in a dialectical process that long has played a role in both buttressing and altering society's spatial formations. Recent changes in the technologies, governance structures, and intensities of transportation and communication flows therefore should be viewed within a historical context, from a perspective that appreciates ongoing and continuing contradictions within the spatiality of capitalism.

Territory vs. Nonterritory

Turning to the third row in Table 1.1, we take issue with the liberal spatial perspective's unproblematic distinction between territory within state boundaries and nonterritory outside state boundaries. According to the liberal perspective, a prime concern of the state is development through the location of fixed investments in its territory. A clear distinction is made between these activities and those that take place outside state territory (whether in nonterritorialized space, in another state's territory, or through an action whose territorial placement is blurred). This distinction, like the two distinctions previously discussed, is dependent on a contextual view of space that fails to appreciate the degree to which social processes shape the spaces through which society operates.

Over the past years, international relations scholarship has come under criticism for its failure to problematize state territoriality. Building upon a frequently made critique that the discipline artificially separates domestic and international politics (Keohane and Nye, 1998), critical scholars assert that the territorial state is a relatively recent innovation, its power within its territory rarely has been complete, the mechanisms and meanings of state territoriality have changed significantly over time, and states always have attempted to exercise power outside their borders (Agnew, 2005; Kratochwil, 1986; Mann, 1984; Ruggie, 1993; Taylor, 1994). They note that much of the state's authority within its territory comes not from having a "monopoly of violence" within the space it controls but from participating in a mutual sovereignty pact wherein states recognize each others' territorial claims and thereby construct the territorial state system. This recognition has led Taylor (1995) to suggest that the basic unit of analysis in political science should be the *states,* not the *state.* Thomson (1994) adds a further element to this critique, asserting that the state system, although normally associated with political control of territory within state boundaries, historically was not complete until its systemic authority could be asserted in the spaces beyond formal state borders. Rounding out this line of criticism, discourse theorists assert that the legitimacy of the state as a sovereign authority governing territory is buttressed by linguistic practices that "naturalize" the state–society as a geographical "fact" (Agnew and Corbridge, 1995; Der Derian and Shapiro, 1989; Ó Tuathail, 1996). Through discursive strategies, civil interventions within state space come to be seen as natural and acts of governments and militaries designed to protect state space are portrayed as reflexive acts of self-defense.

As an alternative, recent contributors to the literature suggest that society's institutions thrive amid a dialectic between territorialization and movement: "Statecraft oscillate[s] between the desire for order and stability and the facilitation of flows" (Doty, 1999, p. 605). As such, rather than focusing on stabilizing acts of territorialization and destabilizing acts of deterritorialization, it makes more sense to consider a continual process of *re*territorialization through which both the inside space of the territory and the outside space beyond the territory are constituted (Albert, 1999; Mandaville, 1999). State attempts to regulate activities outside territorial containers (e.g., international transportation and communication flows) should not be seen as qualitatively different from attempts at regulating activities within state territory. To assume that extraterritorial processes (and their regulation) fundamentally differ from those that occur within state boundaries is to fall into the "territorial trap," wherein one forgets that the territorial state is itself a social construct (Agnew and Corbridge, 1995). To build on Rosenau and Czempiel's (1992) distinction, "government" may be reserved for activities within the bounded territory of the state, but "governance" is a global social phenomenon and one that we feel is constitutive, as well as reflective, of global society. Furthermore, as Murphy (1994) has shown, historically the global-scale governance of economic activities has played an important role in constituting the modern political–economic system.

Politics vs. Economics

It follows from all of these critiques that we must also object to the liberal spatial perspective's division between political and economic state interests. Incorporating a "mixed ontology" inherited from Hobbes and Smith, mainstream international relations theorists view the natural competition of economics as fundamentally at odds with the social mediation necessary for the formation of a polity (Inayatullah and Rupert, 1994). Economics thus is seen as something to be transcended, manipulated, or both to promote the polity. States attempt to achieve and express their authority by gaining control of and increasing the wealth of their territories, but economic development is perceived as fundamentally a means to a political end.

This politics-versus-economics conception of state transportation–communication policy is intertwined with the three axes of tension critiqued above. Spatially fixed acts of production and consumption that occur at points within a static state territory are taken as the essential acts of society and therefore the basis of political state power. Other economic activities—those that occur outside state territory, those that involve trade, or those that more broadly concern capital mobility—may be engaged in if they are deemed supportive of the essential polity-building activities (a possibility considered fairly likely by neoliberals but less likely by neorealists), but most political scholars agree that states will refrain from these subordinate activities if it is believed that they will be detrimental to the state's primary political objective of maintaining authority over territory.

Because we reject the three axes of tension upon which the politics–economics distinction is based, we reject this distinction also. Just as politics involves the simultaneous construction and transgression of boundaries, the same is true of economic activities. Although it is convenient to think of the infosphere as a free space of mobility that exists beyond boundaries, in fact economic actors themselves erect boundaries (which users then pay to cross) and these acts of boundary construction and crossing assist and are facilitated by the construction and crossing of state boundaries. The two domains of boundary construction and crossing (or reterritorialization) thus are inseparable.

A Constructivist Perspective on Spaces of Movement

In this book we offer a conceptualization that rejects the liberal perspective on space and that instead focuses on the historic processes by which spaces (including those outside state territories) are constructed amid an interplay of political–economic imperatives. In particular, we focus on the dialectical spatial tendencies implicated in those competing political–economic imperatives: the tendency toward establishing regimes that enable capital fixity in space, and the tendency toward establishing regimes that enable capital mobility. Space is not a grid within which investments are placed, areal units emerge as states, and societies trade; rather space itself, and its many areal units, are produced discursively and materially through continual (and conflictual) action (Lefebvre, 1991; Soja, 1989, 1996).

From the moment transportation–communication spaces first serve this function, they begin to be regulated. At the onset, their regulatory system likely involves little direct intervention by states as it is oriented solely toward constructing the spaces as domains of mobility.

Nonetheless, this minimalist regulation is itself an act of sociospatial construction. As the space's uses intensify and diversify, and as fixed investments are made to enable the "annihilation of space with time," the regulatory system likely will become more complex and states will play a more direct role so as to facilitate the placement and security of fixed investments as well as continuing to preserve the space's functionality as a domain of flows. As uses of the space for movement and uses of the space for locating fixed investments both increase, the institutional structures supportive of each tendency are likely to conflict, and a crisis of regulation will ensue (Steinberg, 1999).

Working from our spatial constructivist perspective, we focus not on the perceived *diametric* tension between in-state and trans-state processes depicted in Table 1.1, but rather on the *dialectical* tension between spatial fixity and movement that constructs and reflects institutions within, across, and outside state boundaries. Although the concepts represented in the columns in Table 1.1 are in opposition to each other, they also complement and contribute to each other's constitution. Therefore, rather than seeking to determine the conditions under which states compromise (or enhance) their essential political objective of territorial development by cooperating with others to facilitate movement across nonstate space, our research questions revolve around ongoing changes in the intensity of regulation, the specific mechanisms implemented (including how those mechanisms relate to formal state power), and how shifts in regulation reflect and impact political–economic dynamics, particularly in the context of the ongoing dialectical relationship between the need to foster capital fixity and the need to foster capital mobility. These shifts are examined specifically with reference to the ways in which individuals and institutions adopt, adapt, and regulate technologies to construct the world of electronic interconnections that is the infosphere.

The Infosphere as a Space of Management

Because the infosphere is a space of movement that is constructed by and within society, any analysis must focus on how social actors construct the infosphere (or locate themselves in the infosphere) in order to achieve specific ends. In line with this research agenda, some scholars have studied the ways in which governmental and nongovernmental entities have worked together to build and regulate technology and physical infrastructure (e.g., Kahin and Nesson, 1997; Kahin and Wilson, 1996; Mueller, 2002; Mulgan, 1991; Murtha, Lenway, and Hart, 2001; Rosenau and Singh, 2002). Others have examined the ways in which the infosphere has reproduced existing dimensions of social and spatial hierarchy, between and within national societies (e.g., Brunn and Leinbach, 1991; Castells, 1996; Dodge and Kitchin, 2001; Mosco, 1996; Schiller, 1999). A third group of scholars have turned their attention to the ways in which users of the infosphere have formed new communities and identities that transcend the usual markers of community and identity such as class, gender, and geographical location (e.g., Brook and Boal, 1995; Fornäs, Klein, Ladendorf, Sunden, and Sveningsson, 2002; Jones, 1995, 1997; Shields, 1996; Swiss, 2000; Turkle, 1995), or new venues for education (Haynes and Holmevik, 2001) or social and political activism (McCaughey and Ayers, 2003). Still others have focused on the ways in which the infosphere has been seized upon by localities and nation-states as a route to social and economic development (e.g., Heeks, 2001; Mansell and Steinmueller, 2000; Mansell and Wehn, 1998; Singhal and Rogers, 2001; Wilson, 2004), or ways in which firms and governments are reshaping the online experience of individuals (Elmer, 2004).

In this book, we adopt a perspective that simultaneously considers individual actions, collective actions, and public policy choices and avoids the limitations of a purely structural or technologically determinist analysis. One cannot, for instance, analyze how "netizens" use chat rooms to construct alternative identities and communities without simultaneously recognizing how the infrastructure through which these communities are being formed is regulated by companies seeking profit and by governments seeking power. Conversely, one cannot analyze instances of technology choice and protocol adoption by Internet providers without understanding user preferences (and corporations' plans for constructing users and consumer needs). In other words, our aim is to apply a perspective to the infosphere that combines the view from Appalachia (i.e., the infosphere as a space of places wherein individuals unevenly have access to and adopt communication technologies), the view from Hong Kong (i.e., the infosphere as a special administrative region that both supports and pushes against the limits of dominant forms of sociospatial organization), and the view from the ocean (i.e., the infosphere as a special space of movement in which the boundaries imprinted through social construction are kept to a minimum in order to preserve the image of a friction-free transit surface).

By revolving our study around the concept of *management*, we add a situational component to perspectives that focus on determinant (or restrictive) structures, enabling technologies, or agent-centered cultural change. Our focus on management leads to a recognition that human decisions are made and actions are taken within specific contexts given the goals of actors; it opens up a discussion of the choices in governmental, organizational, and individual practice that are shaping the infosphere, rather than assuming that technologies follow their own path; it links "micro" decisions about technology and organizational directions with a "macro" level examination of decisions that shape the broader context; and our focus on management adds an action agenda, leading to questions of what should be done to shape technologies and uses of the infosphere, and how its management can be directed in order to achieve social goals.

In this book we conceptualize management as having three dimensions: *governance*, *culture*, and *technology*. Our first dimension of management is *governance*: management as control and operation so as to facilitate use, security of investment, and profit generation. This is the conceptualization of management identified with Henri Fayol, the founder of what is sometimes called the "governance school of management" (Gray, 1984, p. 5). Fayol, whose 1916 volume *General and Industrial Management* (Fayol, 1916/1949) continues to be referred to in business school textbooks, writes that management encompasses five processes: planning (defining goals and establishing long-term strategy), organization (delineation of tasks, reporting authority, and decision-making), coordination (issuing the commands that entrust individuals in the organization with their tasks), command (establishing the sequence of work), and control (monitoring to ensure that progress is being made toward the predefined goals and modifying the organization and tasks as necessary to ensure that goals are met). This view of management can be summarized as the series of processes that occur when an actor or actors exercise power and apply rational organization and coordination toward a set of predefined ends.

Although Fayol's primary concern was the management of the business enterprise, his conceptualization of management as governance is relevant to other social institutions as well. Indeed, the goal-oriented nature of management-as-governance resonates with the way the term governance is used by international relations scholars (e.g., Barnett and Duvall, 2005; Held and McGrew, 2002; Wilkinson and Hughes, 2002). James Rosenau, for instance, defines governance as occurring when a system—with or without formal governmental institutions—has the capacity "to cope with external challenges, to prevent conflicts among its members or factions from tearing it irretrievably apart, to procure resources necessary to its preservation and well-being, and to frame goals and policies designed to achieve them" (Rosenau, 1992, p. 3). This perspective on management can be applied directly to the coordination of the infosphere, which, although beyond the control of any one state's government, is subject to rational planning. The infosphere is managed by a complex web of formal and informal institutions representing various state, capital, and civil society interests, who seek to use their power to reproduce or transform existing social and spatial hierarchies through achieving specific goals of communication and connectivity.

Although the governance school of management remains the dominant perspective among persons studying how to coordinate business organizations, management encompasses other dimensions as well. Our analysis moves beyond normative prescriptions about how the infosphere should be managed to interrogate the actual practices by which the infosphere is constructed through everyday use. Such a perspective requires consideration of subjectivist interpretations by users as well as objectivist prescriptions by governors and would-be governors. Thus, in contrast to the first dimension of management (governance), which implies control and authority, this second dimension of management refers to coping and creative response. One who "manages to get by" does not exercise power over others for a predetermined end (as does one who manages in the interest of governance). Rather this dimension of management refers to one who assesses the environment and the available resources, piecing together a coping strategy that sustains oneself and one's community. In this *cultural* aspect of management, individuals respond to existing situations and manage their own meanings and roles in the environments in which they are embedded and which they reproduce through their everyday activities. When applied to the infosphere, the cultural dimension of management encompasses acts of coping and response by "navigators" who interpret and assign meanings to signs and places, affirm identities, and construct communities as they travel through the infosphere. From this perspective, an individual navigating through the infosphere is an engaged citizen and not merely a passive consumer.

Occupying an intermediate position between the governance and culture dimensions of management is the dimension of technology: management as the design and implementation of basic protocols and standards. Individuals engaged in organizational governance and those engaged in cultural interpretation are, in effect, managing the relations between technology and society. Thus, issues of technology choice and technology adoption (and adaptation) play a large role in our investigation of how the infosphere is being managed, both from below and from above. As the ATM, wireless telephone, and Caller ID examples from Appalachia demonstrate, technologies are both introduced and adopted selectively, in order to maintain cultural norms, enable governance by bureaucratic or corporate institutions, or reproduce (or transform) structural power relations, at scales ranging from the household to the national or global political–economic system.

The intersection of these three dimensions of management is a theme developed over the course of the book, but a brief example is outlined here: the rise of electronic commerce ("e-commerce") transactions on the World Wide Web. The rise of e-commerce web applications is experienced most apparently as a technological innovation. However, the emergence of these applications reflects (and precipitates) much more than the development and deployment of new technologies. These applications have emerged in response to changes in law and policy that allow for web-mediated transactions to be recognized as binding and thus fall under the jurisdiction of commercial law. Concurrently, as these technologies received increased use, industry groups began to lobby for further changes in the applicable areas of commercial law. At the same time, the use of e-commerce applications has required individuals and groups to make web-based shopping part of their daily lives and practice. This cultural development has led both private- and public-sector actors to engage in ongoing efforts to address tensions in the process of governance, while competition among providers has

spawned efforts to attract and retain users, both through further technological innovation and through the construction of provider-identified
"e-cultures."

Bringing together these three dimensions of management—
governance, culture, and technology—we stress that the infosphere is
a space of action, choice, and collective responsibility. The infosphere
does not have the character it has solely because corporate or state
elites will it as such. Nor is its character solely the result of efforts by
its grassroots users or a function of its technology. Rather, these three
dimensions of infosphere management interact to reconstitute each
other and the infosphere within which the interaction transpires. By focusing on infosphere management as a multifaceted, multidimensional
process, we hope to shed light on this complex arena of twenty-first-
century society.

Managing the Infosphere as a Space of Motion

The central aim of this book is to apply this notion of management, as
a multifaceted process, to the social construction of the infosphere as a
space of motion. As has been noted, we focus on motion in two ways.
First, the processes of change in governance, technology, and culture are
ongoing, and this fluid and constant institutional flux, while exhibiting
some constancy in underlying market dynamics, must be incorporated
as a component of a social theory of the infosphere. This might be called
historical motion, a view that draws upon Fernand Braudel's (1982)
differing notions of time, including the *longue durée*, conjunctural time,
and the time of events. James Rosenau's (1990) idea of "turbulence" is
also useful in providing a sense of the instability in world politics over
the last two decades. Rosenau's concept of turbulence emphasizes the
institutional uncertainties that have come to typify world politics and is
drawn upon in our efforts to outline the historical motion of infosphere
institutions. We argue that instability in the infosphere is related to
accelerated circuits of commerce and the flow of capital.

Second, *geographic motion* is part of the constitution of the infosphere. Among the unstated but common goals of governance, technology choice, and the cultural practices of the infosphere is the effort to
facilitate easier mobility of goods, services, people, and identities. One

part of our overall argument is that although the normal state of affairs in social theory is to view identities, groups, and social institutions as fixed, with interactions and exchanges among these units as marginal or secondary, we should rather view many of the institutions of governance, technology, and culture pertaining to the infosphere as implicitly promoting mobility by constructing infrastructure and fluid institutional and social spaces that encourage and facilitate this movement, a point that has been made elsewhere by students of diasporae, borderland dwellers, and immigrant communities (e.g., Appadurai, 1996; Clifford, 1997; Gilroy, 1993; Ong, 1999; Price, 2004). As has been noted, in some instances, ironically, this movement is facilitated through the construction (and subsequent crossing) of boundaries.

In applying the three dimensions of management—governance, technology, and culture—to the infosphere, we find it useful to revisit the four tensions that are assumed to be diametric oppositions when the liberal conception of space is applied to state-societies (see Table 1.1). Now, however, the diametric relationship portrayed within each element (i.e., each row in Table 1.1) is reconsidered as a dialectical relationship. This dialectical relationship, for each of the four tensions, is worked through (and reproduced) as social actors engage in the three dimensions of management (Table 1.2).

Turning to Row 1 in Table 1.2, we can see how the governance, technology, and cultural dimensions of management all are implicated in the simultaneous production of the infosphere as a space of both production and trade. Much of the value derived from web-based services by producers and users is in the form of meta-information services (such as databases and search engines, or information about information), in transaction services (such as e-commerce), or in information and communication services (reporting, e-mail, marketing). These activities cannot be conceived of as production of value separated from the constant exchange of information and goods and services. For service transactions, production often takes place at the same time as consumption, and the value of the service is based upon what the end user is willing to pay. Cell 1A refers to the structures of governance that facilitate the simultaneous promotion of production and exchange.

Moving to Cell 1B and considering the technology aspect of management, we see that even intellectual property, whether in symbols, images, media content, or production processes and technology (which

TABLE 1.2. FOUR TENSIONS IN THE ORGANIZATION OF POLITICAL ECONOMY,
EXPERIENCED ACROSS THREE DOMAINS OF INFOSPHERE MANAGEMENT

Tensions	Dimensions		
	A. Governance	B. Technology	C. Culture
1. Production/ Trade	1A. Simultaneous promotion of production and exchange	1B. National possession of patents and intellectual property rights to enhance productivity versus access to licensing; Research as form of value creation	1C. Investment in education of workforce; Open exchange of ideas for economic and social development and integration
2. Fixity/ Mobility	2A. Strong institutions governing a place allow for greater mobility of goods, services, information, and people, which develop a place.	2B. Investments in infrastructure upgrades and new network technologies to enhance mobility	2C. Cultural hybridity; Ambiguous online identity; Migration of people and ideas
3. Territory/ Nonterritory	3A. States expand and contract territorial control according to historical and strategic considerations, ceding power to or claiming power from civil society.	3B. Access to knowledge and technology in other countries; Open flow of technology; Suspension versus exercise of state control	3C. Debates over content control in domestic space and other countries; Representations of national space; Construction of geographically defined versus transgeographic communities
4. Politics/ Economics	4A. Economic considerations not always second to political; Infosphere as a special administrative region	4B. Strategic and controlled technologies versus maximum benefit from technology sales	4C. Create locational advantage through social and cultural institutions to attract people and capital

is often seen as a core factor of national production and improvement in productivity), is connected with exchange and trade. Rather than exploiting intellectual property within nationally based firms, intellectual property rights may be licensed to other firms on a global basis. Licenses may even be released to competing firms. Early release of software code for operating systems by Microsoft, for instance, allows other firms to create applications that work with new operating systems (enhancing Microsoft's market position), as well as making it possible for firms to create software programs that may compete with some of

Microsoft's offerings. Other firms have separated their research and development units from the main operating company, in part to isolate the risk of lost investments from failed innovations. Conversely, the patents arising from research into new technology may be made available for license or sale and become a form of value creation apart from a direct link to actual production.

Moving to Cell 1C, we see that the tension between production and trade also appears in social and cultural concerns. In the 1990s, former U.S. Secretary of Labor Robert Reich (1991) argued that governments should accept the main features of global trade and investment and capital mobility. He urged governments to invest in the education of the workforce and in high quality infrastructure, two inputs into national production processes, in order to attract mobile transnational investment capital to locate in their countries. At the same time, social and economic policy makers in liberal market economies emphasized that open exchange of ideas and information, including access to recent and up to date management, technical, and scientific knowledge, is essential for economic and social development. Although the specific strategies and decisions may differ in time and place, production and even the human factors of production or social capital cannot be separated from exchange and trade.

The reproduction and working through of these tensions through the three dimensions of management are evident when one looks at the other three rows in Table 1.2 as well. Turning to the second row (the tension between fixity and mobility), we see that strong institutions governing a place allow for greater mobility of goods, services, information, and people, which in turn serve to develop a place. The institutional arrangements that facilitate transactions, property rights, and the movement of information and capital are at least as important as electronic communication networks and technologies in creating spaces of mobility. Continuous investments in infrastructure construction and upgrades, and new technologies in communication networks, enhance and support the institutional and physical capabilities that allow for this mobility.

Access of citizens and consumers to infosphere services and technologies allows the infosphere to enter more fully into everyday life through uses such as e-commerce, social communication, and workplace applications. In addition to providing opportunities for the creative construction of identities and communities (e.g., through blogs, social networking websites, online photo albums, etc.), these technologies also allow for more active and accurate profiling of individuals' activities. The tension between fixity and mobility is also reflected in the migration of people and ideas, the formation of new forms of community in online settings, and debates about ambiguous online identity and cultural hybridity at a transnational level.

Turning to the third row, we observe that territorial and nonterritorial boundaries and scopes are malleable and changing, not unmovable and impermeable as absolute images of state sovereignty would suggest. States expand and contract their territorial control following historical and strategic considerations, in some cases creating geographic economic development zones where certain laws and taxes may not apply, or allowing some sectors of the economy and society to be zones of more or less autonomy. States may at different times cede power or claim power from the private sector, civil society, or even other states and international organizations if necessary.

As with the benefits deriving from the open flow of information and technology, states may choose to deny strategic technologies to other countries. Alternatively, states may choose to limit superficially or suspend their authority in order to encourage the rapid diffusion of new technology and to seek a specific mode or path of development for the technology.

Culturally, debates over content control on web-based services, whether in domestic or international spaces, further illustrate the ongoing and difficult choices encountered in the management of the infosphere as a space of mobility. Direct state control is sometimes replaced by industry self-regulation or efforts to develop filtering software to achieve public goals. Although infosphere technologies supposedly do not depend upon physical spaces, many countries invest heavily in the construction of a national space and image on the web. This may be to advance tourism, by defining and projecting an image to potential visitors. Also e-government activities may require the construction of brands associated with the services being delivered by public sector agencies. In other cases, the construction of nationhood in the infosphere seems more important than the actual physical territory or present population.

Turning to the fourth row, we argue that economic considerations are not always secondary to political considerations. The example of special administrative regions has been noted, and the infosphere has been compared to these economic development zones where some laws and taxes may be suspended. The moratorium that was introduced in the United States on sales taxes on online purchases is another example of the economic goals of a specific sector or overall economic growth being balanced against the benefits of more direct control.

Examples from the domain of technology management further illustrate this point. Just as more economic benefit may accrue to companies by licensing their technologies to others than by only exploiting technologies in their production activities, so too countries must balance the relative power that may be gained by limiting technology exports and monopoly control with the economic benefits to be gained from selling goods, services, and technology or from licensing intellectual property rights.

Culturally, efforts to enhance educational, social, and cultural attributes of a region or city may serve to attract people and capital. The openness to movement of people, ideas, and capital demonstrated by world cities is among the core attributes that define these places, as well as serving as the basis for cultural and economic development. However, this openness frequently conflicts with national governments' will to control space, secure borders, and root national identity.

Outline of the Book

The next five chapters of this book present a series of cuts across Table 1.2, as we examine specific issues or controversies in one or another domain of infosphere management and how they work through and reproduce tensions between production and trade, fixity and mobility, territory and nonterritory, and politics and economics. In the next chapter of this book (Chapter 2), we turn our attention to the technological dimension of management. We consider a number of explanations for how and why technology change occurs, from macroscale functionalist explanations that focus on structural needs to microscale behavioral explanations that focus on user preference. These debates about technology change overlap with a larger debate between those who view technology as largely autonomous of government policy and others who view it as a tool for promoting national development. Thus, in Chapter 2, we integrate specific issues surrounding technology choice within the broader problematic of managing the infosphere as a space of movement.

In Chapter 3, we focus on the governance dimension of infosphere management, as we examine the contradictory elite interests and policy programs that emerge as governing bodies attempt to align their governance initiatives with the other two dimensions of management (technology and culture). Here, we address the tensions among different levels of government in the United States that have arisen as a result of efforts to introduce new technologies rapidly in the telecommunications sector, as well as efforts to make greater use of market mechanisms.

In Chapter 4, we shift our focus to the cultural dimension of infosphere management, as we critique dominant interpretations of the role of communications technology in cultural consumption which hold that information simply crosses space in order to reach its spatially fixed audience. The cases of tourism and travel reveal that, for cultural practices that involve mobility, the assumed distinction between mobile information and fixed consumers does not hold. Consumption itself involves mobility, and thus the movement of information across the infosphere is an aspect of consumption and not just information transmission. This chapter thus connects a concern with the way in which the world is being transformed by economies and spaces of movement with larger debates about the management of culture, technology, and markets.

In Chapters 5 and 6 we look at a number of issues relating to Internet domain name conventions. Naming plays an important role in the spatial construction of the infosphere by providing the common understanding that makes technology, governance, and culture possible. When naming conventions are associated with states, they serve both to reassert the authority of the state and to enable the fusion of state and corporate power that is necessary to protect intellectual property. Likewise, names can provide the common identifiers around which communities coalesce and, by "fixing" addresses, they make navigation possible. In Chapter 5, we look at issues concerning the assignment and use of country code top-level domain names (ccTLDs) to investigate the broader question of how the infosphere is transforming the relationships between state, capital, and both place-based and nonplace-based institutions of civil society. The politics of naming in the fluid domain of the infosphere is discussed further in Chapter 6, in which we look at ICANN, the principal organization governing the assignation of names on the Internet. In this chapter, we analyze how, despite the appearance of democracy, some of the major institutions of infosphere governance implement neoliberal ideals as they devolve management from national governments to civil society.

We conclude, in Chapter 7, by raising several claims that should contribute to a reassessment of some of the core concepts assumed and used in the examination of the infosphere. In this chapter, we address the connection of infosphere applications to transnational trade and investment, the features of the global "space of flows," the mobility of offline and online identity, and the amorphous features of control in the infosphere. Moving toward responsible management of the infosphere necessitates understanding the full range of choices that are available to different actors and demanding more accountability to relevant publics in those choices.

Lastly, the approach that we take to study infosphere management in terms of governance, technology, and culture is historical and critical. The approach is historical in that concepts and theories refer to a range of institutions and practices across specific times and places. It is critical in that the purpose of the theory and research underlying this book is to inform decision-making at various levels and to contribute to the construction of communication environments and opportunities that are more open to all citizens.

2 Managing Technological Change

nfosphere technology is in a constant state of flux, leading some to observe that no sooner is a technological advancement or product created than it is immediately obsolete. Depending on the scale at which technological change occurs, governments and organizations, designers and developers, and individuals manage this ever-present stream of motion in a variety of ways that combine a range of social, economic, and political objectives and constraints. In this chapter, the phrase *managing technological change* refers to the processes by which various affected parties direct and respond to technological innovations, changes in hardware and software, on an ongoing basis. In using the term *technology*, and its derivations, we subscribe to Frederick Ferré's (1995) definition that technology reflects "practical implementations of intelligence" (p. 26).

More specifically, our focus is on those technologies that combine to produce the infosphere. Because technological change affects a wide variety of groups and individuals in different contexts, we have selected four prominent contemporary theories that examine the effects of technological change at different scales of management (macro to micro levels). By addressing the different scales at which technological change is managed, we acknowledge the complexity of the issue and are positioned better to discuss the management of this change in the context of the four tensions explored in this book: production/trade, fixity/mobility, territory/nonterritory, and politics/economics.

The four theoretical perspectives that form the framework for this chapter include: social shaping of technology, technical code, diffusion of innovations, and social construction of technology. Social shaping, in the usage we present here, generally operates at the macro level to focus on how governments and large institutions, such as markets or national/multinational corporations, manage technological change to reflect their economic, political, and social agendas and practices. Stepping down a level in scale, the technical code perspective focuses on the role that designers and developers play in creating the look, feel, and functionality of technology products and services. Narrowing further, diffusion of innovations examines the processes by which a new product or service is adopted over time among members of a social system. At the micro level, social construction emphasizes the role that individual and groups of consumers play in making meaning of a technology based on personal uses, values, attitudes, and beliefs. Although these scales of focus, as presented, imply a linear progression from macro to micro levels, in reality these scales of management frequently occur simultaneously and are interrelated, as will be demonstrated throughout this chapter.

For the purpose of maintaining continuity across the scales of management examined in this chapter, we primarily limit our discussion of these theories to the example of networked computing (i.e., the Internet), a subset of the infosphere definition provided in Chapter 1. The chapter concludes with a synthesis of these differing perspectives with respect to managing technological change based on the four tensions identified previously.

Social Shaping of Technology

The social shaping of technology perspective holds that technologies reflect broad and long-term institutional power. Technologies are designed and deployed to meet the needs of powerful institutions and social groups, specifically governments and large private sector corporations. The specific technologies that are chosen are selected because they meet the longstanding goals of these organizations and the actions they undertake within institutional configurations, such as pursuing national security within the interstate system, controlling the production processes in the labor market, seeking greater efficiencies in distribution and exchange in the market economy, or trying to gain greater control over intellectual property and other forms of property in media markets (Lievrouw and Livingstone, 2002; Park and McDowell, 2005; Volti, 2001).

The social shaping of technology takes place at various points in the development cycle of new technologies (Edge, 1995). Not only are design and development of new technologies shaped by the goals and purposes of powerful public and private sector organizations and institutions, so too are the deployment of technologies shaped by investment decisions and strategies of organizations within specific contexts. Robin Mansell's (1993) analysis of how firms in the 1980s and 1990s acted strategically to design digital telecommunication network and switching technologies demonstrates how they attempted to retain the high-value-added activities and services on the network for themselves, while reducing the range of control of these activities by users. Existing media systems, such as terrestrial broadcasting, cable television, or the Internet, can be viewed in a similar light. They exist not as full blown realizations of technological possibilities, but rather as the outcome of historical bargains among the public sector, the private sector, and audiences on the appropriate coverage, content, pricing, and use of media technologies and systems. These relationships may become stable, but also may be disrupted by a number of changes, including new financing and marketing strategies, new content formats to reach different audiences, and the adoption and use of new technologies in program production, distribution, or reception.

As Roger Fidler (1997) notes, new media technologies are also introduced into a context of existing technologies. Not only does the use of new technologies by service providers and users disrupt the existing arrangements and practices, these pre-existing media also shape the ways in which new technologies are applied, the choices about the places and populations to which they are deployed, and the uses to which they are put. The social shaping approach taken here, then, argues that the most relevant actors and institutions that should be examined to understand the development of infosphere technologies are those shaping the production, distribution, and use of media technologies and systems that are already in place.

The social shaping perspective may best be exemplified by the paragraph with which Patrick Parsons (2003) concludes his study of the development of the cable-satellite distribution system in the United States:

> The idea of, and concrete proposals for, a cable-satellite system, in short, arose logically from prior technical, economic, and regulatory development. Social structures in place at the time helped constrain and guide development. Costly terrestrial distribution options motivated cable operators and broadcasters to look to satellites, while changing FCC policy with regard to satellite ownership and smaller critical issues, such as allowable dish size, served to channel and regulate the pace of development. Within the given set of social and economic parameters, a multitude of players, . . . each with their own resources and agendas, engaged in a process of contestation and negotiation (p. 14).

As Parsons's example indicates, there may be conflicts between different actors and institutions that place greater weight on national development and security or on achieving the benefits of the rapid deployment of new technologies and those that do not. As is discussed in Chapter 1, on the one hand, those who write about the emerging "information society" typically highlight a new, postindustrial mode of production, likening activities occurring in the infosphere to those that were associated with farms, workshops, and factories during previous modes of production. This production-oriented perspective has been used to guide trade and investment policies oriented toward building and furthering the dominance of specific financial centers, as well as the states within which they are located (Leyshon and Thrift, 1997; Sassen, 1991). On the other hand, proponents of a global infosphere champion it as an arena of trade, a friction-free space of flows that transcends state boundaries and exists outside the essential domain of the state, much like the transportation-space of the ocean; indeed, some advertisements for telecommunication and finance firms use images of the ocean to highlight their space-annihilation designs for the infosphere (Steinberg, 1999). Effectively, these two views encapsulate the perspectives represented in the left and right columns, respectively, in Table 1.1.

In a similar vein, authors who examine technological change typically view technology either as a series of developable state resources or a self-propelling force that defies state control. According to the former group, technological know-how is a naturally occurring national resource. There are differing policy perspectives among members of this group—neoliberal institutionalists (e.g., Libicki, 1996), for instance, would recommend the open sale, sharing, and exchange of technology for the maximum benefit of all, whereas neorealists would attempt to control strategic technologies as a national asset—but neither has a well developed sense of the role of public policy in encouraging technical development or use. According to this view, technology and technical change are aspects of national production systems that emerge naturally and that may be thought of as the equivalent of fixed property (state attributes that fall on the left side of Table 1.1). Others, by contrast, such as Wriston (1992), view technology change as accelerating, inevitable, and more or less outside the control of state power or private control (in which case it falls on the right side of Table 1.1).

Despite the obvious ways in which the expansion of communication technologies transcends state boundaries, no analysis of communication technology development can be complete without recognition of the important role that states have played in technology, for a variety of reasons and through a variety of means. In the United States, for instance, a primary mode of promoting technological change has been the assignment of intellectual property rights. The United States has this enshrined in the Constitution, which gives Congress the power "to promote the Progress of Science and useful Arts, by securing for limited Times to Authors and Inventors the exclusive Right to their respective Writings and Discoveries." In addition to providing public support for copyrights and patents, public funding has also been used to guide technology change. These mechanisms might include government procurement, contracts and grants for new technology development, tax credits to support research, and trade policy. Among other types of direct or indirect modes of technology policy and governance are standard-setting, competition policy, and regulation of monopoly utility or network industries. Moreover, many of the decisions and actions shaping technology design, development, adoption, and use are not public policy decisions. Technologies may be designed by engineers and researchers, adopted by managers in organizations or users in their households, and applied in various settings by individuals and groups. These are also important forms of managing technological change.

In addition to placing technology change within the rubric of economic development, government support for technological innovations has often been driven by military concerns. United States defense planning has been notable in the last 50 years for using extensive support for technology research and development in aeronautics, ballistic missiles, satellites, and data processing to gain strategic advantage militarily. In the 1980s, for instance, massive parallel computer processing applications were promoted to meet the data processing needs of the Reagan administration's proposals for ballistic missile defense, or the Strategic Defense Initiative. The so-called "Star Wars" program reinvigorated by the Bush administration in 2001 is justified by pointing to the support for technology research and development that it will provide as much as by the actual ability to achieve its mission (which has not been demonstrated and is very much in question). The U.S. government allowed an exemption to antitrust laws in order to encourage the formation of a national consortium of companies (SEMATECH) to cooperate in basic research in silicon chips or semiconductors, despite a general aversion to picking technology winners. Government support for semiconductor research and high-performance computing has been justified on national security grounds. The U.S. government also became involved in international standard-setting debates over high-definition television (Dupagne and Seel, 1997; Galperin, 2004), supporting a U.S. standard over European and Japanese proposals. In Europe, the development of the GSM standard for digital wireless telephony followed a decision by the European Union member states to develop a European standard at the European Standards and Technology Institute (ESTI) and to use one standard in the deployment of second generation or digital wireless technologies throughout Europe. In China, as well the government has played a strong role in developing communications technologies for national security ends. For instance, by establishing a limited number of gateways in order to monitor and control Internet usage, it has furthered its aim of preventing information flows and uses of Internet technology that might undermine national political order and stability (Kalathil and Boas, 2003).

Indeed, although mobility and the crossing of borders appears at first glance to exist in opposition to national security concerns, state leaders have asserted the essential nature of these communication networks and technologies and have equated them with other essential resources that are more typically associated with national prosperity and survival. In 1996, the U.S. government formed a President's Commission on Critical Infrastructure Protection with Executive Order 13010 (July 15, 1996). Its preamble states:

> Certain national infrastructures are so vital that their incapacity or destruction would have a debilitating impact on the defense or economic security of the United States. These critical infrastructures include telecommunications, electrical power systems, gas and oil storage and transportation, banking and finance, transportation, water supply systems, emergency services (including medical, police, fire, and rescue), and continuity of government. Threats to these critical infrastructures fall into two categories: physical threats to tangible property ("physical threats"), and threats of electronic, radio-frequency, or computer-based attacks on the information or communication components that control critical infrastructures ("cyber threats"). Because many of these critical infrastructures are owned and operated by the private sector, it is essential that the government and the private sector work together to develop a strategy for protecting them and ensuring their continued operation (United States President's Commission, 1996).

This emphasis upon designing and deploying information and communication technologies in ways that ensure security of communications networks and data, and also strategies to monitor and track the use of infosphere technologies by enemy groups and citizens, has taken on greater priority since 2001. The broad social goal of security enhancement has been supported by increased expenditures for these purposes, with these purposes and relationships being reflected in new media.

The ongoing involvement of states (as well as other institutions) in shaping technology in the infosphere suggests that the infosphere is neither a pure "global" phenomenon beyond the nation-state nor simply the sum total of state-based territorial development initiatives. Strategies pursuing national production or international trade are not so much selected from a slate of policy options as they are connected to existing ways of thought, practices, and institutions. If the infosphere is being constructed as "global," that construction is occurring through a series of private choices, institutional practices, and state actions undertaken with the intent of deploying technologies and pursuing trade and investment strategies for specific purposes (Schiller, 1999). Alexander Wendt (1999), for instance, presents a *Social Theory of International Politics* as an application of constructivism in international relations, drawing upon "structurationist and symbolic interactionist sociology" (p. 1). Technology choice in this instance reflects the goals of large corporations in profit maximization through cost reduction, product differentiation and marketing, and labor control, as well as governmental goals of monitoring, surveillance, security, and public administration and management. Fixity and flows are both part of information production and exchange in the information economy debates. Although some factors of production may be more footloose than in the past, the persistence of the fixity–mobility dialectic is indicative of a general continuity with the systems of production, trade, and investment characteristic of industrial society.

Technical Code

The technical code perspective focuses on how social, economic, and political values and assumptions are literally designed into the structure and functioning of technologies. Andrew Feenberg (1995) defines technical code as "those features of technologies that reflect hegemonic values and beliefs that prevail in the design process" (p. 4). Although these social, economic, and political values and assumptions are built into a technology, the members of a society—both designers and users—are not necessarily aware of this process because these values and assumptions "like culture itself ... appear self-evident." Thus, technologies reflect not only the choices of designers and developers, but also the broader social, economic, and political values of the historical setting in which they are designed. These assumptions shape the architecture of different technologies, but, after being incorporated, place parameters or constraints on what can be done with the technologies and the types of uses that are most readily available.

For instance, currently, the hierarchical switching and ownership structure of the existing telephone network compared to the more open and diffuse routing and ownership structure of the Internet are examples of different technical codes at work. In the case of the traditional telephone network in the United States, large corporations generally maintain control of the infrastructure in terms of its ownership, planning, access, and functionality. Customers pay to access the telephone network and its services, but their opportunities to create networks of their own or to modify existing telephone technology are more restricted compared to the opportunities currently offered by the Internet. In the case of rural telephone cooperatives in the United States, constructing networks first requires extensive political efforts and institutional changes. Still, the limitations inherent in the traditional telephone network illustrate the underlying social, political, and economic values of hierarchy and top-down corporate control. By contrast, in the case of the Internet, although large corporations own vital portions of the infrastructure (e.g., fiber optic cables, major data switching hubs), individuals are currently better able to create their own smaller computer networks (e.g., local area networks, wi-fi) that tap into the backbone.[1] Additionally, open source software allows individuals to customize operating systems and servers within their networks. The greater flexibility offered to businesses and customers alike with respect to the design and functioning of the Internet reflect broader social, political, and economic values related to freer access to information, greater participation by the citizenry, and free-market practices that ideally foster increased competition and choice.

Lawrence Lessig's *Code and Other Laws of Cyberspace* is perhaps the most widespread and popular articulation of this perspective (Lessig, 1999). Lessig argues that decisions made by designers are usurping what are often seen as political or policy decisions concerning network technologies. Among these choices are the selection of open source or proprietary software and technology standards, the openness or enclosure of networks, the features in software protecting the security of transactions, the use of surveillance of network activities and the extent of privacy protection, the protection of intellectual property, and the extent of national jurisdiction over networks. Designers may make their own decisions about the resolution of these questions and the values that should inform their choices, and may proceed with or without examining the assumptions they hold about these values. The result may be a crystallization of certain capabilities of functionalities within software, hardware, or networks.

Thus, the technical code perspective, like that of social shaping, stresses that technologies are not conceived of or designed in a vacuum. Various players—designers, business owners, politicians, lobbyists, and consumers—provide input into the design process, often vying to have their particular interests represented in the final product, which ultimately becomes some combination of the social, economic, and political expressions of these groups and individuals. Hence, recognition of these underlying values and assumptions helps us to understand better how these social, economic, and political perspectives shape the technologies with which we interact.

Farinola, Farinola, and Metzer (2000), who focus on the role of the United States in the Internet's development, consider the technical code of the network specifically, arguing that the values of openness and interactivity inherent in the society in which it was, in part, created are reflected in its design. They apply Feenberg's technical code to assess the hidden values and assumptions that are built into the Internet and the World Wide Web. The authors conclude, "The fact that the Internet was developed in a democratic country is reflected in its very design, which emphasizes such democratic ideals as freedom and equality" (p. 421).

Furthering this line of discussion, the ideals of freedom, openness, and equality with respect to the Internet appear in early conceptions of its design and use. One Internet pioneer, J.C.R. Licklider (1960), a prominent American scholar and scientist, initially envisaged the technology as an open network of computers designed to foster increased access to the data of geographically separated researchers in the United States. This early conception of the network[2] that later manifested itself in 1969 as the ARPANET experiment, is similar to the ocean space model in that it intended to create a friction-free channel or surface for data transit (Hafner and Lyon, 1996; Waldrop, 2001). Eventually, Licklider predicted, this network would diffuse to the general public whereby individuals would log onto "thinking centers" using "broadband, leased-lines" (Licklider, 1960, p. 7). Thus, the social, economic, and political ideals of free and equal access to information as well as self-regulation and market-driven control combine to form the Internet as many of us experience it today. Had the Internet been developed, for example, in China, whose government is less receptive to the aforementioned ideals, it is likely that these values and assumptions would not be present in the technology and its uses would not be the same. This point is illustrated in the Chinese government's recent insistence that search engines, such as Google, use content-filtering software if they are to have access to Chinese markets.

At this point in our discussion, it is important to acknowledge that the values and assumptions (e.g., free access to information, democracy, capitalism) reflected in the Internet's design and functioning are largely ideals rather than concrete realities. As Graham (1999) notes, the United States, despite its general claim, is not an absolute democracy in which every citizen has equal and direct input into the decisions and practices that govern the country. It is a representative democracy because the country's founders saw this particular political structure as necessary, due to its sheer size and concerns about the qualifications of leaders as well as the processes of leadership in a democracy. As with other political models, this institutional arrangement comes with its own set of challenges and limitations. Thus, in light of contemporary claims, although the Internet possesses the potential to increase citizen input, bringing it closer to a true democracy, it has yet to modify the current structure of the U.S. political system, which remains a representative model. Likewise, the potential of the Internet to foster increased access to information and communication resources, to "level the playing field," is another ideal based on the value of open access that has yet to be realized.

To date, the Internet's diffusion is not occurring evenly across segments of the United States or the world. The digital divide is a primary example of this failure, but it mimics (pre)existing divisions in technology access in the United States (and beyond) that are tied into economic conditions, which the Internet also has not changed. Nonetheless, the Internet was and continues to be premised on the ideal that it can function as an equalizing technology by offering higher levels of information and communication access to larger numbers of people than was previously possible. Hence, we witness an interesting tension being played out in a technology that is situated somewhere between the ideals of the society in which it is created and the reality of the day-to-day operations of that society, a tension that is played out most directly in debates over Internet governance, discussed in Chapter 6.

Further complicating matters, the Internet within a few short years has grown from a predominantly United States–based technology to a worldwide technology. Because the Internet is now largely a global phenomenon, its United States–inspired technical code creates a number of tensions in that not all countries, governments, and societies hold similar values and assumptions as those built into the technology by American designers. Issues of access, content control, and ownership become sites of contention on the international scene as governments struggle to impose their own sets of values and assumptions on how their businesses and citizenry should be allowed to interact on and with the Internet.

Summing up, the technical code perspective challenges us to pause and reflect on those underlying social, economic, and political values and assumptions that influence our everyday decisions and actions, especially in the design and development of technologies. In a world that is becoming increasingly globalized on many fronts, technical code implies that a myopic focus with respect to technology design and development may lead to unforeseen tensions when such technologies are used by other groups holding different values and assumptions, particularly with reference to the degree to which the Internet should be bound by national laws and serve as an instrument for national development.

Diffusion of Innovations

In general, diffusion of innovations examines "the process by which an innovation is communicated through certain channels over time among the members of a social system" (Rogers, 2003, p. 5). Although the term innovation may evoke images of specific technologies such as computers and electron microscopes, the term covers a much broader range. An innovation is defined as "an idea, practice, or object that is *perceived* as new by an individual or other unit of adoption" (p. 12, emphasis added).

In its most basic form, diffusion of innovations attempts to explain how and when individuals and groups decide whether to incorporate, or adopt, an innovation (in the context of this chapter, examples include cell phones, web services, operating systems, databases, portable digital devices, etc.) into their daily practices. Factors considered in the process of innovation adoption include the characteristics of the innovation, of the potential adopter (individual or group), and of the communication or social network(s) to which the individual or group belongs. Importantly, diffusion of innovations recognizes that not all innovations successfully diffuse (e.g., the metric system in the United States) and that those that are adopted are not done so uniformly; rather, the diffusion of an innovation is frequently uneven with the affluent segments of a society more likely to adopt before those who are less affluent, especially when monetary cost is a factor. A case in point is the digital divide, which highlights the inequality between those who have reliable and up-to-date access to digital technologies as well as the skills to use them in comparison to those who do not. In June 2005 there were 42.9 million high speed Internet connections to homes and businesses in the United States (Federal Communications Commission [FCC], 2006). Internet connections per 100 inhabitants were highest in Iceland in 2005 (26.7/100 inhabitants), South Korea (25.4/100 inhabitants), and the Netherlands (25.3/100 inhabitants), with the United States ranking 14th among advanced economies at 16.8 per 100 inhabitants (Organization for Economic Cooperation and Development [OECD], 2006). These numbers are in contrast to the total number of Internet hosts in other parts of the world, as reported by the International Telecommunication Union (ITU). In 2004, the number of Internet host computers (those with an Internet protocol [IP] address) stood at 1.74 per 100 inhabitants in Africa, 34.49 in the Americas (76.22 in the United States, and 69.82 in Canada), 6.35 in Asia, 28.48 in Europe (68.47 in the Netherlands), and 50.72 in Oceania (with Australia at 68.90) (ITU, 2006a).

High-end technologies, such as computers and other related devices, are frequently maximally priced upon their early release, in part because of initially high research, development, and production costs coupled with low initial demand. As more people adopt these technologies and information about the innovation is circulated through the various formal (e.g., media) and informal (e.g., opinion leaders) communication channels, economies of scale emerge, and prices drop, which allows more people to afford the purchase.

In market-driven economies, upon initial public release businesses are often the first recipients of new technologies and individual customers are the last; likewise, urban areas are more likely to receive new technology services before rural areas, as noted in our discussion of Appalachia in Chapter 1. Broadband deployment is one example. The new entrants into markets to provide advanced telecommunications services in the United States in the late 1990s (the so-called competitive access providers) focused mainly on offering services to large organizations with high revenue potential, and in denser urban areas. Even by 2005, many urban areas in the United States had seven or more providers of high speed services, whereas most rural areas had between one and three providers (FCC, 2006b, p. 23). Although this segment has focused on market-based economies, it can be argued that similar dynamics of a general nature occur in developing countries and in nations using alternative forms of government where some combination of the more socially, politically, and economically affluent are typically the first to gain access to new technologies than are those who are less affluent.

Thus far we have focused on adoption decisions made by individuals; however, diffusion also occurs at the organizational level, with slightly different dynamics. At the group level, the decision to adopt an innovation typically occurs in one of three ways: (1) optional decision, (2) collective decision, and (3) authority decision. Optional decisions allow the individual to decide whether to adopt independently of the group. Collective decisions are based on group consensus about whether to adopt. Authority decisions occur when relatively few members of the group who possess power, status, or technical expertise make the adoption decision for all members.

Underlying these group level decisions is the degree of "innovativeness" of the organization itself. An organization that embraces change is more likely to adopt new technologies than is an organization that resists change. Given the rapid pace of obsolescence in the computing industry, the ability of an organization to effectively serve its customers and the very survival of the organization itself may hinge not only on the type of group adoption decision outlined above but also, and perhaps more importantly, on the willingness of its members and customers to adapt to change in general.

In the early years following the Internet's public release, one example of an adaptable and innovative organization was the University Libraries' Inter-Library Services (ILS) Department at Virginia Polytechnic and State University (Virginia Tech). Foreseeing the potential of the Internet as a means to streamline internal work processes and to simultaneously improve patron services, the Virginia Tech ILS Department designed and implemented ILLiad, Inter-Library Loan Internet Access Database, an employee and customer web-based interface used to request materials from other libraries. The system was officially launched in March 1997 (Kriz, 2006).

Regarding the characteristics of the innovation, ILLiad had a relative advantage over the paper-based system in that it was more convenient; requests could be made from any networked computer and did not require a patron to visit the library. The system also allowed patrons to edit, cancel, and track the progress of their requests, thus reducing the volume of status request calls to the ILS Department. The system was compatible with the paper-based system in that it included information fields on the online form that were similar to those on the paper form; the main difference was that the form was filled out electronically instead of on paper. Additionally, the library had automated its card catalog in the late 1970s, and a simple web-based ILS form had existed online for two years prior to ILLiad's release, so patrons were already witnessing a shift to electronic formats in the library setting. Complexity was, perhaps, an initial limiting factor of the system because it required patrons to create a username and a password and to set up a user profile. For patrons new to the computer and online environments, this may have been a slightly intimidating prospect. ILLiad did not go through a formal trial period with library patrons; however, during its development, patrons were consulted for input and ILS staff members were involved in the design phase of the system prior to its public release (Kriz, Glover, and Ford, 1998). Lastly, with respect to observable results, customers experienced reduced request submission times, increased feedback on the status of requests, and faster receipt of materials. ILS staff experienced faster processing of requests, fewer requests to correct data entry errors, and the elimination of paper files.

Within the library, the decision to replace paper-based requests with an online interface was an authority-based decision—that is, library administration supported and mandated the shift to an online interface based on information it received from ILS staff about the new system's merits (e.g., faster processing of orders, ability of patrons to customize and track orders online, reduced paper waste). Importantly, although ILS employees were required to adapt to the new system, library patrons were given optional decision power.

Patrons who were reluctant or who simply refused to use the web interface had the option to continue using the paper-based request system, at least initially; however, this option was not widely publicized because ILS wanted to go completely paperless. Although these individuals were few in number compared with those who readily adopted the online request system, from the patron perspective, the overall effect was positive in that the transition to the new system did provide accommodations for the different patron adopter types, namely the "late majority" and the "laggards." From the employee perspective, the authority decision made by the library was less accommodating for those individuals who were slower to adapt to the technology change. The end result was that a small segment of employees was marginalized in the transition and shifted to other less technically skilled tasks. Thus, in this particular case, we see how the decisions made by an organization affect different groups in different ways with respect to an innovation's adoption success. Refinements to the request system coupled with the widespread adoption of the Internet within the United States and marketing efforts have fostered the diffusion of the request system to other libraries. As of 2006, ILLiad is in use in more than 600 libraries, handling about 42 percent of electronic requests (Kriz, 2006).

Broadening our view of the diffusion of innovations perspective, we see that the U.S. government also functioned as an adaptable and innovative organization with respect to the Internet's release to the American public in the early 1990s. In 1991, the National Science Foundation removed commercial restrictions previously imposed on the Internet, and in 1993 the Clinton Administration, foreseeing the network's potential as an information and communication resource, promoted the creation of an Information Superhighway (Hafner and Lyon, 1996; Pavlik, 1998). This is an example of an optional decision occurring on a grand scale; citizens and businesses alike had the choice to adopt at the time of the Internet's commercial release. Although large governments are typically characterized as being "behind the times," this is one instance in which government played a pivotal role in widely and rapidly diffusing a technology, a development that illustrates potential links between the diffusion and shaping perspectives on technology.

Although it may appear from this summary that the diffusion process is dichotomous—an innovation is either adopted or rejected—the process can be more complex. Adoption of new technologies may contribute to the construction of space and mobility, which can then have wide-ranging social implications. Organizational roles may come under pressure in broader contextual shifts that are associated with the adoption of new technologies. For instance, just-in-time production and virtual organizations refer to processes that reconfigure the relationships of time, space, and place. Technology that may be designed to serve business processes (e.g., word processing, group decision support systems, spreadsheets, e-mail, order processing) may be the vehicles through which more fundamental transformations of organizations take place.

In addition, a practice known as reinvention may take place in the implementation stage. Reinvention occurs when adopters modify the innovation in a way that changes its original intent in actual design, function, and meaning or some combination. This process is closely linked to the social construction of technology perspective, which will be addressed in the following section. For now, it is sufficient to recognize that, although governments, corporations, designers, and developers have certain goals in mind about a technology's role and function, the members of society who come into contact with that technology potentially have the power to alter its role and function based on how they use and make sense of the technology in their daily lives.

Social Construction of Technology

The social construction of technology perspective explains that technology is used and understood differently by individuals and groups in different cultural and social settings. These cultural and social contexts, and the understandings and interpretations associated with technologies in these different contexts, ultimately define both how people use new technologies and how they interpret and understand that use (Fischer, 1992). Thus, the wireless telephone, the Internet, and so on, may be used in distinct ways and mean different things in different social contexts.

For example, the rise of e-mail as the most widely used Internet application is in part a story of social construction. An early version of e-mail was developed by Ray Tomlinson of Bolt, Beranek, and Newman (BBN) in 1972, and BBN was the company that built the ARPANET in the late 1960s (Hafner and Lyon, 1996). Although it was not a part of the network's original mission, Tomlinson reasoned that researchers might wish to exchange text messages with one another over the network.

He modified and spliced together two separate software programs to create an early version of e-mail whereby messages were sent over the network and dropped into a file on another computer, today what we call the "inbox." Tomlinson is most noted for his decision to use the @ sign in e-mail addresses; he reasoned that messages were sent to people *at* certain locations, and the @ sign is now a part of U.S. popular culture. Although email was almost an afterthought, it was this application that users embraced, defined, and redefined in their own ways.

Tomlinson's e-mail program is a form of reinvention mentioned previously in the diffusion of innovations discussion. That is, he took an existing technology and modified its use by creating an application that was not part of the network's original plan. His invention was based on a perceived need that tied into his understanding of how others, including himself, might better or alternatively use the network. Interestingly, Tomlinson's role as a software engineer also ties into the technical code perspective in that he functioned as a designer to build the e-mail application that would (unknowingly) become one of the most widely used features of the network based on values and assumptions he held about the importance of open communication. Likewise, his introduction of the @ sign integrated into the Internet code a perspective that the Internet, while a boundary-free arena of communications, was also a space of distinct locations. Notwithstanding these encoded properties, however, the Internet, as a communication channel, may have different meanings and uses within and across cultures. It is at this point that users contribute to the Internet's social construction, as, for instance, when users construct the Internet as a place of community that cuts across geographic and cultural boundaries.

Sherry Turkle's (1995) early work revealed how various online subcultures formed by using the network as their place of interaction. In these online communities, individuals explored a range of experiences including anonymity in text and avatar-based environments, gender-switching, and the therapeutic benefits of role-playing. Gaming environments were constructed to satisfy entertainment needs, with the original MUDs (multi-user dungeons) paying tribute to the real-time Dungeons and Dragons role-play game of the offline era. Recently, social networking sites, such as Facebook, Friendster, and MySpace, have become popular by allowing millions of individuals to create and share their personal profiles with others around the globe. The creation of these sites has given rise to a new term, "publizen," which is used to describe "the very public citizen" who does online "everything for all the world to see" (Weeks, 2006, p. D01). None of the above-mentioned applications were intended or foreseen in the original design of the Internet; rather, they evolved after the network diffused to the larger public, in part, because of the ideal of openness (technical code) upon which the design was based.

Grassroots political organizations, such as MoveOn.org (2006), currently with more than 3.3 million members, may also be considered to be examples of social construction in that these groups have modified the use of the Internet to coordinate and promote political activism in the United States. These uses of the Internet have perhaps been even more significant in other countries, such as South Korea. Still other individuals use the Internet to justify additional avenues of inquiry, such as Paul Levinson (2003), who uses the Internet as a springboard in arguing for the need to increase space exploration. In later chapters of this book, we explore other examples of infosphere users constructing spaces, including the spaces of tourism (Chapter 4) and web surfing (Chapter 5).

Managing Technology Change and the Four Tensions

In this discussion, we have considered briefly four dominant perspectives—social shaping of technology, technical code, diffusion of innovations, and social construction of technology—that examine the ways in which technology change occurs and is managed. Many technology studies focus on one of the perspectives of technology change, and the relevant factors, processes, and dynamics of a relatively narrow scope of activities. However, in recognizing the importance of each of these views, we argue that bringing together a consideration of governance, technology, and culture will contribute to a fuller understanding of how technology change is governed, as well as ways in which groups, individuals, and governments can act to shape this change.

The role of individuals and groups in decisions about technology change has primarily been seen as that of adopters of technologies, who in consumer markets make the final decisions about whether a technology will be purchased. Beyond consumption choices, individuals and groups incorporate communication technologies into their lives and daily practices. They are developing their own meanings and cultural practices associated with new technologies, leading some to argue that we should look at cultural practices and understandings prior to looking at new technologies. Because the choices we make at this level are consumption choices that may seem to be of little importance, and since the cultural practices are contingent on and unique to specific times and places and seem to be given rather than made, these choices are not often seen as technology choices.

Governance impinges upon individuals and groups of users in trying to redirect and prohibit some of the patterns of use that have emerged in the infosphere. Many of the communication regulatory decisions in the period of monopoly regulation focused upon limiting the market power of monopoly companies in order to protect the public and the public interest. As more firms were allowed to enter telecommunications markets, the focus of communication governance in the 1980s and 1990s moved toward finding ways to make competition fair for new entrants and incumbent companies. Competition would serve the public interest. With the deployment of new technologies by software, equipment, and service firms, many smaller organizations have gained access to new tools. These advances were initially celebrated in the 1990s as allowing viewers to become creators, readers to become authors, listeners to become producers. As concerns arose about copyright infringements, child pornography, spam, and computer hacking and viruses, the focus of communications governance has shifted toward controlling the behavior of individuals and groups in the infosphere. This has extended to efforts to shut down service companies providing file-sharing software and to civil lawsuits against users to make an example of them and to dissuade others.

The responses to and debates about the management of new technology uses are evidence that, as David Edge (1995) argues, the different types of decisions about technology are constantly interacting. The infosphere was once seen as a space where there was little need for governance of behavior; it was a space of freedom, a virtual world almost divorced from the real world and its problems and woes. Stakeholders and communities would emerge spontaneously, and would balance short-term and long-term interests in solving problems and in setting up conflict management institutions. Additionally, apart from the lack of need to regulate infosphere behavior, it was held to be impossible to regulate the infosphere. The dispersed nature of the technologies (with millions of increasingly powerful personal computers supposedly able to act as copiers, or Internet servers) and the dispersed and redundant network structure and network access points meant that regulation was not possible. The Internet's immunity to regulation was believed to be compounded by its international scope, beyond the reach of national laws.

Nevertheless, there have been tremendous efforts made by companies and governments to introduce more effective ways of regulating Internet behavior. As has been noted, these efforts have been oriented both toward constructing the Internet as a space of movement (which itself requires degrees of regulation) and toward constructing it as a space of boundaries and territories and as a resource for economic development. The contradictory goals of states, corporations, and users for the Internet can be seen in attempts to manage the four tensions illustrated in Table 1.1.

Turning to the first of these tensions, we see that the management of technology change reflects the tension between production and trade. Knowledge and intellectual property, especially that connected to infosphere technologies whether in symbols, images, media content, or production processes and technology, are often seen as core factors of national production and improvement in productivity. At the same time, the movement of information and communication technologies and their exploitation and deployment by public agencies and private firms is a central component of national commerce and international trade. However, as discussed earlier in the chapter, states have a clear choice, whether to pursue the statism- and production-oriented types of policies (such as control over access to technologies), or to promote national corporate champion firms based upon technological advantage. Alternatively, states are under pressure from transnational firms to allow the free flow of knowledge, technology, and information among units connected in transnational production and to allow open exchange and trade in intellectual property rights and technologies through sale or licensing to other firms on a global basis.

The ongoing interplay between fixity and mobility is also evident in the governance of technology change. The institutional arrangements that facilitate the development of new technologies, the contract laws that ensure open and predictable transactions among research firms, the property rights for the different technologies that may be incorporated into specific products or services, and the movement of capital into the high technology sector, together create spaces in which ideas and information can be exchanged. Similarly, continuous investments in infosphere network infrastructure create forms of fixed property that allow for the enhanced mobility of information and commerce.

The territory versus nonterritory tensions are perhaps most evident in choices made to control technology flows and movement into and out of a country. In some cases the United States has denied strategic technologies to specific countries, while also trying to retain the overall openness of technology flows, capital that has served as one element of the basis for U.S. economic growth and preeminence. In some cases, such as the support for SEMATECH, national strategic goals and those of members of a specific economic sector come together. In other cases, such as the devolution of Internet governance tasks by the United States to a private corporation, ICANN (see Chapter 6), the U.S. government has limited or suspended some state authority in order to encourage the rapid diffusion of new technology.

In efforts to balance the support for technology development, control, and use, tensions are being worked out as political processes where economic policies, foreign policies, and national security policies intersect. In the last decade, the United States has seen a massive swing from a general emphasis on openness as a strategy to encourage technology development toward the emphasis on network security as a political goal. Although economic benefits may accrue to companies that sell high-technology products, offer services based upon the use of their networks, and license their technologies to others, governments may opt to limit technology exports or allow monopoly control by a national company to best serve the national interest.

In this chapter, we have examined different theoretical approaches to technology change in order to enhance the consideration of the spatial construction and governance of the infosphere as a space of mobility. Each approach emphasizes a different dimension of management, as laid out in Table 1.2: governance, technology, and culture. The management of technology change includes efforts in a variety of contexts and in different levels of organization. Questions of governance arise hand in hand with questions of cultural practice and meaning. Hence, we argue that any account of technological change must include reference to multiple perspectives that address governance and culture as well as technical decisions. As change occurs over time, any account of technology management must also deal with historical differences from place to place and in different periods. Like other technology systems, infosphere technologies and Internet backbone and applications have been developed over time, and hence any single mode of explanation is unlikely to account for the numerous changes over 40-plus years.

Similar to the Internet that it encompasses, we see that the infosphere integrates a variety of technologies and networks that interconnect, and we also recognize that the infosphere is not owned by one group; rather, it is composed of a set of technical protocols and standards that allow for the interconnection of many networks, devices, and applications that are owned and managed by many groups ranging in scale from individuals to national governments. Hence, identifying a single technical code for the infosphere becomes difficult because it is not a single entity, and its ownership does not reside with a single or easily identifiable authority. With efforts to control Internet usage more closely, technical code also becomes a matter for ongoing debate. The core software and telecommunication standards that set the basis for technological interaction are sometimes proprietary and sometimes open source or nonproprietary. Whether undertaken formally through governments, intergovernmental organizations, or industry working groups or in a *de facto* fashion through firms seeking and obtaining market dominance, technical standard setting is a high stakes political and economic struggle affecting both revenue potential and the path of subsequent development and change. The Internet is not controlled by one government or firm, so the question of social shaping becomes more complex. All of these considerations point to both the need to try to understand the processes of managing technology change and the need to draw upon a variety of historical and empirical perspectives in exploring the management of technological change and the construction of new spaces of mobility.

3 Scales of Governance, Governance of Scales

I n shaping the spaces of mobility, governance, technology, and culture come together in a variety of ways in planning for infrastructure investment and services at the local level of city and municipal governance. For citizens, offline activities in daily life are increasingly tied to those making use of infosphere technologies and networks. Access to these networks is shaped by public and private infrastructures and investments, and this access can be mapped in geographic space. Some of the governance decisions structuring the access to and use of infosphere technologies take place in a local geographic scale and in local settings, but these decisions occur in the context of national policies that also shape the linkages to and participation in wider national and transnational economic, technical, and cultural networks. This chapter explores some of the debates that have arisen as cities and local governments in the United States try to work through questions of advancing the prosperity and quality of life of their communities by guiding investment in and deployment of digital services and networks, networks that facilitate connections both locally and globally.

The relationship between economic, cultural, technical, and policy developments of different geographic scopes has puzzled numerous social science researchers and theorists. This was so especially during the 1970s and 1990s, periods that were typified by a process of globalization in a number of market, investment, political, and social institutions. The exact character of globalization, however, is a matter of some debate. Interpretations range from globalization as the standardization of all experience, resulting from an invincible process, to a new configuration of local and world production networks called "glocalization."

Undertaking research on these questions is complicated in several ways that are related to different scales of space and time. First, although globalization sometimes is used to refer to processes by which common elements are manifest in different parts of the world, the conflicts, relationships, and institutions supporting global patterns of flows of information and exchange are evidenced at a variety of local and regional sites and in relationships that are not abstract, general, or broad. Second, whereas the goals of some actors to build more global markets, property rights, and cultural practices may result in fundamental structural change over time, this process is actually an aggregate of more short-term conflicts and specific place-based steps that both reflect and reinforce longer-term processes.

Although much attention focuses on worldwide processes, many scholars have focused on cities and regions that are reconfigured to be part of new patterns of trade, production, and finance. The use of infosphere technologies and applications for electronic commerce, for instance, has been seen either to provide access to some services normally not available outside of urban regions or to enhance the advantages of cities (Kotval, 1999; Pons-Novell and Viladecans-Marsal, 2006). Others have speculated about the end of cities (Winger, 1997). The conflicts over processes associated with globalization and the introduction of new technologies, as well as the impacts of economic changes, are felt not only in the changing composition of national economic sectors, but in wrenching shifts and transformations at the local level. Although the conflicts between local and national governance have existed for some time, they can be understood in the context of more fundamental and structural changes in global political economy: the shifting spatial organization of production and consumption at a global and local level (Cox, 1987; Drache and Gertler, 1991; Harvey, 1989; Mosco, 1996), and the role of cities and regions in the global economy (Brunn and Leinbach, 1991; Graham and Marvin, 1996; Hershberg, 1996; Wallis, 1996). The regionalization and localization of production has and is occurring alongside global coordination (Civille and Gygi, 1995;

Estabrooks and Lamarche, 1987). This transition has been labeled post-Fordist production, flexible accumulation, or just-in-time production (Amin, 1994; Jones, 1997).

In this economic environment, typified by increasingly mobile global capital, it is argued that enhancing place-based characteristics of infrastructure, education, and lifestyle are the few remaining goals that government may realistically undertake. However, national or state governments may not be the best positioned to advance these objectives, given the supposed aversion in the United States to industrial policy at the national level, despite the focus on creating effective national information infrastructure policies (Drake, 1995; Kahin and Wilson, 1996). Cities or regional governments may have a more appropriate role in providing communications, transportation and other physical infrastructures, and educational, research, and technology institutions (Amirahmadi and Wallace, 1995; Celeste, 1996; Coburn, Berglund, and Usher, 1996; McClelland, 1998), and a lifestyle to attract a trained and capable workforce that will attract and retain mobile global capital (see Fox, 1996; Saxenian, 2006). Cities and local governments have noted these developments in their planning (Barnes and Ledebur, 1994), and have promoted the use of telecommunication infrastructure as a locational advantage (Hepworth, 1990; Kasarda and Rondinelli, 1998; Kellerman, 1993; Peck, 1996) and the use of advanced telecommunications to enhance educational programs.

Although this type of analysis assumes a rather instrumental use of public institutions and the population to enhance productivity and economic growth, there are also good reasons for enhancing the role of cities, drawing more from democratic and critical analysis (Doheny-Farina and Herwick, 1997; Morley and Robins, 1995; Van Tassel, 1996). As global capital becomes more mobile and standardized in what Manuel Castells (1996) calls the "space of flows," the unique and immobile attributes of historical places may become more important for identities and culture. Similarly, if national governance institutions are becoming more attuned to the requirements of global trade and investment, local governance is seen by some as the site where democratic deliberation and the public sphere can be reinvigorated (Bird, Curtis, Putnam, and Robertson, 1993).

For instance, returning to two of the examples with which we began this book, Hong Kong is in a sense the paradigmatic "world city," a term that vividly illustrates the relationships and tensions in the construction of global patterns from local elements. Hong Kong's ascendancy in many ways has been facilitated by the growth of global communications technologies that support commerce, finance, transportation, and the mobility of labor, but the continual advancement of these technologies jeopardizes existing patterns of trade and investment and perpetually threatens the city's position as a global nexus. Likewise, at the other end of the urban spectrum, Mountain City briefly industrialized as a manufacturing venue in the 1960s thanks to improved transportation and communication technologies, but further improvement in those same technologies has now reduced its attractiveness relative to overseas locations, and Mountain City is now looking for opportunities to further connectivity as a basis for a new round of economic development.

In other words, an investigation of municipalities' telecommunications policies and growth strategies reveals another facet of the ongoing tensions between fixity and mobility. This chapter focuses upon regulatory and policy changes related to the introduction of new communication technologies at the local level of government in the United States, covering the decade after the enactment of the Telecommunications Act of 1996. Important elements of these changes have been played out at the local level, and in conflicts with local governments. These conflicts illustrate some of the tensions in constructing the infosphere as a *space of mobility*. As well, the conflicts among federal, state, and local governments across the country illustrate quite starkly the interactions among governance, technology, and culture.[1]

Cities and Communication Networks

Although local communities are often seen as sites of production, their economic and social development depends upon integration with other national and international economies through transportation and communication networks. These two complementary aspects of the city—as developable planes but also points that exist within paths of movement—illustrate the dynamic tensions between fixity and mobility and between territory and nonterritory that are prominent features throughout this book.

Transportation and communication networks that intersect the city facilitate flows of capital, goods and services, and technology, as well as the exercise of management decisions. Local government officials must often try to promote the locational advantages of their cities or regions in the *production* process, but must also facilitate low cost *trade and commerce* to support economic growth. These are long-standing types of efforts, present along with strategies of cities and the early introduction of electronic communication networks (Abler, Adams, and Borchert, 1976; Pred, 1973, 1980). These might include characteristics such as the quality of physical infrastructure and utilities (airports, roads, water, electricity, broadband telecom), governmental programs (tax incentives, zoning, planning and other permitting procedures), public institutions and services (schools, libraries, hospitals), workforce attributes (cost, skills, education), and cultural amenities (museums, sports teams, parks and recreation, live performances). Attracting production activities to certain locations is related to management's ability to lower the costs of some factors of production, to find other production resources (such as specialized and high-skilled workers and managers), and to facilitate the rapid exchange of goods and services.

Local governments might attempt to leverage certain characteristics to attract and retain private investment in a world of highly mobile capital. The *fixity* of local capital investments in an era of distributed and coordinated production is in constant tension with the *mobility* of capital, goods, and services. These mobilities include the constant flows that integrate regions and economies. Encouraging the growth of clusters of specific types of economic activity may be part of an economic development strategy. For instance, enhanced infrastructure might allow for people to move rapidly to and from a region, or office parks or special economic zones might allow for interaction among firms in a specific sector. Deploying broadband services would also enhance the environment for businesses. In the late 1990s, for instance, many states and regions tried to emulate the success of Silicon Valley; the Route 128 loop around Boston, Massachusetts; and Austin, Texas (Saxenian, 1994). In Florida, the terms "Silicon Coast" (Fort Lauderdale) and the "I-4 Corridor" (Orlando to Cape Canaveral) were popularized. Broadband deployment was also a popular policy for cities in Europe (van Winden and Woets, 2004). Connections to public institutions, such as hospitals and universities, may also be part of an intensive local economic development strategy.

The *territory versus nonterritory* tension may also be seen in the choices facing local governments. In the U.S. federal system, states have a constitutional role and certain powers. Cities and local governments are the creation of states, and they have no formal role in national sovereignty or absolute control over territory. Although citizens may vote in local, state, or national elections, and the town hall meeting is celebrated as the archetypically and unique form of American politics, at the same time, the government closest to home has no fundamental legal role or protection. This lack of formal power has also been constrained by political tradition and practices that limit the role of local government to providing services, allowing for land development, and not competing with the private sector. Despite this lack of formal power, and the use of policies and programs to attract rather than control capital, local government is often the partner in national programs that deliver essential services to communities. These governments and communities work within the context of national and state law to achieve comparative locational advantages.

In some cities, local governments have some conditional jurisdiction, in that their powers may be altered by state legislatures if they so desire. Even in these areas, such as the ability to impose property taxes and sales taxes, to require land use consistent with zoning laws and development planning, and to issue building permits and allow for the use of rights of way on streets and roads, local governments may choose not to exercise these authorities in order to attract capital. Or, special economic development zones may be created to attract investment, and in these zones more focused tax incentives or other suspensions of local governance requirements may be available.

The interplay among governance, technology, and culture comes into the foreground with the kinds of issues with which local governments must deal. As the examples discussed in this chapter will show, even the limited governance authority that these governments have are hotly debated in efforts to introduce new communication technologies and services, because in many ways these governments control the routes of access for communication networks at the local level (Bertot, 2006; Borins, 1998; Clift, 2004). At the same time, it is to local government that individuals and communities turn to resolve and address important questions related to housing, education, emergency services, parks and recreation, policing, and healthcare. The demands for governance and service provision are often incommensurate with the formal authorities granted to local governments.

The tension between *politics* and *economics* is also evident at the local level. Local governance has most often been seen as a place in which economic and cultural considerations should take precedence over the enhancement of political power (which is the role of national governments). When local power is mentioned in the history of the United States, it is often in response to centralized and corrupt control of political party machines in large cities (New York, Chicago, St. Louis). Local abuses of power in planning, policing, or procurement have also been part of U.S. history. For economists, local power and control has often led to market distortions, and, beginning with the Constitution and the Interstate Commerce Commission 100 years later, the thrust of much economic policy in the United States has been to break down local practices that might distort economies and create a more friction-free internal national market (Horwitz, 1989). Notwithstanding the attempts to free local economies from the distortions of politics, the quality of local governance—such as efficiency, transparency, and accountability—are important components of cultural life and of economic growth and prosperity. Local governmental initiatives have played a key role in developing cities, both as places of investment and as nodes within circuits of flows.

Richard Briffault (1990a, 1990b, 2000) examines both the political and legal claims about localism in the United States, as well as the complexities and variations of the actual practice of localism. He argues that cities must also be seen in the context and as a part of economic regions.

Contemporary normative advocacy of localism proceeds from two different models, one linking local autonomy with the greater opportunities for popular participation in public life said to exist in smaller units of government, the other claiming that decentralization of power, by enabling large numbers of government units in the same region to make decisions concerning spending, taxing and regulation, increases efficiency in the provision of public sector goods and services. Although these associations of local autonomy with participation and efficiency are persuasive in theory, both models ignore central attributes of existing localities, the effects of local actions on people outside local boundaries or on a region as a whole, and the implications of significant interpersonal and interlocal wealth inequalities for the distribution of power between higher and lower units of governments. Today, most local governments do not govern discrete communities as the models of localism presuppose. Rather, most local governments are fragments of larger, economically interdependent regions (Briffault, 1990a, p. 5).

Local governments and the deployment of communication networks may work to construct spaces of mobility in several ways (Sheller and Urry, 2006a). Social network theorists argue that the strength and quality of networks, whether local or remote, give us a way to conceptualize cultural connections and the emergence of similarities and differences over time (Johnson, Oliveira, and Barnett, 1989). Along with linking to national and world production and trade, or extending to other regions, local governments may work to construct spaces of mobility at the local level (Britton, Halfpenny, Devine, and Mellor, 2004). These are the places in which people live, work, and share cultural experiences, practices, and meanings. Planning for development that links the promotion of transportation and communication infrastructures to allow for movement and exchange within communities is a more intensive use of infosphere technologies. Communication networks can be used to enrich and strengthen local linkages, enliven community life at the neighborhood and local level, build cultural expression and practices, and create spaces of mobility that are hybrids of the infosphere and the physical geography of place (de Sousa e Silva, 2006), similar to a local newspaper reporting on cultural activities in its region. Crossing social barriers to build local communities and economies, rather than crossing the barriers of distance, is emphasized in this vision.

At the same time, much of the excitement about the possibilities of infosphere technologies has focused upon what new media offer to bring people together in new ways. Some "cyber-society" reflections (Jones, 1995, 1998) consider how connections might be made among people in different geographic locations who share specific interests or questions over identity. This phenomenon is evident in the meteoric growth of social networking programs such as MySpace and Facebook. Community activists, however, typically focus on how these technologies can be used to build social and economic linkages among people sharing local geographic space. Some of the earliest online communities, such as the Whole Earth 'Lectronic Link (WELL) or the Public Electronic Network (PEN) in Santa Monica (Kling, 1996), represented new ways of connecting people at the local level, as did the "Freenet" project. These efforts continue with community networking organizations' and programs' efforts to enhance access, such as in Montreal, Canada (Powell and Shade, 2006) and in Austin, Texas, in the United States (Fuentes-Bautista and Inagaki, 2006).

Similarly, research on economic development has emphasized the importance of decisions that firms make about the location of production facilities. Just as city and regional planners promote facilities such as airports, sports teams and leisure activities, good schools, and cultural institutions in order to make their city or county attractive to corporate managers, in the late 1990s and early twenty-first century, some of the biggest challenges for economic development have been related to planning and building advanced telecommunications networks, and making these available as quickly as possible to all local residents. In all these instances, an expanded range of responsibility and leadership is called for from local government leaders to promote economic and social development.

In the following sections of this chapter, we look at telecommunications policy issues being confronted by municipalities (cities and counties) in the United States in light of these broader questions about globalization and infosphere technologies. We discuss specific policy issues confronted at the municipal level of government following the passage and implementation of the Telecommunications Act of 1996, an Act that aimed to introduce new services and competition in existing local services. These issues often entail reworked or conflicting relationships between cities and state and federal governments, and with firms providing telecommunications services. The conflicts also have aspects that are more of a long-term and fundamental nature, especially regarding questions about the nature of the duties and property rights of local public bodies.

Although conflicts between different levels of government are longstanding in the United States, these cases are especially important in light of the 1996 Telecommunications Act's goals of promoting competition in local telephone services, encouraging new entrants into telecommunication markets, and stimulating the rapid deployment of new technologies. Additionally, these issues arise in the context of broader shifts in scope and form of telecommunications governance at the national and international level. These conflicts also reflect and have implications for the shifting role of cities in the spatial reorganization of production and culture on a global basis. It is the local level at which access is gained to the networks and services making up the infosphere, and access occurs through physically and geographically distributed networks. It is also at the local level that many infrastructural decisions are made that may distribute access to services among residents of different neighborhoods, with some groups served first in the roll-out of new networks, and some groups served later or not at all. The economic growth and viability of cities and towns, furthermore, are part of larger processes of social and economic change that are part of the construction of mobility in the infosphere.

Selected Cases and Issues in Contention

In February 1996 a reworking of the U.S. Communications Act of 1934 was signed into law as the Telecommunications Act of 1996 (United States, 1996a). The stated goals of this legislation were to introduce competition in all parts of the communications industry and to allow for the more rapid introduction of new technologies and services, while at the same time preserving and enhancing the ability of all U.S. citizens to gain access to existing and new technologies. The Act promised to promote competition among existing industry players and easier entry for service providers using new technologies. Three changes were of special importance for the telecommunications industry, for local governments, and for the provision of services to the public: (1) the Act's attempt to promote competition in the provision of local telecommunications services; (2) changes in the amounts that long distance carriers would pay to connect with local carriers to complete calls (access charges); and (3) reorganization of the institutions and mechanisms that promote universal access to telecommunications services. Decisions and initiatives on each of these questions are interlinked in that those made in one area will shape the resolution of the other issues.

As has been true of federal government efforts in the past in the United States to introduce, widen, or enhance market exchanges, these actions had significant implications for state and local governments, and were met with concern and resistance (Horwitz, 1989; Teske, 1995). Particularly, some of the governing roles, decisions, and rules of city and county governments were presented by industry groups, even during the formation of the Act, as posing impediments to the promotion of competition in telecommunications. The introduction of new services would, in the context of the 1996 Act, disturb the formal institution and informal patterns of relationships among different levels of telecommunications governance. Overlapping rules regulate communications service providers at national, state, and local levels. For instance, the use of rights-of-way along streets is treated differently for cable companies and telephone companies, with cable companies receiving municipal rather than state franchises. Municipalities set zoning laws, but their range of action has been constrained by the federal Act of 1996. The licensing of the radiomagnetic spectrum remains under sole federal jurisdiction. Taxation of seemingly similar communications services differs among various services and between municipalities. A small selection of reported cases is listed below to demonstrate the extent to which the conflict between telecommunications companies and municipalities has occurred on a number of fronts (Table 3.1).

One case in Huntington Park, California, arose as a result of a local ordinance that was designed to reduce illegal activities such as drug sales and calling card fraud. The ordinance sought to make pay telephone usage more difficult, and prohibited pay telephones on private property unless they were located completely within an enclosed building and were at least ten feet from any public door. The California Pay Telephone Association filed a petition on December 23, 1996 calling for the Federal Communications Commission (FCC) to pre-empt the local ordinance on the grounds that it restricted competition between different services. The FCC considered the petition, and in a decision released July 17, 1997, declined to intervene in the case. It concluded that the record did not provide sufficient evidence that the Communications Act had been violated (FCC, 1997b).

The case of TCI Cablevision and Troy, Michigan has also attracted much national attention. TCI had initially sought relief from an order from the city, pre-emption of a local decision by the FCC and a declaratory ruling by the FCC that the city of Troy had exceeded its local government authority. TCI argued that Troy had

TABLE 3.1.   SELECTED LOCAL TELECOMMUNICATIONS CASES

City	State	Issue	Source
Amherst	New York	Cable franchise fees	Lakamp, 1998
Anchorage	Alaska	Railway easement	Kowalski, 1998
Atlanta	Georgia	Access to private buildings for new entrants	Competitors…, 1997
Berkeley	California	Local low power broadcasting	National Lawyers Guild, 1997
Chattanooga	Tennessee	Telecom franchise fee	Tabin, 1988
Cleveland	Ohio	City-owned cable	Beauprez, 1998
Deltona	Florida	Prepayment for digging	Perotin, 1998; Shaw, 1997a
Denver	Colorado	Telecom fees	Estrella, 1997
Huntington Park	California	Pay telephone siting	Federal Communications Commission, 1997b
Maitland	Florida	Investment and service requirements	Florida House, 1997
Peoria	Arizona	Rights-of-way fees	Nelson, 1997
Phoenix	Arizona	Rights-of-way fees	Fiscus, 1997; Maerowitz, 1997
Prince George's County	Maryland	Local telecom taxes	Schwartz, 1998
Troy	Michigan	Licensing requirements	Ilka, 1997; Van Bergh and Tabin, 1997
Tucson	Arizona	Payments for use of rights-of-way	Fischer, 2000

exceeded its authority by seeking commitments that new fiber optic cable installations by TCI would not be used to provide telecommunications services until TCI had received permits and licenses as required by federal, state, and local authorities. TCI had offered only cable television services before this. The FCC decision of September 19, 1997 (FCC, 1997c) was viewed as a partial victory for both sides in the dispute. The FCC did find that the city had exceeded its scope of local franchising authority (the authority to grant franchises to cable television companies to operate in the city), "by placing a telecommunications condition on its grant of cable permits," although Congress "clearly intended to separate the functions of cable franchising from the regulation of telecommunications services" (FCC, 1997c, p. 4). The FCC kept this decision narrow in most respects. It did not agree with TCI's claims that it had been required to obtain a franchise to provide telecommunications services, as TCI was not providing and did not intend to provide telecommunications services. The FCC found that "the City has not sought to restrict the discretion granted to TCI" to choose the transmission technology and subscriber equipment used in the cable system (FCC, 1997c, p. 4). Whereas the FCC declined to issue a broader declaratory ruling to implement federal pre-emption of the entire local ordinance, the memorandum, opinion, and order did state:

> [w]e are troubled by several aspects of the Troy Telecommunications Ordinance in the context of the effort to open local telecommunications markets to competition. While Congress mandated a role for the Commission and the states in the regulation of telecommunications carriers and services, we are concerned that Troy and other local governments may be creating an unnecessary "third tier" of telecommunications regulation that extends far beyond the statutorily protected municipal interests in managing the public rights-of way and protecting public safety and welfare.... In particular, we articulate our concern regarding how redundant and potentially inconsistent levels of regulation ... may deter or discourage competition (FCC, 1997c, p. 4).

A Maitland, Florida, case involved a municipality, the Florida Public Service Commission (PSC), and the Florida House of Representatives. The issues in this case are instructive in that they mirror in some respects those issues encountered with the federalist division of governance. The case initially arose because the City of Maitland had included a provision in an ordinance that required the telephone company to provide the same level and quality of services, including advanced services, in Maitland that it was providing at other locations in its service area. The telephone company interpreted this as an infringement on its license to operate in the state and sought a ruling by the Florida PSC that the city was in violation of Florida statutes. The Florida PSC considered the case and in the summer of 1997 decided not to overrule the city. The firm sought legislative assistance, and, in late 1997, a bill was introduced in the Florida House of Representatives that sought to limit the ability of cities to place certain requirements on those making use of rights-of-way (Florida, House of Representatives, 1997). The bill would have also limited the amount charged for franchise fees to the management costs incurred by the city. A hearing was held on January 6, 1998, but no further action was taken on the bill that year (Florida, House of Representatives, Committee on Utilities and Communications, 1997).

The conflicts highlighted by these three cases arose in part because the Telecommunications Act of 1996 was designed to encourage the rapid introduction of new technologies and services. Whereas the radiomagnetic spectrum is public property that is regulated, and its use is allocated by the federal government in the United States, the streets and public rights-of-way are under the control of city and county governments. Communications firms that made use of wired networks in the past (e.g., telephony, cable) were now considering investments in new technologies that would use both wired networks and the radiomagnetic spectrum (wireless telephony, wireless cable, or multipoint multichannel distribution systems). Hence, although the federal government was attempting to encourage competition and the introduction of new services, municipalities and telecommunications corporations were attempting to manage public property that the federal government did not fully control.

Some representatives of local governments saw the 1996 Act as a sweeping usurpation of local authority, because the Act reduces state and local governments' power by limiting their control over zoning, taxing, and franchise fees for some new services. Questions at stake include the applicability of the franchise fees charged for use of municipal rights-of-way to various service providers, zoning authority over the placement of towers to provide wireless services, state and municipal taxation of communications services, the provision of telecommunications infrastructure and services by city governments, and the role of local institutions—such as schools, libraries, and hospitals—in efforts to promote access to advanced telecommunications services. Although these jurisdictional issues may appear arcane, attempts to shape the organization of geographic space and telecommunications networks at the local level play a crucial role in negotiating the balance between mobility and fixity. The next five subsections provide a detailed analysis of some of the major infrastructure and policy issues faced by varying levels of government, industry, and their respective publics.

Franchise Fees and Rights-of-Way

In order to build telecommunications networks, one must make fixed investments in the physical space of the city, which leads to an ongoing question faced by municipal utility regulators: What should be the appropriate level of the fees charged for use of municipal rights-of-way to various service providers, and any other building permit or administrative requirements for the use of rights-of-way? Rights-of-way along streets and city land are publicly owned, but are necessary for terrestrial telecommunications networks and other infrastructures to use in order to provide a number of services. These networks may include roads and sidewalks, water services, sewers, storm drains, and natural gas, electricity, telephone, cable television, and wireless networks. Subscribers' dwellings may need to be physically connected to these networks to gain access to these services. Additionally, these networks are necessary to provide other public and private services, such as postal service deliveries, garbage collection and recycling, or emergency police, fire, or ambulance services. Municipalities have taken the main responsibility for building, maintaining, and governing the network upon which many essential services are based.

Some transportation and utility networks are owned and operated by local government, even if private companies initially built them. Other networks have been built and operated by private companies, which pay fees to make use of the public rights-of-way. Arrangements for local infrastructure construction and management have developed slowly, often with the prodding of state and federal governments interested in speeding the pace of economic development or in removing local barriers to commerce (Horwitz, 1989). Apart from periodic building booms and initial construction, the pace of construction of communication and other infrastructure networks was relatively slow and stable throughout much of the twentieth century. The enthusiasm for investment in new communication technologies and services in the 1990s was more akin to the excitement for railroad building in the nineteenth century and road building in the mid-twentieth century.

Some argue that public rights-of-way are a resource to be made available for open access and use by the general public and private companies, even if revenue generation is minimized. Others claim that the public rights-of-way are the property of cities, which must act in the interests of all resident constituents, even if that means enhancing the revenue to be derived from use of those resources to the detriment of some users. When municipal utilities are publicly owned, the differences among these perspectives may be less important because the argument can be made that increased municipal revenues would benefit even those city residents who remain "off the grid." With the recent increase in private service provision, however, the divide between these two perspectives takes on new saliency as telecommunications companies, for example, argue that rights-of-way should be seen as a public trust, open to use by all entrants in the private sector at a minimal cost. The price for use of the rights-of-way, they contend, should be based on the actual "cost" of management fees, rather than a source of revenue generation for cities (even though it is impossible to determine the precise cost of a service when, as is often the case, multiple services are provided on one network).

Legislation was introduced in 1997 and 1998 in several states (e.g., Florida, Arizona, Indiana, Washington) to attempt to enforce a management fee structure on cities and counties for use of rights-of-way. The Indiana bill would have prohibited public utility payments for the use of public rights-of-way. Furthermore, to prevent any challenges to the law, the bill would prevent payments for any costs of litigation to challenge the bill itself or to challenge any local ordinance consistent with the bill (Indiana, 1998). The Florida legislation would have reduced the ability of local governments to require permits for the use of the rights-of-way, as well as limiting the fees for use of rights-of-way to one percent of gross revenues or the management costs associated with that specific use of the right-of-way (Florida, House of Representatives, Committee on Utilities and Communications, 1997).

In contrast, cities and counties take the view that rights-of-way are public property, and that those groups of people making use of those public rights-of-way must pay fair rent or usage fees. This revenue will provide benefits to all members of the public, especially those who do not make use of a particular communications service. For instance, although communications companies claim that municipal charges will be passed on to the consumer and hence raise the cost of communications services, these costs will be passed on only to the consumers who choose to purchase a service. If only two-thirds of households with television subscribe to cable television, or if only a small portion of businesses make use of the services of an alternative local exchange carrier, is it appropriate that these users alone bear the costs of using public rights-of-way? If not, the whole public will subsidize the use of advanced communications services by certain small subgroups, justified by the assumption that the use of these services provides either direct benefits to some or at least indirect aggregate benefits for all.

Zoning Authority and Cell Tower Placement

The appropriate authority of local governments over the siting of towers to provide wireless services has been the highest profile and most hotly contested local political issue in communities across the country. Prior to 1996, the FCC had auctioned off licenses for the use of the radiomagnetic spectrum for wireless digital subscription services, most notably cellular telephones. From December 2004 to December 2005, subscriptions to wireless telephone and subscriber services in the United States rose from 185 million to 213 million (FCC, 2006b). The auctioning of a public resource to raise revenues, and the spreading out of the period of payments, means that the FCC assumed two new roles. Revenue generation was now added to regulation in the public interest as a goal the FCC must try to meet (Butterfield and McDowell, 1998). The FCC had an incentive to maximize revenue, and hence to maintain the spectrum to be used by new technologies and services as a valuable resource. Prestle and Miles (1997) claim that the FCC has conflicting interests because (1) it is both a regulator of the industry and local government authority and (2) Congress has mandated that the FCC raise money by selling off spectrum licenses for cellular service.

Following up on this, the initial drafts of the Telecommunications Act of 1996 included strong provisions to pre-empt the power of local governments to limit the placement or installation of antenna towers to provide digital cellular telephone service. Even while the 1996 Act was being debated in the U.S. Congress during 1995, representatives of local governments raised concerns about the infringement of local government authority that the bill contained. The National League of Cities worked to limit the authority to pre-empt the powers of local governments that was present in early drafts of the bill (National League of Cities, 1997). As digital cellular services operate using lower power than analog cellular services use, they required higher towers and closer tower placement than would be required for analog services. Like the analog system, however, the digital system required a network of terrestrial towers in order to achieve seamless coverage over a service area, and, if service demand were to become greater, cells would have to be divided into smaller geographic areas, requiring even more towers.

As with rights-of-way, as a result of citizens' concerns over the effects of the placement of towers on land use and planning, cities and counties were very active in opposing the strong version of the pre-emption of local power that appeared in early drafts of the bill that became the 1996 Telecommunications Act. The final bill included language that limited the ability of the FCC or the states to pre-empt or override local authority without clear reasons. Many cities placed moratoria on new tower construction during 1997 and 1998. More recently, cities have worked with telecommunication companies, encouraging them to use city land, to share towers with other companies, and to camouflage towers for aesthetic reasons. Telecommunications firms have also sought to have the FCC make a broad ruling on pre-emption, rather than having to fight out every case with local governments, and in April 1997 the FCC (1997a) did issue a notice of proposed rule-making to further explore the issue of a broad set of pre-emption rules.

Thus, in the construction of cellular telephone towers, as in many issues concerning local governments and the infosphere, local governments were caught between opposing goals: the need to construct the city as a *place*, an environment for living and working, and the need to construct the city as a node within networks of movement and communication. On the one hand, communication links were crucial for fostering local development. On the other hand, however, the fixed infrastructure that would be required to maintain these links could ultimately detract from the construction of the city as an attractive environment for its inhabitants and for potential investors and residents.

Electronic Commerce

Local attempts to foster electronic commerce similarly illustrate the continuing tendency of capital toward both mobility and spatial fixity, and how these tensions are negotiated and structured in the development of institutions that govern movement. In the United States, a moratorium has been placed on new state taxation of online commerce (Anonymous, 1998). The argument made in support of this policy is that such taxes would not be collectable and enforceable. Electronic commerce is thus posed as one of those "trade" activities on the right side of Table 1.1 that challenges the state system by limiting the state's ability to collect revenues.

Applying the neoliberal tenet that state-transcending mobility functions (the right side of Table 1.1) may be co-opted as resources to aid fixity-oriented state development (the left side of Table 1.1), some scholars and legislators have argued that the United States could encourage the development of these new high technology activities by forgoing tax imposition for at least several years. This would help the industry grow quickly and establish international leadership in the online commerce sector. The period of learning, experimentation, and growth would provide a head start, making it difficult for others to unseat the dominance of U.S. firms after certain protocols and industry patterns had been established.

Others note, however, that the tax moratorium is a public subsidy, often offset for the purchaser by shipping and handling fees, that is used to expand the spatial scope of consumer markets. In the short term, it generates a significant revenue stream for overnight express and expedited delivery companies, supporting over the long term the construction and operation of air transportation infrastructure that restructures choices facing consumers, workers, and firms. The local firm, which pays property taxes, employs people, and may contribute in other ways to the community in addition to remitting sales taxes, sees a public subsidy introduced that works against it.

We see then that the debate over the state sales tax moratorium closely parallels the debate over local control of cellular telephone tower placement. In both cases, municipalities (and states) face strong pressure to invest in infrastructure and make policy decisions that facilitate mobility and connectivity, even though the transformations that emerge from this new round of connectivity may ultimately have a negative long-term impact on the city's quality of life, revenue potential, and attractiveness as a location for investment.

Thus, even as tax holidays in cyberspace annihilate distance (by facilitating interaction across space) and places (by limiting state territorial authority), they concurrently contribute to the constitution of places (by fostering state development). Furthermore, as they construct places, they restructure the distribution of social power within these places by privileging transactions across space over those undertaken between proximate buyers and sellers. If global cyberspace emerges as a realm of commerce that undermines state authority (through reduced tax revenues), it will have less to do with the characteristics of the technology than with the policies of leading states as they attempt, on the one hand, to facilitate the commerce that enables growth of the world economy through the annihilation of space while, on the other hand, to produce and develop discrete places so as to increase the quantity of production occurring within state territory. Such an outcome would not be a triumph of economics over politics so much as it would be the latest instance of space construction in which state regulation is nuanced so as to promote the balance of fixity and mobility required for continuity in the global system of international political economy.

Universal Service Provision

Another arena in which information policy has served to structure the local spaces within which individuals conduct their everyday lives has been the ongoing debate over universal service provision amid the explosion of infosphere technologies. Prior to the 1990s, the telephone pricing mechanism in the United States, which combined unlimited local calling for a flat monthly fee with charges by distance and time for long distance calling, contributed to a strangely bifurcated structure of this sector of the infosphere. Local service prices were kept low in the early twentieth century by AT&T to drive out competition from other firms. Revenues from higher-priced long distance services were used, when AT&T was one large integrated monopoly, to make contributions to the costs of local calls. Because local networks were needed to complete those calls, after the breakup of AT&T and the divestiture of local telephone companies in 1984, access fees were charged by local telephone companies on a per minute basis in order to complete long distance telephone calls. A portion of interstate and international long distance calling revenues were also used to support universal service in high-cost regions of the country, or for low-income subscribers.

Low and stable pricing of local services, a goal supported by state regulators, has also been a key ingredient of the universal access strategy at the federal level in the United States throughout the past sixty years. Other mechanisms to promote universal access included the Universal

Service Fund to offset operating expenses for high-cost telecommunications companies and Rural Electrification Administration program loans to telephone companies. These programs were more effective in addressing unequal access across geographic regions than in providing services for low-income populations. Low-income subscribers living in urban areas were unable to take advantage of programs that supported rural telephone companies and lowered rates to achieve universal access and service in rural and remote regions. Although telephone companies obtained this support and passed along lower prices to all subscribers in rural areas, Communications Lifeline and Link Up America support for poor persons required subscribers to sign up individually for programs.

The 1996 Telecommunications Act includes sections that seek to preserve and promote universal access to telecommunications services, while at the same time introducing competition in the provision of local telephone services and allowing for the introduction of new technologies and services. The Act sets standards for basic household services and identifies schools, libraries, and rural hospitals as agencies that should have subsidized access to advanced communications services. The 1996 Act also attempts to restructure the programs that have kept local telephone rates low and supported lower rates in high-cost regions. It aims to make subsidies more explicit, rather than being buried in the cost structure of local, enhanced, or long-distance services. States are allowed to set their own policies to promote universal service, as long as they do not run counter to the federal policy. As well, public institutions at the local level, rather than private households alone, are now supported by the universal service policy mechanisms.

At the same time, the basis for pricing services and providing revenues to support universal service are also under challenge. Competition in the long-distance sector has led to declining revenues from interstate and international calls, reducing the base upon which contributions to universal service funds are drawn. Wireless telephony pricing plans make the distinction between local and long distance meaningless for subscribers, who are charged for bundles of minutes. The growth of wireless subscriptions and of long-distance calling on wireless services has also contributed to reductions in access charges paid to local operators, because some calls are completed without using the local wired network. Similarly, pricing for Internet access services are insensitive to time considerations, if a local call can be used for dialup access. Internet access services are considered to be an information service under federal regulations, so Internet Service Providers do not make per minute contributions to the costs of local calls. Broadband services offered by telephone or cable television networks were slower to roll out in the United States, with levels of subscription increasing rapidly only in 2005 and 2006 (FCC, 2007). The introduction of Voice over Internet Protocol (VoIP) services on broadband networks, which are classed as an information service, also may result in reduced revenues for long-distance services and lowered contributions to the Universal Service Fund (Leahy, 2006). All of these developments call into question the future of revenues from access charges and from long-distance services that go to support universal service.

With the introduction of Internet services, much research has been undertaken on the different rates of access and adoption among groups in the population (FCC, 2007; Horrigan, Stolp, and Wilson 2006; National Telecommunications and Information Administration 2004) or on the idea of and approaches to a "digital divide" (Gunkel, 2003; Rodino-Colocino, 2006; Selwyn 2004; Stewart, Gil-Egui, Tian, and Pileggi, 2006). The spatial coverage of networks also leads to efforts at specific geographic and social tracking of backbone investments, service offerings, and access levels (Grubesic and Murray, 2005; Malecki, 2004; Moss and Townsend, 2000; Strover, Chapman, and Waters, 2004). The provision of telecommunications infrastructure and services by city governments and the role of local institutions—schools, libraries, and hospitals—has served as one way to promote access to advanced telecommunications services. The "E-Rate" program provides subsidies for the costs of broadband services for these local institutions. With the pressure on other mechanisms that support universal access, local governments, which want to ensure the effective and efficient delivery of public services, have become key actors in the implementation of universal service support mechanisms aimed at increasing access of disadvantaged groups, especially to broadband services.

Thus, the introduction of new technologies has led to a reassessment of the universal service program. The program had been based on assumptions about the spatial fixity of telephony users (which then had allowed for policies targeted at specific geographic areas) and on stable assumptions about the nature of distance (which then had allowed for pricing policies that allowed for a definitive distinction between "necessary" local and "luxury" long-distance calling). Now, with mobile users constructing new vectors of connectivity across new geographical spaces, these policy options are no longer so readily available, or, to the extent that they are available, they no longer meet their objectives so comprehensively. In response, a variety of actors and institutions, across a range of scales of governance, have attempted to recast the universal service provision to match the requirements and challenges of new technologies, in the process recasting the spaces within which and through which individuals communicate and, indeed, recasting the meaning of "local."

Building Public Broadband Networks: Wired and Wireless

One area of concern for local governments as they have attempted to construct the infosphere has been the relatively slow growth of local broadband networks. Private-sector broadband service offerings were rolled out slowly after the Telecommunications Act of 1996, with only 4.3 million high-speed subscribers by June 2000 (at least 200 Kbps in one direction). This had risen to 42.8 million subscribers by June 2005 (among these, 34.3 million were advanced services lines, with over 200 Kbps in both directions) (FCC, 2006b), further rising to 64.6 million lines by June 2006 (FCC, 2007). These figures (both in terms of subscriber levels and transmission speeds) lag behind those of a number of other advanced industrialized countries in Europe and Asia (Organization for Economic Cooperation and Development [OECD], 2006).

In response, many municipal governments have sought to establish their own broadband networks. As of December 2003, "[f]rustrated by a slow or spotty rollout of high-tech communications services, 357 municipalities ha[d] dug up streets to build their own networks and compete against companies that they in some cases also regulate" (Shiver, 2004, p. 1). However, because they represent an expansion of government responsibility, these initiatives have spurred debate over the need for and evaluation of the effectiveness of city networks. By 2005, at least twelve states had passed or were considering legislation prohibiting municipalities from offering telecommunications services directly to the public (Stone, Maitland, and Tapia, 2006).

Although most of these municipal networks have been restricted to individual cities, in the state of Utah, a proposal for a multicity network, the Utah Telecommunication Open Infrastructure Agency (UTOPIA), was debated during 2003 and 2004, and had over 5000 customers in six cities by 2006 (Oberbeck, 2006). UTOPIA is a consortium supported by 18 cities to build a fiber optic broadband network to serve businesses and residences in these cities. *The New York Times* called it, "a 21st century twist on Roosevelt-era public works projects" (Oberbeck, 2003a). Despite its public core, UTOPIA has a strong private component. The actual construction was undertaken by private firms. UTOPIA does not offer services directly to the public, but sells the use of the network on a wholesale basis to private sector service providers such as AT&T, MSTAR, SISNA, Veracity, and XMission, which in turn offer services to the public. The inclusion of private sector service providers was both a practical device and a legal accommodation. Practically, cities would not be responsible for providing services or determining what services could or could not be offered if they were not the retailer. Legally, this arrangement would be permissible under a U.S. Supreme Court decision of March 2004, which ruled that states were within their rights to prevent municipalities from offering services to the public (Hall, 2003; Oberbeck, 2003b; Suzukamo, 2004).

The cities in Utah said that they were forced to build these networks because the cable television company (Comcast) and telephone company (Qwest) had not made broadband services available to their communities. With the exception of Salt Lake City, most were small cities or towns. Advanced broadband services were seen as essential to preserve and build local economies and to attract investment for further economic development. In December 2003, UTOPIA announced that AT&T had signed on "as the first provider of voice, video, and data services" (Oberbeck, 2003c). A private venture capital firm also offered in April 2004 to take on risk and profit in the project (Snyder and Fattah, 2004). However, the telecom companies argued that the public sector would provide unfair subsidies through its support of UTOPIA. Qwest opposed the plan, but also promised to accelerate its investment in broadband services in Salt Lake City. Telecom firms also supported a bill in the state legislature that would require cities to obtain approval from their voters before promising sales tax revenue to guarantee UTOPIA financing (Oberbeck, 2004).

The debate became more heated when municipal loan guarantees for UTOPIA debt were sought. Although there would be no cost to the cities if the business plan for UTOPIA was successful, the municipal guarantees would reduce the risk of the loans for bondholders and allow investment funds to be raised at lower interest rates. However, several city councils, including that of Salt Lake City, balked at being made liable for potential shortfalls in revenue to cover debt obligations should they arise. The project received a loan of $66 million in 2006 from the U.S. Department of Agriculture to assist infrastructure development in six small cities (Oberbeck, 2006).

Many other communities have also implemented or proposed wireless coverage, either offered free or on a subscription basis through a retailer leasing public networks. This has been reflected in an increasing number of city initiatives, with the struggles in Philadelphia, Pennsylvania, attracting much attention across the country (Brietbart, 2006; Wireless Philadelphia, 2007). Many other major urban centers also have initiated free wireless programs, (Arends, 2007; Dell, 2007; Grant, 2007; Helft, 2007; Lai and Brewer, 2006 Stross, 2007). Industry groups, especially companies (that are not telephone or cable television service providers) providing equipment and services, offer a wide range of products, and also support forums for policy discussion and network innovation (BelAir Networks, 2006; Digital Communities, 2007; Intel Corporation, 2007; MuniWireless, 2007; Tropos Networks, 2007). Wireless umbrellas in parks or city centers are seen as a way to improve the convenience or quality of life, but make what had been a scarce, market-allocated resource into a public good. Adrian MacKenzie (2005) argues that WiFi uses should be examined for the potential of "infrastructural inversion" and can be analyzed as "an ongoing event that articulates different types of spatial and informatic movements together (p. 282).

The cases of municipal proposals to provide broadband services illustrate several tensions in the governance of the infosphere. Although telecom regulation and policy in the United States is reserved for federal and state governments, the federal government is increasingly taking the pre-eminent role. At the same time, local governments are closest to the needs of communities and have expertise in planning and managing development, maintaining and operating infrastructures, and providing service. Local officials can see the potential benefits of broadband services, if only because local government may also be a large consumer of these services. Combined with schools, hospitals, and other public services, local governments may also be able to identify the benefits of aggregating sufficient demand to justify investments. They also have the historical experience in stepping in when private sector investment has been insufficient or in cases of market failure. As Washington-based telecom lawyer Jim Baller commented, "This is like the history of electrification all over again and communities realize that if they don't roll their sleeves up and get involved, they are not going to get broadband and other advanced communication services" (Shiver, 2004).

At the same time, the private sector providers deploy a rhetoric that restricts the role of government, decries the use of inappropriate public subsidies, and claims that public funds would be placed at risk. The Progress and Freedom Foundation, a Washington think tank, has issued several reports questioning the effectiveness of these networks (Lassman and May, 2003; Lenard, 2004). By comparison, a series of reports from the Massachusetts Institute of Technology takes a more positive view of the feasibility of these networks, and considers the different approaches that cities are taking to municipal broadband networks, whether as user, financer, rule-maker, or infrastructure provider (Gillett, Lehr, and Osorio, 2003; Lehr, Sirbu, and Gillett, 2004, 2006; Strover and Mun, 2006; Tapia, Maitland, and Stone, 2006). Media activists have also expressed concerns about industry efforts to prevent municipalities from offering broadband services (McChesney and Podesta, 2006; Scott and Wellings, 2005).

As each of the examples in this chapter has demonstrated, the construction of local places has shaped access to communications infrastructure which, in turn, has played a central role in developing strategies for the additional construction of local places. Amid this cycle of place and network development, local governments, in addition to the private sector and other levels of government, play an ongoing and crucial role.

Local Issues and Restructuring Spaces of Mobility

Although conflicts between different levels of government are long-standing in the United States, the cases and issues that have been discussed in this chapter are especially important in light of the 1996

Telecommunications Act's goals of promoting competition in local services, encouraging new entrants, and stimulating the rapid deployment of new technologies. Additionally, these issues arise in the context of broader shifts in scope and form of telecommunications governance at the national and international level, and the shifting role of cities in the spatial reorganization of economic production and culture on a global basis.

Litigation contesting regulatory decisions, originated by companies claiming that their ability to expand services or offer new services was limited, has provided the opportunity for cities and counties to make the case for a very narrow and limited set of circumstances in which the FCC should pre-empt local authority, despite the call by firms and trade associations for more widespread and declaratory rulings. Thus far, the FCC has been restrained in its use of whatever additional preemption authority was given to it by the 1996 Act, possibly seeking to avoid a prolonged cycle of appeals to federal courts by local governments and firms, as has happened in other FCC decisions implementing the 1996 Act.

The FCC Intergovernmental Advisory Committee (formerly called the State and Local Government Advisory Council) has provided one mechanism or forum for reviewing these issues, developing some clarification of the questions at stake, and providing advice to the FCC and to state and local governments in dealing with a number of these questions. When the Local and State Government Advisory Council formed, both the FCC Chair William Kennard and the Associate Bureau Chief of the FCC Cable Services Bureau emphasized the need for consultation and cooperation among different levels of government. Kennard (1997) stated that the FCC would attempt to operate with common sense: "Common sense means writing rules that are clear and understandable and deal with real problems. It means finding practical solutions to problems. And it means forging a relationship between the FCC and the states that allows us to do that." Associate Bureau Chief Barbara Esbin (1998) spoke directly to the issue of land use and zoning policies: "... the Commission's approach to the pre-emption issues in each of these actions [is] cautious, measured, and mindful of the shared obligations of federal, state and local governments under the Act." The December 2003 formation of the Intergovernmental Advisory Committee was intended to "reflect greater balance between state, local and tribal representation, and urban and rural representation, as well as to gain expertise in homeland security and rural matters" (FCC, 2003).

In contrast, although the FCC has centralized legal authority, and large telecommunications firms have more concentrated resources and expertise than do cities (which may have to hire outside experts or join in collective cases to undertake telecommunications planning—see Armstrong, Miles, and Pestle, 1997; Fidelman, 1997; Leibowitz and Associates, 1998), the huge absolute number of cities and counties would tax the institutional capacity of the FCC and courts to deal with all the cases that might arise. Additionally, the myriad of rules, permitting processes, licenses, taxation, and fees that local governments administer and can manipulate could result in numerous cases arising in each city, if even some of the mathematical possibilities for litigation were to materialize. Hence, there are strong incentives to use a consultative and cooperative process as much as possible, even though the FCC holds formal rulemaking authority.

One possible substantive change in the role of local governments that may arise from these consultations is that local governments increasingly will be seen only as service delivery vehicles, although overall policies will be set in the national and international forums or in consultation with national agencies (Bonnet, 1998; Christensen, 1997; Dinan, 1997). For instance, Brenda Trainor (1995), while defending the role of local governments in telecommunications, does so by referring to local government expertise and experience in service delivery:

> What does local government do best? Traditional powers of public safety, health, and welfare are well organized, and local governments provide direct service in these areas consistent with national policy. Local transportation and right-of-way management policies are implemented in concert with federal, state, interstate and regional coordination. Take garbage, for instance. Trash is collected under appropriate franchise or delegated powers of local government and hauled regionally to regulated trash sites under state and federal mandates. Why should telecommunications be any different?

Hence, much discussion of the shaping and use of infosphere technologies by local governments has revolved around designing, implementing, and assessing electronic government initiatives (Bertot, 2006;

Brown, 2005). However, if major policy and planning decisions shift predominantly to the infosphere, appropriate and legitimate roles for self-governance at the local level may be lost, and along with them, the ability of local government to serve as a unique and proximate public forum to discuss, deliberate, and respond to the variety of issues and problems with which people living in specific places must deal.

At the same time, however, local governments are increasing their capacity and assertiveness as actors on the global stage, in the infosphere and elsewhere (e.g., through international trade missions, foreign policy declarations, etc.). In other words, the strategy of promoting extraterritorial links (through infosphere connectivity) to promote territorial development is coupled with one in which territorial development is used to foster municipal presence and power outside the city's borders. As the examples in this chapter have shown, however, these efforts at deterritorialization (and the subsequent reconfiguring of space) have been resisted by state and federal authorities as well as by private corporations, all of whom depend on territorial control.

Yet, the conflict is not so simple as one in which local governments' efforts to transcend boundaries are in opposition to more entrenched territorial forces. Any local government action seen to cause friction with private sector communication firms is equated to local protectionism and obstructionism, a charge that labels the local government as being inappropriately territorial. Local taxation, charges for the use of rights-of-way, zoning, service provision, and efforts to promote access all have been challenged by industry groups. Usually, these industry challenges have been supported by state legislatures and federal officials.

The moratorium on taxation of e-commerce combined with changes in the taxation of telecommunications services as discussed in this chapter mean that local communities take a double hit. E-commerce already has the potential to move economic transactions away from the local vendors who provide jobs and pay property taxes. The space of mobility for e-commerce is defined extensively, rather than as offering possibilities to intensify local linkages. The limitations imposed on local governments in taxing communication service providers for use of local rights-of-way further reinforce this definition of the space of mobility.

These local conflicts encountered in a redefinition of national telecommunications governance also reflect a public policy commitment and industry objectives to rapidly introduce new technologies in ways that contribute to an extensive space of mobility. New communications technologies and services—such as radio pagers, personal communications systems, video services offered by telephone companies, and direct broadcast satellite—integrate multimedia services and wired and wireless modes of delivery in new ways (Baldwin, McVoy, and Steinfield, 1996; Jameson, 1996). During the twentieth century, separate and complex divisions of governance among federal, state, and local bodies arose for radio/wireless, telephone, broadcasting, and cable television services. For instance, although the FCC allocated spectrum for use by broadcasters in the 1930s, it sought to achieve a goal of localism (Horwitz, 1989; McChesney, 1993). New services and technologies may disturb these governance arrangements and face conflicting regulations from various levels of government.

Firms also have some cross-cutting interests on these questions. In the Troy case discussed earlier in this chapter, the incumbent cable company sought to remove certain stipulations from its permits for construction of fiber optic cable networks. Although these services were limited to cable television for residences, there were also telecommunications services being offered for public institutions. In other cases, it is new firms that seek permits from cities and from private property owners to provide services that compete with those offered by incumbent carriers, sometimes in partnership with municipal utilities.

Conclusion

The examples in this discussion of scales of governance explore ways in which the debates and decisions over the role of local governance have contributed to constructing spaces of mobility in certain ways. This is the management of the infosphere, literally at the street level and the retail level, and management that encompasses and shapes governance, technology, and cultural practices. A global space of mobility is made up of some large policies reflected in international organizations and treaties, but also by a series of discrete decisions and initiatives. Although the outcomes of the debates discussed in this chapter shape physical mobility at the local level, they also form the terms and conditions of connections and linkages with the national political economy, as well as global trade, investment, governance, and culture. Questions about shaping the infosphere and the types of mobility of information and communication are implicit in each of these debates. Local governments and communities, like Mountain City or Hong Kong, in debates over rights-of-way, universal service, and broadband services, are also defining to some extent the conditions of their connections with other local places, with the spaces of flow discussed by Castells (1996), and the surfaces, pathways, and borders of mobility in the movement of goods, services, information, and people. As noted, however, in the federal system of governance in the United States, the role of local government is quite curtailed and is often presented as a barrier to open trade and commerce. The four tensions proposed in this book—between fixity and movement, territory and nonterritory, production and trade, and politics and economics—are continuously mediated at the local level in conflicts and cooperation among citizens, local governments, private firms, and state and national governments. Efforts to attract firms and production facilities through the emphasis on locational attributes may accentuate local communication services and the availability of a high-tech workforce. Fixed investments in communication infrastructures and services can allow for a space of mobility connected to global flows, or intensify local linkages. Whereas formal sovereignty rests at other levels of government, local authorities face similar tasks of identifying some powers from which they might forebear in exercising full control, reducing full territorial jurisdiction. These decisions may be local in scope; however, they are also about the modes of articulation (Cox, 1987) with global political economy, and the parameters of infosphere cultures, technologies, and governance.

These are governance and technology issues, but given the ways in which local government decisions shape physical space and core services, many of these decisions are central to the lives of people. The spaces of mobility, whether extensive or intensive, are made real and accessible to people by the management of concerns closest to home. The next chapter considers the infosphere and spaces of mobility that cross national borders, exploring the representation and structuring of mobility in the interactions between infosphere applications and uses and international tourism.

4 Communication Technology, Mobility, and Cultural Consumption

Notwithstanding the ongoing importance of place in the construction of the infosphere, which was emphasized in the previous chapter, the experience of living in the infosphere, in a fundamental sense, involves moving across space and transgressing the boundaries of place. Watching television programs from different parts of the world has become part of daily life for many people in the twenty-first century, with television coming to more and more remote villages (Johnson, 2000). For a much smaller group, leisure travel across state borders is an expectation either every year or during one's life, just as pilgrimages might be for some groups. These cultural activities have distinctive spatial dimensions, both in the paths and ways that media messages move and in the travel patterns of travelers or tourists.

The interaction between cultural practices and understandings, the development and use of new information and communication technologies, and the processes of economic globalization have all attracted significant attention in the last decades. The collapsing of time and space in international trade, investment, and financial flows, and in international communication and transportation, are presented almost as immutable forces arising from globalization and the introduction and use of digital media technologies.

The international tourism sector provides one glimpse of the complex processes at work in the management of mobility in contemporary global political economy and in trade in services, and of applications of international media of various forms. International tourism promotion and operations combine the use of media representations, information networks, and transportation services to facilitate the mobility of persons across state borders. Movement is promoted and experience is guided and filtered by representations in media portrayals of places through advertising, news, and entertainment. Although international data networks support both the providers of travel and financial services and state security efforts, in the past decade web-based interactive applications have been increasingly used to offer travel and accommodation services directly to the public. Tourism can also be tied to efforts to encourage and facilitate mobility of cultural identities, as travelers move to different national jurisdictions, exploring even for a short time new roles outside of work, family, and community, as well as national legal frameworks (Pennings, 2002).

This chapter draws connections to larger debates on the interaction of culture, technology, and governance in the infosphere by considering the spatial dimensions of the production and consumption of communications products and tourism services. Tourism is a cultural practice that also highlights the role of media (Mazierska and Walton, 2006), the consumption choices of individuals and groups, and the intercultural interactions of national belonging or foreignness. International tourism flows are built upon and dependent upon investments that have been made in a number of networked technologies and applications, whether communication, transportation, financial services, insurance, or local utilities. Because crossing borders is at the core of defining international tourism, governance of that crossing, as well as the conditions of transnational investment, are also a crucial part of constructing this form of mobility. The relationships between tourism and media have emerged as an important focus (Beirman, 2003; Jansson, 2002; Neilson, 2001), with international research conferences on tourism and media being organized by the Tourism Research Unit at Monash University in Australia in November 2004 and December 2006 (Frost, Croy, and Beeton, 2004; Gammack, 2005; Monash Tourism Research Unit, 2007).

This chapter draws upon concepts developed in international negotiations on trade in services, looks at the ways in which mobility is being constructed, and aims to examine inter-related dimensions of the spatial organization of one segment of global cultural activities, specifically by looking at ways in which the tensions outlined in Chapter 1 are being managed in the media construction and cultural construction of tourism places and in the debates over trade in tourism services. A spatial constructivist approach is applied to conceptualize the tensions in governance, technology, and culture that underlie efforts to promote mobility and/or fixity. The role of infosphere applications in the representation, facilitation, and experience of international tourism are explored to illustrate more fully the possibilities and implications of advancing a spatial constructivist perspective on the management of mobility in the infosphere.

Drawing on a critical examination of governance, technology, and cultural dimensions that contribute to spatial construction, this chapter argues that processes in the design, deployment, and use of communication networks respond to sometimes complementary and sometimes competing efforts to promote either the mobility or the fixity of capital, goods, services, information, and persons. The ways in which communication networks are shaped and managed create spaces of mobility, allowing for movement of information and people in specific directions and types, while inscribing parameters on other activities. This management takes place through policy, technology design and deployment, and cultural uses and understandings of network-based services. Whereas our consideration of these issues arises from an examination of management of mobility in the infosphere, a more general analysis of these issues arises in the area of mobility studies (Sheller and Urry, 2006b).

Culture as Commodity: Trade in Services

Over the last decades, large corporations, some national governments, and many international organizations have made great efforts to promote more open global trade and investment in goods and services. Perhaps the most significant conceptual shift has been the application of trade disciplines, such as progressive liberalization or continuous efforts to open markets and nondiscrimination among trading partners (or most-favored-nation status), to think about and guide services transactions. The upshot of these efforts would be to open up service sector activities to international trade and investment. This is a major change in direction, because many service activities had national ownership requirements or required national credentials for service providers. These shifts occurred as part of the development of international trade and investment agreements in the World Trade Organization (WTO; up until 1996 called the General Agreement on Tariffs and Trade [GATT]). Prior to the new focus on services, trade ideas guided the negotiations over international exchange in goods. New trade-in-services concepts developed in the 1980s were applied first to services activities—such as finance, insurance, transportation, and communication—then to cultural activities such as audiovisual products. Background papers were prepared on trade in tourism services by the WTO Secretariat in 1990 and 1998, and for a special workshop on trade in tourism services in 2001 (see Honeck, 2001; WTO, 1998, 2001). In proposing that an "Annex on Tourism" be added to the services agreement, the Dominican Republic, El Salvador, and Honduras noted that many developing countries lack the infrastructure to participate fully in international tourism offerings.

This chapter does not deal with the implications and limitations of treating culture as a tradable commodity, an issue that has concerned many cultural policy analysts and has led to efforts to create a cultural diversity convention that was formalized by the United Nations Educational, Scientific and Cultural Organization (UNESCO) in 2005. Rather, this chapter considers spatial and mobility implications of two different forms of cultural production and consumption: media and tourism.

International trade in services was initially conceptualized in the late 1970s and early 1980s, after extensive research programs and negotiations, as the provision of services across national borders (McDowell, 1994). Service transactions do not result from the production, exchange, or possession of a tangible good. In fact the consumption of a service, such as a visit to the doctor for medical treatment, often occurs at the same time and place as that service's production. Communications technologies may allow for the delivery of information-intensive services across space and time, such as online sales of downloaded music, so that the provider and consumer do not have to be in the same place at the same time. A telephone counseling service would also be an example of this type of transaction. Transportation technologies and services also allow persons to shift national locations, so that services may be delivered to them in another country.

International trade in services, because the exchange involves parties in two countries, is governed by a number of different legal and institutional relationships between the provider and the consumer. According to the framework developed in the GATT Uruguay Round negotiations (GATT, 1994), international trade in services may include cases where: (1) a foreign provider with a business establishment in a country may sell services to a national consumer (foreign direct investment); (2) an international provider with no base in a country may sell services to a national consumer using electronic means or temporary agents (nonestablishment, conventional export–import of services); (3) a consumer of services may enter a country and purchase services from a national provider (such as education, a medical visit, business travel, or leisure tourism); (4) both the provider and consumer of services may not be based in a country where the service transaction takes place (transportation or accommodation services purchased from an international firm) (GATT, 1994).

These different modes of international service provision and exchange illustrate some of the tensions in the ways in which mobility is constructed, as discussed in Chapter 1. First, the *fixity versus mobility* tension or dynamic is evident in services transactions in cases when movement by either producers or consumers takes place to facilitate an international service transaction, or the movement of information might also occur to support the services transaction. For instance, a hotel chain might invest in tourism activities in different countries, and provide services both to nationals as well as to international tourists. Consumers, or international tourists, may move within their own country or to a different country to consume tourist services.

Mobility is an essential part of tourism services production and exchange for service transactions where travel services are the core service or in cases where the seller and the buyer of tourism-related services must be in the same place at the same time. Put another way, the media space of tourism is as much a space of mobility as it is a space of places wherein the production and consumption of culture occurs. Movement of tourists is not a secondary activity that supports production and consumption. Rather, movement lies at the essence of tourism (Jansson,

2005). As such, like the example of the ocean discussed in Chapter 1, tourism engenders a particular form of management that enhances both its nonterritorial and its territorial properties and tendencies.

Second, the different ways of thinking about trade in services reorder somewhat the conceptual bind in the *production versus trade* dynamic. Some services, such as professional or personal services, are produced at the same time as they are consumed, collapsing the production-versus-trade distinction. Trade in services starts with selling and buying as the core relationship in understanding services provision, and works backward to consideration of the location and mode of service production and consumption, or of the producer and consumer of services. In a sense, because trade in services addresses many activities or exchanges where no physical good has changed hands, the conceptualization of international trade in services requires one to look at the exchange process and the ways in which the act of exchange adds economic value to the service. These may include cases in which an infrastructural resource has been used (transportation, communication), a professional's time has been spent addressing a problem (law, accounting, banking, healthcare), or a human service has been provided (retailing, restaurants, accommodation, maintenance). These may be standalone service activities, or the service function may add value to a transaction that also includes an exchange of goods. In all cases, the production-versus-trade relationship is complex, and the mobility of services and their consumption may be constructed in varying ways.

Third, the *territory versus nonterritory* tension is central to thinking about international trade in services, especially tourism services. The four categories or modes of service delivery outlined above illustrate ways to conceptualize transactions that do not fit into the predominant view of economics, that goods are produced in national spaces and then traded outside of these spaces in a secondary international space. International trade in services can occur in spaces loosely linked or only nominally connected with national spaces, such as offshore banks or shipping companies using flags of convenience. Furthermore, many international service transactions may be among subsidiaries of the same transnational firms, rather than between distinct and separate firms. The transnational organization of service investments and service production within the same firm means that the territory versus non-territory distinction is also diffused in these cases.

Fourth, the supposed distinction between *politics versus economics* is also addressed in negotiations on trade in services. Economists and trade lawyers have noted in the course of trade-in-services negotiations that many of the barriers that prevent full international trade and investment in service activities are not trade rules, but national regulations and certification requirements. These might include the rules governing professions, such as national certification for doctors, lawyers, and teachers, which in the view of some may reflect entrenched political power more than a desire to ensure high-quality services to members of the public. Similarly, public regulation of the prices and practices of utility service providers, such as transportation, communication, electricity, or water, or national ownership rules for these sectors, may prevent the full benefits of international trade and investment in service activities from being realized.

Although the conceptual framework for agreements on trade in services for specific service sectors was finalized at the conclusion of the Uruguay Round, an agreement on an annex on telecommunications was completed only in 1997. Talks on trade in financial services were also extended because U.S. negotiators did not think that significant trading partners had made sufficiently liberal offers. International aviation proved difficult to redesign around a trade framework, especially given the long-term ownership of landing rights at key international airports, which have proven to be bottleneck facilities. Audiovisual services have also been considered (Kakabadsiie, 1995), as have trade-related intellectual property rights. Services negotiations are ongoing under the General Agreement on Trade in Services (GATS), a parallel agreement associated with the WTO.

Communication Technology and the Spaces of Cultural Consumption

One form of services consumption occurs when services are delivered across borders and geographical space to the final consumer. This is typified by the purchase of cultural products embodied in a particular medium, such as books, magazines, recorded music, or software.

However, the consumption of communications and cultural products and services can take place in a number of other forms as well, each with its own trade and spatial characteristics. The purchase of the right to use certain cultural products under license—such as movies for public exhibition, foreign television and radio programs, or advertising campaigns by broadcasters—represents another form of trade. Using telecommunications networks to gain access to foreign information service providers, such as online or information services, constitutes yet another mode of delivery or consumption.

Notwithstanding the varied ways in which the consumption of media images (and, more generally, services) intersects with physical movement across space, the bulk of communications research on the topic is derived from what might be called a broadcasting model, epitomized by Shannon and Weaver's sender–message–channel–receiver typology (Shannon and Weaver, 1949). Although this model is broadly critiqued, it continues to be taught in communications textbooks, and its underlying assumptions still prefigure much of communications studies. According to this model, the purchase, reception, participation in, or consumption of communications products, services, and activities is conceived of as taking place in a static and stationary geographic setting or locale. Persons and groups are depicted as living in national or local political and social orders, where geographic space is somehow coterminous with the boundaries and distinctions among different political and cultural spaces. Communications and cultural services are then delivered across time and space using various electronic media, such as radio or recorded music, films, television and audiovisual services, or computer software. Or, conversely, consumers empowered by new technologies may use interactive electronic media to seek out and obtain certain products and services. In short, the broadcasting model assumes a fixed point at which an image is produced and another, distant, fixed point at which the image is consumed. The broadcasting model thus envisions three distinct moments—the moment of content production, the moment of transmission across channels of communication, and the moment of content consumption—and each moment is associated with a distinct space.

When one utilizes this model to analyze contemporary global media flows, one typically celebrates (or bemoans) the boundary-free character of new, place-transcending media channels (Crothers, 2007). Under the old order, according to scholars using this model, national institutions or markets were able to facilitate or serve as intermediaries or distribution mechanisms for traditional media such as books, magazines, films, sound recordings, and television programs. By contrast, new technologies of transmission, such as transborder computer communications connections, direct broadcast satellites, and low-earth orbital telecommunications satellite networks are often conceived of as offering a unique, inevitable, and invincible threat to national institutions (for discussion see Comor, 1998; Webster, 1984).

We take issue with several aspects of this perspective. Our critique of the broadcast model focuses on four areas: infrastructure, policy, content reception, and the organization of production and distribution. In contrast to the broadcast model, we contend that the technologies, dynamics, and spaces of mobility do not simply emerge from the intersection of place-based actors and cultures. They too are spaces of dynamism that are continually constructed through policy decisions, and these decisions may impact associated places and cultures as much as they impact the act of movement. For instance, the content of television, radio, and recorded music has significance and immediacy only because of the substantial investments in technological infrastructure that are required to distribute these messages.

The conceptual distinction between, on the one hand, content, consumption, and culture and, on the other hand, transmission and mobility, weakens when one considers the investments required to deliver a communications service. Certain forms of service provision and consumption are made possible only by large, geographically extensive, and sometimes very concentrated investments in technical infrastructures. These investments significantly reshape the physical and social spaces in which everyday life and consumption occur (Graham and Marvin, 1996; Mitchell, 1996). Infrastructure investments that are necessary for communications and cultural services consumption might be found in communications networks, transportation facilities, or public buildings. Hence, the ability to consume the infrastructure component of communications and cultural services is limited not only by the resource constraints of consumers, but also by the physical access of consumers to infrastructure investments in a specific geographic space. These technical media systems might include television broadcast stations, telephone lines, cable television distribution systems, or wireless towers (Baldwin, McVoy, and Steinfield, 1996). Consumption of the services available through this infrastructure, furthermore, can often be undertaken only through significant levels of private investment in equipment, such as consumer electronics.

The spatial configuration of access to services is likely to be very different depending on what type of investment strategy is chosen. Public policy objectives and regulatory constraints have resulted in traditional electronic communications investments in North America being spread out geographically to provide universal access to postal, telephone, radio, and television services (Horwitz, 1989; McChesney, 1993). Some of the contemporary and planned investments necessary to provide advanced telecommunications services will be in the form of wired networked technologies, which require incremental on-the-ground investment to reach new groups of consumers (Bernt, Kruse, and Landsbergen, 1993; Hadden and Lenert, 1995). Other investments, such as satellite or radio broadcasting systems, are more of an all-or-nothing proposition that will reach all potential users in urban areas and rural areas within the service region.

The feedback relationships between investments in communications infrastructure, media content, and cultural transformation are further elucidated when one examines the example of television. In *No Sense of Place*, Joshua Meyrowitz (1985) argues that the intimacy and immediacy of contact with a variety of very different settings and stories destroys an audience member's sense of being grounded and situated in a specific geographic or social setting. Arguably, this contention, which was made over twenty years ago, could be made even more forcefully today, with the advent of direct broadcast satellite transmission, which facilitates place-transcending identities and affiliations, sometimes through the broadcasting of programming across national borders. However, direct broadcast satellite systems require ground-based receiving and transmitting technologies and billing systems, and these, in turn, require national legislation and regulation (e.g., contract law). Hence, direct broadcast satellite systems construct places and rely on the existing fabric of places even as they demolish them. Further complicating Meyrowitz's argument is the fact that, in addition to contributing to a loss of sense of place locally, television also may have the role of enhancing consumers' familiarity with ob-tainable "foreign destinations" to which viewers then may travel as tourists or immigrants. Thus, television, which at first glance serves only to move images between fixed locations (and thereby dimin-ish the distinctiveness of those locations) may have a number of unintended secondary effects. It may also foster viewers' sense of place-distinctiveness (for distant destinations) and, in the long term, it may work to encourage the physical movement of people through space to those distant destinations (Frost, 2006; Mercille, 2005). This link between the movement of place-images and the movement of people, and the simultaneous and ongoing construction of the info-sphere of movement through travel is considered more directly later in this chapter. The eventual blurring that occurs between the con-struction of a media image of a nation and its actual physical con-struction (through tourism and immigration) is discussed at length in Chapter 5.

In general, we find that the more successful attempts at under-standing the role of new media in global society (and in the continuing importance of place) integrate these questions with broader investiga-tions of spatial trends in international political economy. For instance, it is widely noted that there has been a long-term movement in in-ternational political economy away from international trade between nationally organized vertically integrated firms engaged in mass indus-trial production for mass consumer markets. The past two decades have seen shifts toward production and exchange that are organized on a "post-fordist" and "global" basis (Amin, 1994; Mittelman, 2000; Tonkiss, 2006). There is less focus on mass production for mass mar-kets and more emphasis on production for fragmented and niche mar-kets. Firms are urged and forced to become agile, flexible, and more specialized (Harvey, 1989). Economic production is also typified by a larger role for service and information production, in what is often la-beled a postindustrial society or an information economy. These new forms of production, designed as they are to encourage, or serve, new forms of consumption, raise important questions for students of com-munication: Have new investments in and uses of telecommunications technology played any significant role in facilitating these changes? Are there emergent forms of spatial and temporal organization that typ-ify emerging forms of production, exchange, and consumption in an era of widespread use of computer communications (Hassan, 2003; Mosco, 1996)?

Questions about the importance of changes in telecommunications technology for the geographic centralization or dispersion of social life (or audiences) form a second overarching contemporary problem. For instance, it is widely argued that the declining cost of telecommunications and computer technology, new uses of computer-communications services by business and social groups, and the combined uses of broadcasting, computing, and communications services have led to new social uses of communication with distinctive spatial configurations (Harasim, 1993; Jones, 1995, 1998).

The production of communications and cultural products is being constantly reorganized to lower costs, gain access to skilled personnel, make use of new production technologies, and construct new audiences. This has resulted in a shift of much audiovisual production organized by major studios in California and a pattern called "runaway production" (Elmer and Gasher, 2005). A brief review of some of the literature on the spatiality of the film industry reveals some of the issues related to these questions. Michael Storper (1994) examines the industry organization in U.S. film-making (see also Storper and Christopherson, 1987). Sharon Strover (1995) also considers global and regional patterns in film coproductions, arguing that nationally identifiable characteristics are declining in products that seek to reach audiences in various countries and cultures. Paul Attallah (1996) notes the ambiguous and blurred references to places and the formulaic mix of characterizations emerging in international coproductions.

Joseph Straubhaar (1991) argues that regional linguistic agglomerations of film and television production and viewership are emerging which challenge notions of global markets for audiovisual programming, and which also lead to questions about the continued dependency of certain nation-states on flows of communications and cultural products from the North (see also Straubhaar, 2006). Michael Salwen (1991) looks at uses of media to challenge assumptions about the extent and shape of cultural imperialism. At the same time, as Beverly James (1995) points out in her study of Hungary, an important part of the media experience in countries that are in the process of becoming integrated with world markets is "learning to consume." What is apparent from these studies is that both the production and consumption of audiovisual services is becoming less nationally based. At the same time, new ways of integrating national audiences as segments of the global audience are being developed. As the example of the film industry demonstrates, the broadcast model, with its conceptual separation between production, transmission, and reception and its concomitant separation of channels of communication from content, is of limited utility for understanding the emergent spatial organization of cultural consumption.

In the remainder of this chapter, we turn our attention to the tourism industry, a component of the infosphere which, like the film industry, blurs the distinctions between the movement of people and the movement of images, between the reproduction of place and its transcendence, and between sites of production, transmission, and consumption. Following a brief introduction on the significance of tourism as a global industry based on the dual movement of people and images, the industry is analyzed in light of some of the infosphere characteristics that have been discussed previously in this book.

Travel and Tourism

Returning to the GATT typology of international trade in services, tourism fits into the third class of services (when a consumer of services enters a country and purchases services from a national provider) or the fourth (when both the provider and consumer are based in a country other than that in which the service transaction takes place, as when one stays at a hotel owned by an international hospitality services firm). As in the case of media, movement of tourists is not a secondary activity that supports production and consumption. Rather, movement lies at the essence of tourism.

In addition to these conceptual links between the flow of media images and the flow of tourists, these industries are materially linked as well. Indeed, it is difficult to imagine the tourism industry existing without communications media. Information and communications services support tourism in various ways, whether through promotion of tourism in advertising and marketing of prospective destinations and experiences (Trauer, 2006), the use of free media in press relations by tourism officials, news stories that cover stories in different parts of the world that are tourist "destinations," or the information and communication systems that are used to complete travel- and tourism-related transactions or to fulfill business process operations. Put another way, the tourism industry is as dependent on the flow of images from tourism destination areas to tourism source areas as it is dependent on the flow of people from tourism source areas to tourism destination areas.

World Tourism: A Growing Industry

The World Tourism Organization, a specialized agency of the United Nations, has been collecting and publishing data on international tourism since 1950. In 1950, international tourist arrivals (excluding same-day visitors) recorded at all international borders were just over 25 million. This rose to 69 million by 1960, and to 166 million by 1970. The largest rates of growth occurred in the 1950s (10.61 percent annual growth for the decade) and in the 1960s (high of 16.13 percent annual growth in 1964, low of 1.09 percent annual growth in 1968). Although the rates of growth in the mid- to late-1980s were lower, it should be emphasized that rates of growth in the 1980s were based on a much larger base of international tourist arrivals. For instance, in 1989 the level rose by 9.44 percent over 1988, but this number reflected an increase from 400 million arrivals in 1988 to 429 million arrivals in 1989. These rates of growth represent, in the 1990s, a huge absolute level in the annual number of international tourist arrivals (WTO, 1995b). Tourism rose in the 1990s, with international tourist arrivals growing from 455.9 million in 1990, to 550.4 million in 1995, to 687.3 million in 2000. The attacks on New York and Washington in 2001 and the conflicts that followed resulted in a decline of 0.5 percent that year to 684.1 million arrivals, but this was followed by an increase of 2.7 percent in international tourist arrivals in 2002 to 702.6 million arrivals (WTO, 2003, p. 1).

It is also notable that the levels of international tourist arrivals are quite variable. They roughly follow levels of overall economic growth (with their rate of swing, or increase and decrease, amplifying changes in the economic growth or recession). For instance, periods of slow economic growth also see very low levels of increase in tourist arrivals: 0.42 percent increase in 1980; 0.84 percent increase in 1981; and 0.01 percent decrease in 1982 (the only decline in international arrivals in the last 47 years until 2001). A similar, but not as severe slowdown in the rate of increase was seen in the early 1990s: 1.61 percent increase in 1991; 8.59 percent increase in 1992; 2.03 percent increase in 1993; and 3.02 percent increase in 1994 (WTO, 1995b, p. 193).

Receipts from international tourism (excluding international fare receipts) have increased even more rapidly. The year 1950 saw $2.1 billion in receipts, increasing to $6.9 billion in 1960. These levels of growth in receipts exceeded 20 percent throughout most of the 1970s. Even more accentuated patterns of rapid changes in rates of growth are seen in receipts. For four years (1977 to 1980), rates of growth averaged more than 23 percent. These figures fell, however, to a 2.06 percent increase in receipts in 1981; a decrease of 6.38 percent in 1982; and an increase of 2.61 percent in 1983. The late 1980s and early 1990s saw continued growth, but with levels varying from 21 percent in 1990 to 2.5 percent growth in 1991 (WTO, 1995b, p. 194). In 1990, international tourism receipts stood at $264.1 billion, and this number rose to $473.4 billion in 2000. With a slight decline in 2001, the overall receipts were estimated at $474.2 billion in 2002 (WTO, 2003, p. 3).

The regional patterns of tourist flows show a concentration of arrivals in European and North American Organization for Economic Cooperation and Development (OECD) industrialized countries, with 1993 arrivals led by France (60 million), the United States (46 million), Spain (40 million), Italy (26 million), Hungary (23 million, up from

TABLE 4.1. TOP TEN INTERNATIONAL TOURISM ARRIVALS, 2002

Country	Arrivals (millions)	Percent Change (2001 to 2002)	Share (%)
World	703	2.7	100
France	77.0	2.4	11.0
Spain	51.7	3.3	7.4
United States	41.9	–6.7	6.0
Italy	39.8	0.6	5.7
China	36.8	11.0	5.2
United Kingdom	24.2	5.9	3.4
Canada	20.1	1.9	2.9
Mexico	19.7	–0.7	2.8
Austria	18.6	2.4	2.6
Germany	18.0	0.6	2.6

Source: World Trade Organization (2003, p. 3).

TABLE 4.2. TOP TEN INTERNATIONAL TOURISM
RECEIPTS, 2002

Country	Receipts (billions $US)	Percent Change (2001 to 2002)	Share (%)
United States	66.5	–7.4	14.0
Spain	33.6	2.2	7.1
France	32.3	7.8	6.8
Italy	26.9	4.3	5.7
China	20.4	14.6	4.3
Germany	19.2	4.0	4.0
United Kingdom	17.8	9.5	3.8
Austria	11.2	11.1	2.4
Hong Kong (China)	10.1	22.2	2.1
Greece	9.7	3.1	2.1

Source: World Trade Organization (2003, p. 3).

9.4 million in 1980), the United Kingdom (19.5 million), and China
(19 million, up from 3.5 million in 1980) (WTO, 1995a, p. 12). The
rate of tourism to East Asia and the Pacific region grew the fastest in
1994, by 10 percent for the year, whereas Europe and the Middle East
were up 5 percent. North American arrivals increased by 3 percent for
the year, with Africa showing the smallest growth of tourist travel of
0.2 percent (OECD, 1996, p. 7). The same countries dominated in international arrivals in 2002, as shown in Table 4.1; with the exception of
China, they were all located in Europe or North America. Most of the
same countries were also world leaders in tourism receipts for 2002, although Canada and Mexico, both top ten countries in terms of arrivals,
are replaced by Hong Kong and Greece on the receipts table (see
Table 4.2).

Moving Images, Places, and People

Although our study joins research on media flows with that on the flow of
tourists, traditionally, the study of these flows operates from very different perspectives. Mass communications studies typically have focused
on the larger market, institutional, and organizational patterns of media
production, transmission, and consumption (the broadcast model discussed earlier in this chapter), with an emphasis on outlining structural patterns and forces (although cultural studies have often started
by looking at "practices"). The examination of tourism and travel

decisions and behavior, in contrast, typically begins by assuming a pre-eminence and freedom of individual decisions and discretion, rather than by looking at the systems of demand creation for travel and tourism (see Nash, 1995 for further discussion). The analysis below presents an integrated view of the spatial construction of mobility by connecting mobility in the infosphere to physical mobility in tourism and cultural consumption.

Infosphere technologies and services facilitate the physical mobility of information, things, and people in numerous ways. Existing transportation and communication infrastructure investments reflect past decisions in favor of certain forms and paths of mobility. These investments make specific forms of physical and information mobility possible, reducing the costs of some forms of mobility to certain destinations. Infosphere information and e-commerce transaction applications also facilitate travel by assisting planning and reducing uncertainty in tourism decisions, and the use of these technologies has contributed to massive change in the travel services sector.

Media, including news, entertainment, and gaming, contribute to the social construction of places and spaces of movement. They spark interest in newness and novelty of foreign destinations. We come to know of experiences and services that can be consumed only in distant locations. However, travel and tourism also reflect a dissatisfaction with mediated experience. The real place is sought in contrast to that experienced in media constructions in the infosphere. Managing the brand of a country or destination thus becomes a significant public relations problem for people in the tourist industry and for government officials (see also Chapter 5). Although safety and predictability are valued by travelers, international travel entails crossing borders and boundaries, heightening the sense of mobility by accentuating difference and uniqueness of distinct places.

The various forms of mobility are interconnected. We have focused on the mobility of information, goods (trade), investment, and finance; however, the movement of people for leisure, business, or long-term migration is also part of the spatial construction of mobility. These relationships lead us to ask whether the infosphere is a parallel space of mobility, a space supportive of mobility, a space of mobility inseparable from other spaces of mobility, or another distinct space of movement outside the physical world.

Technology, Infrastructure, and Restructured Spaces of Tourism and Cultural Consumption

The spatial reorganization of production and cities, it has been widely noted, is a process that is driven to a large extent by the availability of inexpensive, reliable transportation and communication. Peter Gould notes that technologies have a geographic impact in that they change the experience of the relationship between different places. An "accessibility surface" could provide a mapping of the time and cost required to travel to any geographic place. However, the "geographic impact of technology and the way it alters time and space relationships between places" (Gould, 1991, p. 6) differs among people with different levels of income and wealth. The cost of air travel may be minimal relative to expenditure power commanded by one individual or group, but may be so high for others that these services are essentially out of reach. Depending on the transportation infrastructure (seaports, airports, roads) and the services that are offered, the time and cost to reach places of similar distance from a given point may vary significantly. These structured patterns of space form, in Gould's view, a "backcloth" upon which collective and individual human experiences of the structures of physical space are set.

Gould argues that geography is not just about unrelated points and places, but that the consideration of the communication, transportation, economic, and cultural connections between different places is essential. "Without 'communication' there can be no 'geography of.' You cannot have a geography of anything that is unconnected. No connections, no geography. No connections means mere checklists without any relations between the items" (Gould, 1991, p. 4). Whereas "space" seems to refer to an abstract measurement of distance, "place" is seen to refer to the specific historical and cultural attributes of a location. A renewed sensitivity to spatial dynamics points to the structured relationships among different places, and "a place, or a region, only takes on human and geographic meaning in relation to other places and regions, and relations mean, once again, connections over geographic and all sorts of other spaces" (p. 4).

In the past 150 years, changing experiences of time and space have accompanied the development and availability of new transportation and communications technologies. The cost and time associated with travel has changed drastically, with more rapid and less expensive transportation technologies making the choice of transportation and travel as a form of consumption more available to nonelites. The ease, time, and cost of reaching particular tourist or travel destinations is affected both by the available technologies and by the level and type of investment in transportation infrastructure, such as canals, railway lines and stations, seaports, highways, or airports. Fernaud Braudel's (1984) history of the development of the world economy and of everyday life notes the importance of transportation and communications for the expanding extent of markets. Harold Innis's (1951, 1972) work provides an even broader survey of historical examples to demonstrate the connection between the strengths of various media in communicating across time and space (time-biased media, such as sculpture, being stronger across time; space-biased media, such as electronic broadcasting, being stronger across space) and the exercise of imperial power and control.

Attention to more specific or thematic historical and cultural studies of communications in the nineteenth century also provides insights into these shifts. Transportation and communication innovations, such as creating, building, and using railways, electrical services, and telegraph and telephone networks altered the geographical extent of markets and the spatial range of social and political life during that time period. James Carey (1988) argues that, in the mid-nineteenth century, truly national markets were created in the United States for the first time by the interrelated development of electronic communications and the introduction of standard time zones, both of which were partly efforts to organize and control railways. "[T]elegraphy [generated] the ground conditions for the urban imperialism of the mid-nineteenth century and the international imperialism later in the century" (p. 212). Daniel Headrick (1991) relates the expansion of European and British imperial power in the late nineteenth century to repeated efforts to lay worldwide submarine cable networks. Stephen Kern (1983) notes the importance of a number of transportation and communications technologies, such as the railway, the bicycle, the telegraph, and the telephone, in prompting a sea-change in conceptions and experiences of space in the nineteenth century, as do Daniel Czitrom (1982) and Peter Hugill (1993, 1999). Carolyn Marvin (1988) considers the ideological and moral content of the ways in which the annihilation of space and time was first conceived. These historical treatments of the development and use of communications technology and their relationships to the spatial reorganization of economic, social, and political life allow us to place contemporary theoretical debates in a longer term perspective. With the post-1945 growth of the automobile culture and physical infrastructure (Kunstler, 1993), and with the decline in airline ticket prices and increased traffic in major hubs (Matsumoto, 2007), there are resources available to a minority of the world's population that allow them to make national and international travel a significant part of annual household budgets.

In other words, advances in transportation and communication technologies that have made tourism (relatively) accessible to the masses are inseparable from advances that have both facilitated and responded to changes in the organization of production (and these changes, in turn, have increased leisure time that has further enabled the growth of tourism). The operation of "flexible production" or "just-in-time production" requires more reliable communications and transportation networks and services to move information, raw materials, parts and components, and semimanufactured goods throughout the world. Although post-Fordism demonstrates specific patterns of production and exchange, the emerging spatial patterns of consumption of communications and cultural services, as evidenced in tourism, can also be explored along these lines.

Infosphere technologies also provide for logistical support to coordinate and plan tourism and transportation, just as communication, information, transportation, finance, and consumption were connected in the development of the industrial economy in the United States (Beniger, 1986). Services consumed may range from a meager subsistence for the backpacker or the person who visits friends, to a full package of transportation, information and guides, sports, cultural events, entertainment, shopping, food, accommodation, and communication, offered separately or in a package. Cruise lines combine interstate mobility with predictable levels of accommodation, food, and entertainment. The airline industry coordinates the logistics of transportation through interconnected passenger information exchange, while also working to meet state requirements to facilitate rapid passage through customs and immigration at national borders.

As new media take on more importance in the daily lives of persons, especially persons in the developed regions of the world, new media and infosphere technologies are increasingly being used in tourism-related information and transaction activities. Already, online booking of travel and accommodations services has become one of the most popular forms of e-commerce, and has led to significant restructuring in the travel agency business. International travelers, in particular, often prefer making reservations via websites as a means of avoiding language difficulties that emerge when one interacts in person or over the telephone. In the United States, the Airlines Reporting Corporation reported in 2004 that "the number of travel agencies nationwide has been cut in half over the past five years,... [a]nd the travel agencies that have survived aren't exactly flourishing" (Quick, 2004).

The relationship between the construction of tourism infrastructure, mobility, and economic development is similarly complex within tourism-destination countries. Claims about the benefits for national citizens arising from infrastructure investments should be examined carefully. The mobility that is facilitated by seaports, airports, roads, and utilities is constrained to the specific physical locations in which those investments are located and may not be fungible into other forms of physical mobility. Infrastructure investments are often geographically specific, and the lack of roads, electricity, and communication services in some regions may not be addressed if the support for international tourism results in uneven investment and geographic distribution of basic infrastructure. For instance, building good roads in one part of a town or country may lead to a failure to provide these services in other parts of the country. Likewise, large international airports, which often are constructed to support rapid international mobility of short-term visitors from other countries, may be less useful to support the mobility of national visitors from within the country or the daily movements of people and things that are required to support economic and social development.

After all of these infrastructural investments have been made, both by international travel companies and destination-country actors, packages are presented to travelers as "choices." These somewhat predictable experiences are marketed as expressions of individual freedom. Prominent applications in the infosphere contribute to the standardization of these services. Together, these investments in place and transportation–communication infrastructure allow the projection of consumer power around the world, constructing spaces of social and geographic mobility.

Media and Socially Constructed Images of Destinations

The shifting of social space along with geographic space may be associated with the historical knowledge and ideological or religious beliefs of a traveler. The significance and experiences associated with a specific geographic location cannot be divorced from these historical and social meanings (Urry, 2002). These meanings attached to a location by a culture or its fragments, however, often are significantly contested and debated (e.g., Berlin, Jerusalem, Sarajevo). The social and historical meanings associated with particular places that serve to define cities, fields, beaches, parks, or the regions of a country or ocean may also carry and deliver across time, through a shared set of cultural stories and symbols, a significance that the empirical and visible characteristics of a particular place do not seem to sustain (e.g., site of Kent State killings, historical battlefield sites).

As noted above, mass communications media may serve an important role in entertainment, news programming, and advertising and in building these shared meanings, whether among national groups (Kirby, 1986) or among global audience members, of what stories or significance are attached to geographic locations and regions such as "Miami," "Orlando," "New York," "Calcutta," "Africa," "Australia" (Frost, 2006), or Tibet (Mercille, 2005). This creation of social meanings of space may also occur more deliberately for manufactured places or destinations as a form of "product placement" in films (Hudson and Ritchie, 2006). Christopher Anderson (1994) argues that the early Disney television programs of the 1950s became essentially extended commercials for the then under-construction Disneyland (see also Cohen, 1995). Places are constructed in part through media representations, likewise travel, touring as an experience (Peel and Steen, 2006), and ethnicity are constructed in varying ways through media representations (Buzinde, Santos, and Smith, 2006; Dorsey, Steeves, and Porras, 2004; Fursich, 2002).

In December 2003, the World Tourism Organization launched a series of initiatives to improve media portrayal of the tourism industry

(UNWTO, 2004a). One initiative, called the "Tourism Enriches" campaign, presents a set of media messages intended to be used in tourism campaigns by national tourism promotion authorities (UNWTO, 2004b). The aims of the campaign are "to promote tourism as a basic human right and a way of life, to stimulate communication about the benefits of tourism as the most prospective economic activity for the local communities and countries, to enhance cooperation between destinations and the tourism industry with the local, regional and international media and to link individual tourism entities to the larger community of international tourism" (UNWTO, 2004a). Among the claims made by the "awareness campaign" literature are that:

> International tourism is the world's largest export earner and vital to the balance of payments of many countries. For small, developing nations, tourism is often the only way they can compete in the dynamically expanding service sector.

> Tourism jobs and enterprises are usually created in the most underdeveloped regions, helping to equalize economic opportunities through-out the country. This also provides an incentive for residents to remain in rural areas rather than follow the exodus to the already over-crowded cities of many developing nations.

> Taxes on hotel stays, restaurant meals, and other tourism-related goods and services fill the coffers of local, regional, and national governments (UNWTO, 2004b).

The campaign documentation also claims that "enrichment is not just economic."

> The environment and local culture receive a boost when authorities restore monuments, open museums and establish parks to lure visitors.

> As tourism increases, so does a destination's need to improve infrastructure to handle the influx. New airports, roads, marinas, sewage and water treatment plants and dozens of other projects are the

result, providing a substantial improvement in the residents' own lives from clean drinking water and speedier communications (UNWTO, 2004b).

The Secretary-General of the World Tourism Organization introduced this campaign by noting, "We are calling upon governments to implement this importance of tourism in practice and invest more funds in tourism development and promotion.... The success of 'Tourism Enriches' also depends in part on its diffusion in the media, so we are inviting them to become the third member in the already established public-private partnership in international tourism" (UNWTO, 2004b).

In his keynote address to the First World Conference on Tourism Communications, held in Madrid in 2004, Secretary-General Francesco Frangialli noted that the last three years of "crisis" had "underscored the importance of the relationship between tourism and the news media" ("WTO calls on media," February 6, 2004, see also Richter, 2003). Frangialli stated:

> This difficult period has made tourism destinations and businesses more aware than ever of the need for effective communications programmes. Advances in communications technology, round-the-clock news coverage, globalization of the news media, and a proliferation of media outlets offering alternative viewpoints are developments that are rapidly changing the communications field— forcing us all to update our strategies and skills" ("WTO calls on media," February 6, 2004).

Frangialli also claimed that, although the media did play a "highly positive role" in encouraging tourism, travelers' concern and "panic" in response to the 2003 Severe Acute Respiratory Syndrome (SARS) epidemic were in part "a reaction to excessive media coverage and to a perceived safety threat that is often way out of proportion with the real situation." Frangialli stated,

> Many tourism officials in Asia are now saying their SARS crisis last year was not an epidemic at all but an infodemic. Traveller panic over these problems is in part irrational. It's a reaction to excessive media coverage and to a perceived safety threat that is often way out

of proportion with the real situation. Seasoned travellers already know this and we can see that the general public is also becoming somewhat desensitized to crisis. . . . This growing insensitivity helps destinations recover more quickly from crisis, as public attention turns to the next big news story. But journalists still need to be aware that the way they interpret and the way they report on an event can have severe implications for tourism. On the other hand, if news coverage is balanced and sober, it can have fewer negative impacts" (Frangialli, 2004, p. 2).

The UNWTO's Code of Ethics, Frangialli notes, calls for "honest and balanced information on events and situations that could influence the flow of tourists. This is what the tourism sector request of you, the media" ("WTO calls on media," February 6, 2004). Furthermore,

tourism by nature is highly dependent on media reporting. The vast majority of holiday decisions are made by people who have never seen the destination for themselves. They select a place to go, they buy plane tickets and reserve hotel rooms based only on what they have learned from their travel agent, from friends and above all from the media. Research has shown that the media is many times more influential in the selection of holiday spots than travel agents and even more influential than the recommendations of friends (Frangialli, 2004, p. 2).

The UNWTO's focus on representations in news stories, rather than in industry-generated media, points to the importance of destination branding in the tourism industry. Destination branding is the point at which the flow of an image (a potential tourist's perception of a place) meets the flow of tourists that (it is hoped) will generate revenue for the tourism-destination country (Azarya, 2004; Fursich and Robins, 2004). As the campaign tacitly acknowledges, destination branding does much more than disseminate information about a potential destination. It also may contribute to uniformity in the types of facilities and experiences that are promised in different countries. For instance, designing na-tional museums for tourism may serve different goals than would be met if the museums were designed to serve the national public and nation-building. Theme parks designed and operated by transnational integrated media and entertainment companies, such as Disney or Universal, may become a more important part of building revenues from international tourism than indigenous local museums and cultural institutions, and, as has occurred in Florida, may in fact become the region's central identifying marker of its "culture" on the world stage (to the point where Florida's state parks have been reduced to defensively branding themselves as "The *Real* Florida").

Along with the shifting of geographical spaces accomplished through international mobility comes a movement among social and political spaces, each with different rules and expectations. The motivations to shift geographic and social spaces may arise because different formal and legal institutions are encountered by travelers, allowing them to gain access to activities that they are forbidden from indulging in at home (Eadington, 1995). As international tourism entails crossing national borders, the traveler encounters a change in social and political space that may be more significant to their experience than any change in geographic space or climate. The escape from certain social roles and practices that one experiences as a tourist may in fact be the primary motivation for consumption across borders. Sex tourism, drug tourism, gambling tourism, or hunting in environments with less restrictive rules may be met by traveling to a different jurisdiction (Enloe, 1989; Richter, 1995). At the same time, while destination branding typically emphasizes difference and distance, too much difference or distance can detract from a destination's attractiveness. For instance, Canada advertises itself to the U.S. market as "the world next door," a slogan that emphasizes nearness (and, especially, safety, in the post-9/11 world) as well as a distinct and diverse ethnic and cultural composition. In a similar vein, Key West, Florida, advertises itself to potential visitors from the United States as "The American Caribbean." Similarly, Frangialli's concern about media portrayals of the SARS epidemic suggests that, although tourists may be amenable to undertaking some risks in travel, other risks are so severe as to dissuade potential visitors.

Conclusions: Relating Spaces of Mobility

The links between media and tourism are strong and long-standing, whether in images in entertainment programming or news reports, in the use of media for advertising and public relations campaigns to promote tourism, or in the use of information and communication technologies to support business transactions in the tourism industry.

The movement of people through travel and tourism, and the experiences they either seek or enjoy, are also connected to the spatial construction of mobility in the infosphere. Although the infosphere can be seen as a parallel space of mobility, in which physical movements are coordinated and controlled by information and communication activities, it is also much more than this. Likewise, the concept of the infosphere as a space *supportive* of mobility, in which images of destinations and the rest of the world are presented as different but accessible, is also only partial. As elaborated in the next chapter, in addition to serving as a space of imagery and logistical support, the infosphere is also a space of imagination, wherein individuals travel to construct their own images of real (but imagined) places. The mobility of the infosphere thus is mutually shaped by other forms of mobility, and the representations, coordinations, and imaginings of physical mobility shape and contribute in important ways to forms and understandings of physical mobility, such as tourism.

5 Internet Names, Semiotics, and Alternative Spaces of Governance

Peter Taylor (1996) begins his book *The Way the Modern World Works* with an observation about hegemony and language in global telecommunications. He asserts that true hegemony is fairly uncommon. A state that has the power to bend others to its will is not necessarily hegemonic. For Taylor, hegemony involves more than being dominant militarily, politically, culturally, or economically. Rather, a hegemon's combined *social* power is so awesome that its values and desires define the field of interaction. A hegemon's identity becomes fused with that of the global system, leaving other states' identities to be scripted only as exceptions.

Taylor buttresses this definition of hegemony with two examples from international communications conventions. Postal conventions developed during the nineteenth century decreed that each state would print its own postage stamps, and that each stamp would bear the name of its issuing state. The exception was the United Kingdom, the stamps of which needed no state identification. The international system was a British system, and British nationality was accepted as the default nationality (or, perhaps, as the "internationality"). To this day, postage stamps issued by the United Kingdom are the only ones that do not contain the name of the issuing state. Taylor's second example comes from the Internet, a medium of the late twentieth and early twenty-first century, in which the United States has been hegemonic. Taylor contrasts his e-mail address at what was then his home institution in the United Kingdom (newcastle.ac.uk) with his e-mail address when he had been a visiting scholar at Virginia Tech (vt.edu). As is the case with the postal system, the hegemon's power is assumed.

Although this vignette demonstrates that the infosphere is a site of uneven social power, it also suggests that the infosphere lies in a border zone between globalism and statism. The Internet could have been constructed as an arena in which every site clearly was associated with a state (in which case each U.S.-affiliated site would contain a .US suffix) and it could have been constructed as a purely nonstate space (in which case every website would have a generic top-level domain name like .COM, .EDU, or .ORG, and country-code top-level domain names like .UK and .JP would not exist). The hybrid system that emerged—with generic domain names predominating inside the United States and country-code names prevalent elsewhere—combines claims to globalism, sovereignty, and the overarching power of the hegemon, much as was achieved by nineteenth-century Britain with respect to the postal system.

It follows that the infosphere is neither a space that is solely the sum of pre-existing state territories nor is it a space where the authority of the state is universally transcended. Rather, as we have argued throughout this book, it is a space wherein the continual tension between globalist flows and statist claims to territorial sovereignty are being renegotiated.

As we asserted in Chapter 1, sovereignty is produced not through the policing of boundaries but through their crossing, and the infosphere is one domain in which these sovereignty-producing spatial practices of reterritorialization are conducted. The management of the infosphere has been, and continues to be, a complicated affair. The infosphere must be understood as a space more complex than simply the space of a new world order, instituted by a global hegemon (the governance dimension of management). Nor is the infosphere simply a space in which the community of states has consensually implemented a technical-bureaucratic fix (the technological dimension). Nor can the infosphere be reduced to the sum of all the grassroots spaces and communities constructed by its users (the cultural dimension). It is all of these and more. The infosphere is managed through a continual process of renegotiation between states, nations, and communities of providers and users. This continual renegotiation occurs on many fronts, and one of these fronts revolves around how one names and represents one's presence there.

It is to this process of renegotiation through naming that we turn in this chapter and in the one that follows. In this chapter we focus on two Pacific Island microstates that, in very different ways, have used their Internet domain names to construct new virtual identities outside the idealized nexus of nation, government, and territory that typically legitimizes state sovereignty in the modern global political system. In Chapter 6, we approach the politics of Internet name management from a different angle, examining the politics of the Internet Corporation for Assigned Names and Numbers (ICANN) and the way that it positions itself between concerns for openness and mobility and the desire to maintain security and territorial stability.

States and Signification

Because an Internet domain name is just that—a name—and not a material country, we launch these two chapters from a perspective informed by semiotics, the study of symbols and signs, particularly as applied to social phenomena (Gottdiener, 1995; Hodge and Kress, 1988). This emphasis parallels the concerns of a number of poststructuralist international relations theorists who stress that the web of power relations that confer authority on the state system and individual states is textual as well as material. A state's power is derived, at least in part, from its designation as a state, and this designation is reproduced as it and other states interact according to the established rules and languages of international relations (Biersteker and Weber, 1996; Der Derian and Shapiro, 1989; Ó Tuathail, 1996).

The role of signification in the maintenance of the state system can be elucidated by expanding on an example provided by de Saussure:

> We assign identity, for instance, to two trains ("the 8:45 from Geneva to Paris"), one of which leaves twenty-four hours after the other. We treat it as the "same" train, even though probably the locomotive, the carriages, the staff etc. are not the same. Or if a street is demolished and then rebuilt, we say it is the same street, although there may be physically little or nothing left of the old

one. How is it that a street can be reconstructed entirely and still be the same? Because it is not a *purely* material structure. It has other characteristics which are independent of its bricks and mortar; for example, its situation in relation to other streets. Similarly, the train is identified by its departure time, its route, and any other features which distinguish it from other trains (de Saussure, 1986, p. 107, emphasis added).

In other words, when we refer to two different trains as "the 8:45 from Geneva to Paris" we are combining the signifier of a train (the word "train") and the signified of a train (our concept of a train) and applying them to the train's functional, rather than material manifestation. This is not to say that the material train does not exist outside of its functionalist representation. However, the referent that emerges from our signification is embedded with functional properties (identity across a regular interval of time) not inherent in the material object. The fact that our language embeds these characteristics within the sign of a train suggests that certain functional properties of a train (its regularity and predictability in space and time) are of high social importance when we interact with the signified concept (the train). It follows from this line of argument that whereas trains are material constructs that exist logically prior to signification, the idea of a scheduled train as a single, regularly recurring entity is a function of our signification. If this act of signification proceeds to shape our expectations (e.g., that trains will run on time) as well as our overall ideal of mobility (e.g., that the world is one that can be traversed with reasonable predictability, given the appropriate mechanical infrastructure), and if individuals and institutions plan their activities around these ideals, then we can assert that signification not only reflects the material world but even plays a role in constructing it.

A similar phenomenon with regard to signification and the construction of concepts as occurring with regularity in time and space pertains to states. As Anderson (1991) notes, the concept of a nation is built upon the (imagined) ideal that there is a community that has continuity across time and permanency in space. When this ideal is merged with that of the territorial state (that a state has uninterrupted control over a swath of bounded land), we see the emergence of the concept of the nation-state: the idealized confluence of government, nation, and territory. The ideology of the modern territorial nation-state is based upon the ideal that the bounds of a state's territory neatly coincide both with the area over which a state government exercises sovereign authority and with the area wherein residents identify as members of a single, indivisible nation. Thus the state is portrayed as a "natural" community, fixed in space and beyond the variability of time.

Although the modern ideal of the sovereign, territorial nation-state is founded on the state's claim to transcend the constraints of present-day exigencies, in actuality all states have clearly defined temporal boundaries, with few going back more than a few hundred years and with even fewer displaying the history of territorial and national integrity implied by the modern ideal (Agnew and Corbridge, 1995; Newman, 1999). Thus, acts of signification play a role in constructing the state ideal, and these in turn underlie the basis of governmental authority. For instance, when we see the Canadian flag (or the word Canada or a map of Canada) we think of it as representing the state known as Canada. But would Canada as a *state*—a concept that embodies an idealized confluence of government, nation, and territory, with some permanency in time and space—exist if it were not so signified? The materiality of Canada—its governmental entities, individuals, and places—would still exist, but one can argue that the state exists, at least in part, as a function of its signification. This signification, in turn, is constructed through the numerous micropractices through which individuals construct the state's discursive power and the identity of its citizen-subjects (Mitchell, 1991). And, as Sparke (2005) notes, these micropractices that reproduce the state ideal occur not only between states and their citizen-subjects. They also occur through the actions of economic actors who cross borders as they negotiate (and reproduce) the state system with its underlying ideal of the unified nation-government-territory nexus (see also Der Derian and Shapiro, 1989; Ó Tuathail, 1996).

Transformations in the signification of statehood are particularly noteworthy because for several decades scholars have been asserting that the traditional bases of the modern sovereign state are under attack, whether from intercontinental missiles that deprive the state of its territorial protection function (Herz, 1959), multinational corporations that prevent states from controlling their economies (Vernon, 1972), or information flows that disable modern notions of citizenship and territorial integrity (Wriston, 1992). Taken as a whole, a convincing argument may be made that increased global flows of information, commodities, and currency are leading to a deterritorialization of the state that is undermining the ideal of the nation-government-territory nexus that historically has provided the ideological foundation for state power. As new levels of global mobility and interaction make the links between nation, government, and territory ever more tenuous, states (and other political actors) scramble to construct new bases for legitimizing their participation in social activities that traditionally have been reserved for state actors (i.e., domestic governance and international relations). Efforts at reterritorialization are likely to involve new ways of conceiving the state, engendering new ways of constructing related concepts such as sovereignty and citizenship, and integrating aspects of social life and methods of signification not traditionally associated with state authority (Albert, 1999; Doty, 1999; Mandaville, 1999).

The infosphere is one such arena of state signification wherein this reterritorialization is occurring. For instance, when a Japanese corporation establishes a website based in France with a .DE suffix but whose referent to Germany refers neither to the territory where the server is located nor the nationality of the site's administrators or users, is the significance of statehood being transformed, transgressed, or reaffirmed? According to the ideal of the territorial nation-state, under which most (if not all) modern states justify their authority, states are affiliated with governments that claim the affiliation of individuals and the control of space. Thus, at the most radical level, one could argue that this discursive construction of statehood represents a fundamental reformulation of state identity. According to this argument, new "states" are being created on the Internet, freed from the nation-government-territory nexus that historically has formed the ideological foundation of states' existence. A slightly less radical version of this interpretation is that, although state signifiers in the infosphere are not constructing new states, they are contributing to a reterritorialization of existing states, as states gather new sets of resources to redefine their scope and foundation. Alternately, the infosphere may be seen as a parallel universe of floating state signifiers that point to virtual states, a development that is one component of a broader trend within postmodern capitalism in which individuals increasingly encounter and consume the "hyperreal" world of signs rather than the real world of materiality (Baudrillard, 1988). According to this interpretation, the existence of nontraditional state signification in the infosphere is indicative of a general trend in the role of signs in society, but it is not necessarily transformative of the referents behind the signified objects (the material states). Another possible interpretation is that state signification in the infosphere represents little change at all, but simply the continuation of a flexibility in state signification that always has been present in the modern state system. Finally, the persistence of state signifiers in the infosphere may be seen as a reaffirmation of state power, given that the arena of electronic communications lacks the territoriality that typically provides a material foundation for state power and therefore could theoretically exist completely devoid of state signification.

In this chapter, we explore these questions concerning the role of the infosphere in the reproduction (or transformation) of the state system. The following section presents a brief history of the Internet domain name system. This history is followed by sections on state signification in the country-code top-level domains of Pitcairn Island (.PN) and Niue (.NU). These sections are followed by a conclusion in which we attempt to assess the import of state signification in the infosphere.

Generic and Country-Code Top-Level Domains

Despite its origin as a communications system for the U.S. military and its later incarnation as a venture of the U.S. National Science Foundation, all indications are that the Internet Assigned Numbers Authority (IANA) envisioned an Internet in which there were no state signifiers and in which, more generally, overt intervention by state institutions or reproduction of state borders would be kept to a minimum. IANA, based at the University of Southern California and headed by Jon Postel, was contracted by the U.S. government to design and maintain a system of Internet domain names. IANA initially created seven generic top-level domain names (gTLDs) that could be used by an entity wishing to register its own second-level domain name: .COM for commercial entities, .EDU for educational institutions, .NET for networks, .INT for organizations established by international treaties, .MIL for the U.S. military, .GOV for governmental entities within the United States, and .ORG for all other registrants.

At the same time that these gTLDs were established, IANA, in "an uncharacteristic lapse of consistency on the part of early Internet designers" (Mueller, 1998, p. 92), established a parallel structure of country-code top-level domain names (ccTLDs). As Postel later recalled, the establishment of the ccTLDs was "pretty much an afterthought after a lot of debate about what the original [gTLDs] should be.... Most of the people involved at that time didn't think the country codes would be used for much" ("What's NU?" 1997). As late as 1998, Postel also noted that for each ccTLD, the administrator "is generally the first person that asks for the job (and is somehow considered a 'responsible person')" (Mueller, 2002, p. 89).

Postel's intentions notwithstanding, within a short amount of time, the gTLDs came to be perceived internationally as U.S. TLDs (hardly surprising given both their history and the fact that two of the seven original gTLDs were reserved for U.S. government entities), and registrants in countries around the world (except for the United States) flocked to their ccTLDs (Mueller, 1998). As of July 2006, about 155 million hosts were registered with ccTLD suffixes, compared to just 76.7 million hosts registered with .COM names (Internet Systems Consortium [ISC], 2006).

Postel and his associate Ann Cooper acknowledged already in 1993 that the TLD system had deviated from IANA's original plan:

> Even though the original intention was that any educational institution anywhere in the world could be registered under the .EDU domain, in practice, it has turned out with few exceptions, only those in the United States have registered under .EDU, similarly with .COM (for commercial). In other countries, everything is registered under the 2-letter country code, often with some subdivision. For example, in Korea (.KR), the second level names are .AC for academic community, .CO for commercial, .GO for government, and .RE for research. However, each country may go its own way about organizing its domain, and many have (Cooper and Postel, 1993).

In this same report, Cooper and Postel announced a reorganization of gTLDs and the barely used .US ccTLD. The ccTLD .GOV would be reserved solely for the federal government, and .EDU would be reserved solely for institutions of higher education. U.S. governmental bodies below the federal level and educational institutions below the level of four-year colleges would adopt names reflecting a geographic hierarchy, ending with the .US ccTLD (e.g., www.dep.state.pa.us for Pennsylvania's Department of Environmental Protection).

In practice, the TLD system has mutated still further since this reorganization, as casual web surfers have learned to hone in on .COM, .NET, and .ORG. Thus, for instance, the United Nations has established its website at www.un.org, not www.un.int (the latter URL is associated with a listing of permanent missions to the United Nations), and the State of Florida has established its website at www.myflorida.com, not www.state.fl.us (although this URL automatically forwards to www.myflorida.com). The Internet Corporation for Assigned Names and Numbers (ICANN), which in 1998 assumed most of IANA's functions, effectively has acknowledged that the distinction between .COM, .NET, and .ORG has been obliterated. A Frequently Asked Questions sheet on the ICANN website contains the following information about these three gTLDs:

- The .COM domain . . . is a generic top-level domain originally intended for commercial businesses around the world.
- The .NET domain . . . is a generic top-level domain used by many types of organizations and individuals globally; it was historically intended for and is still commonly used by Internet service providers.
- The .ORG domain . . . is unrestricted, but it was intended to serve the noncommercial community (ICANN, 2004).

In November 2000, ICANN announced four new gTLDs (.BIZ, .INFO, .NAME, and .PRO). Additionally, ICANN has proposed or implemented a number of sponsored top-level domains (sTLDs), the use of which is to be closely restricted to select users such as firms in a specific industry or providers of a specific service. These include .AERO, .ASIA, .CAT, .COOP, .MAIL, .MOBI, .MUSEUM, .POST, .TEL, .TRAVEL, and .XXX. Meanwhile, beginning in 2002, the barely used .US ccTLD was delinked from U.S. governmental entities and became available to any registrant associated with the United States (NeuStar, Inc., 2002).

When IANA began assigning ccTLDs, it chose to utilize the ISO 3166-1 list, a series of two-letter country codes that the International Standards Organization (ISO) had begun assigning to countries in 1974 in an effort to aid international postal services (ISO, 2004). Although the ISO list primarily is derived from a list of country names published by the United Nations, it also assigns unique codes to a number of inhabited overseas territories. Thus, as of October 2006 there were 192 United Nations member states but 244 "countries" on ISO 3166–1. Not wishing to enter the politically murky "business of deciding what is and what is not a country, nor what code letters are appropriate for a particular country," IANA/ICANN has declared that it will adhere strictly to ISO 3166-1 in assigning ccTLDs (IANA, 2003).[1]

In other words, even though the Internet was envisioned as an arena that would transcend the territorial divisions of the world, the domain name structure reproduces these divisions. As Wilson (2001, p. 64) writes, "Despite the potential to develop as a supranational system, the naming convention for cyberspace reinforces the existing geographic delimitation of space." This finding is in keeping with those of others who have suggested that the Internet, rather than transcending divisions among and within states, reproduces them, whether through its use for state promotion (Brunn and Cottle, 1997), through tendencies for one web page's links to refer disproportionately to web pages associated with the same host country (Halavais, 2000), or through the physical location of Internet infrastructure (Dodge and Kitchin, 2001).

Given the unexpected utilization of ccTLDs (outside the United States), it seems incontrovertible that the Internet, to at least some degree, exists within and reproduces the state system. However, there is disagreement about the extent to which the naming system reproduces U.S. hegemony. Mitchell, Bradner, and Claffy (1997, p. 262) write that the use of gTLDs in the United States and ccTLDs elsewhere is merely a "historical anachronism," and similar positions are taken by Abbate (1999), Mueller (1998), and Wilson (2001). These authors note that, when the Internet began, practically all institutions with a web presence were located in the United States, so there was no need to use the .US ccTLD. As other countries' institutions began to appear on the web, these entities desired ccTLD identifiers. Thus the present system evolved wherein a gTLD effectively is shorthand for association with the United States.

Despite these apparently innocent origins, outside the United States the tendency for American firms to use .COM rather than the .US ccTLD is seen as arrogant (Mueller, 1998; Shaw, R., 1997), and it appears that there is not yet a consensus whether .COM signifies a global or an American presence. Some non-U.S. companies, for instance, have organized their web presence around the principle that .COM represents a global business and they have reserved their .COM address for their global corporate website. For instance, the world headquarters of the Finnish multinational Nokia is at www.nokia.com and the world headquarters of the Italian firm Parmalat is at www.parmalat.com. Firms such as these, who use .COM as a global signifier, then tend to create a second .COM address for their U.S. subsidiaries (e.g., www.nokiausa.com and www.parmalatusa.com). In contrast, other firms recognize that, for much of the world, .COM effectively means "United States" and they have reserved their .COM address for their U.S. subsidiary. For instance, the Japanese firms Honda, Sony, and Toyota all have taken this strategy, as www.honda.com, www.sony.com, and www.toyota.com each point to websites specifically designed for customers in the United States or clients interested in their U.S. subsidiaries.

Firms such as Honda, Sony, and Toyota that use .COM to refer to their U.S. subsidiaries then are left with the dilemma of what to name their global websites, and here each firm has adopted a different strategy. Honda has chosen to reuse .COM for its global site (much in the way that Nokia and Parmalat reuse .COM for their U.S. sites), creating the website world.honda.com. Honda also maintains websites for countries such as Canada (www.honda.ca) and the United Kingdom (www.honda.co.uk). Sony uses the gTLD .NET for its global site (www.sony.net). Toyota represents its global business as an extension of its Japanese roots by including its global corporate information within its www.toyota.co.jp website.

Regardless of whether .COM is used to signify "United States" (the Honda/Sony/Toyota model) or "world" (the Nokia/Parmalat model), multinational corporations seem to agree that, outside the United States, national subsidiaries should be signified by use of that country's ccTLD, even in the corporation's home country. For instance, Nokia's website for users in its home country of Finland is www.nokia.fi and Parmalat's in Italy is www.parmalat.it. This decision seems to be in line with the advice of international business consultant Lee Hodgson, who instructs companies trying to reach customers outside the United States to use ccTLD addresses so that they will appear to be offering "local solutions" (Hodgson, 2001a). Meanwhile, the registrar for the .US ccTLD, which, beginning in 2002 was made available to individuals and organizations resident, incorporated, or with any other "bona fide presence" in the United States, similarly has been attempting to market itself as an option for businesses and individuals seeking an American "local" identity (NeuStar, Inc., 2002). An advertisement for the .US registry proclaims, "Get your .US address and be part of something uniquely American" (NeuStar, Inc., 2004), but it remains to be seen how successful this strategy will be, given that the American public expects their "local solutions" to come from commercial entities that have .COM addresses.

Although it seems likely that the privileging of the United States in the Internet domain name system was unintentional, intent is not necessary for the reproduction of hegemony. Indeed, a key indicator of hegemonic status is that one's authority is so pervasive that dominance is projected in the absence of intent. Given this definition of hegemony, it appears that the Internet naming system has all the signs of reproducing U.S. hegemony. First, the hegemon defines its own naming system as the generic standard. Second, other states are given opportunities to define themselves on other terms, but these other terms are suboptimal for would-be global actors. Third, as entities outside the United States abandon their ccTLDs to clamor onto the .COM bandwagon, the hegemon's standard becomes naturalized as a global norm.

Before one launches an attack on Yankee cyberimperialism, however, it should be stressed that hegemony is a double-edged sword. As with all hegemonic practices, the domain naming system is notable for its inclusiveness as well as its reproduction of hierarchy. Indeed, hegemony reproduces hierarchy *through* inclusiveness. In one sense, U.S. hegemony, on the Internet as elsewhere, offers the promise of democracy. Entities outside the United States are invited to adopt the .COM gTLD alongside U.S. companies, rather than being relegated to the minor leagues of .UK, .JP, and .FR. However, by making this move, these non-U.S. entities acknowledge that success as a global economic actor is dependent upon developing an American-style name, and this involves becoming a late entrant in a system that remains controlled by U.S. firms and institutions.[2]

Whereas the structure of Internet domain names may reproduce the broad contours of the U.S.-led state system, it does so in a manner that calls into question the nation-government-territory relationship that discursively underlies each state within that system. Thus, even as the Internet domain system reproduces hegemony, it simultaneously renegotiates its basis. Perhaps this reconfiguration of the nation-government-territory nexus is most evident in the relatively insignificant role that, especially until recently, IANA/ICANN has given to governments in the administration of ccTLDs.

IANA's original criteria for designating a ccTLD manager were outlined in 1994 in RFC 1591 (Postel, 1994), which decreed that for each ccTLD there must be one individual designated as administrative contact and one as technical contact. The administrative contact must reside in the country of the ccTLD that he or she is managing. Additionally, "The designated manager is the trustee of the top-level domain for both the nation, in the case of a country code, and the global Internet community. Concerns about 'rights' and 'ownership' of domains are inappropriate. It is appropriate to be concerned about 'responsibilities' and 'service' to the community" (Postel, 1994, pp. 3–4). Beyond these requirements, RFC 1591 established a number of other criteria for ccTLD management. "The designated manager must be equitable to all groups in the domain that request domain names"; "significantly interested parties in the domain should agree that the designated manager is the appropriate party"; and the designated manager must possess the technical skills and authority to maintain that country's Internet infrastructure (Postel, 1994, p. 4). A developing country's ccTLD could be assigned to a proxy manager in instances in which the manager was unable to provide domain service to the entire country but where the manager would use operation of the ccTLD to bring service to the country in question.

Significantly, the classic elements that constitute a state (nation, government, and territory) were downplayed or entirely absent from these guidelines. There were no requirements that either the managers or the users of a ccTLD be nationals of the country in question, and governments were given no explicit role at all. Although the administrative contact was required to reside in the territory of the country and the manager was required to competently provide service (or work to bring service) to residents, there were no requirements that either the server that hosts the domain or the users be physically located in the country's territory. A country's government could apply to be manager of its ccTLD—for instance, the manager for .VN is the Vietnamese Government's Ministry of Post and Telematics—and, if a nongovernmental entity such as an individual, university, nonprofit organization, or corporation were designated manager, the country in question could enact legislation that would restrict its operation. However, whereas a state government's authority over internal affairs was recognized, its status as sole, sovereign representative of nation and territory in its relations with other sovereigns was not. Amid this de-linking of state signifiers from the constitutive elements of nation, government, and territory, notions of citizenship become weakened or nonexistent (notwithstanding the attempts of the managers of the .US domain name to equate it with a sense of patriotism). Thus it is unclear whether one's sense of belonging on the Internet is tied to one's domain name, one's Internet Service Provider (ISP), one's physical location, or the global community of Internet users. This ever-shifting locus of citizenship must be considered before one accepts the argument that Internet governance be based on the principal that Internet users are citizens of a global civil society (McDowell and Steinberg, 2001).

Indicative of the status of the Internet as an arena in which the basis of state power is being renegotiated, the past few years have seen a series of attempts to reinsert the formal role of state governments (although not state territories or national identities) into global Internet governance. A 1999 memo, ICP 1, clarified and revised RFC 1591, adding that "the desires of the government of a country with regard to delegation of a ccTLD are taken very seriously. The IANA will make them a major consideration in any TLD delegation/transfer discussion" (ICANN/IANA, 2000). Although this document explicitly noted that governments are legitimate interested parties, governments still were not given anything approximating sovereign authority over operation of their country's domain structure. In practice, even prior to the release of ICP 1, there was an unwritten rule that if a government wanted to directly administer its ccTLD it would receive priority over all other applicants (Shaw, R., 1997). However, even under this unwritten rule and in the guidelines specified in ICP 1, governments were conceived of only as first among potential applicants, not as a special class of applicants with sovereign authority.

Under the most recent revision of the process for designating ccTLD administrators, ICANN has begun to recognize the special role of governments. In 2000, a document issued by ICANN's Governmental Advisory Committee (GAC) proposed a set of principles to guide the role of governments in ccTLD administration. The GAC document reaffirms the role of ICANN in designating ccTLD administrators, but it also justifies extensive government involvement based on the requirement, stated in RFC 1591 and ICP 1, that ccTLD administrators must manage their ccTLDs in the public interest. Because "the relevant government or public authority ultimately represents the interests of the people of the country or territory for which the ccTLD has been delegated . . . the role of the relevant government or public authority is to ensure that the ccTLD is being administered in the public interest, whilst taking into consideration issues of public policy and relevant law and regulation" (ICANN, 2000). The GAC principles, along with RFC 1591 and ICP 1, have been enshrined as the three official documents guiding the designation of ccTLD administrators (ICANN, 2003a).

Guided by this new concern for the role of governments in ccTLD administration, ICANN has developed a model contract for formalizing the relationship between ICANN, ccTLD managers, and national governments. According to this model contract, authority to manage a ccTLD still is to be formally granted by ICANN. However, selection of an administrator is to be made by the country's national government, and ICANN is obligated to reassign ccTLD administration if the government asserts that the manager has violated national laws (ICANN, 2002). This recent assertion of governmental power in ccTLD management is part of an ongoing struggle surrounding the politics of Internet domain name management (Paré, 2003), and it reflects a trend toward an increase in the role of governments in all areas of Internet governance ("Internet Oversight," 2002; Mueller, 2002). To date, however, the incorporation of state governments remains partial. At the International Telecommunication Union's World Summit on the Information Society held in 2005, calls to transfer Internet governance from ICANN to an intergovernmental organization were defeated. Meanwhile, even as there is some movement toward the replication of governmental power on the Internet, the other two components of the sovereign, territorial nation-state—state territories and national identities—remain almost entirely absent. According to one survey of the rules for 159 ccTLD registries, only 69 registries have any "local presence" requirement. For the other 90 ccTLDs surveyed, there are no requirements mandating that an entity hosting a domain name ending with that country's ccTLD be a national or resident of (or, if a corporation, be incorporated or do business in) that country ("To the Point," 2005).

Reflecting on the popularity of ccTLDs, Mueller decries the corruption of a medium that was originally intended to be beyond the politics of the state system:

> By incorporating [ccTLDs] into the domain name space, Jon Postel inadvertently helped to reproduce the political geography of the *ancien régime* in cyberspace. The ISO codes were originally part of a private name space and were intended to be nothing more than an identifier of what country a domain administrator was in. Remarkably, these casual delegations of top-level domains were transmuted into the basis of a sovereignty claim by national governments.... [Governments are making this claim] based on the flimsiest of grounds: an arbitrary semantic relationship, the notion that the ccTLD string "stands for" or "represents" the country, and that that semantic relationship is somehow exclusive and privileged (Mueller, 2002, pp. 243–244).

Mueller is certainly correct that governments are using ccTLDs to assert a presence on the Internet never intended by Postel, as is evidenced, for instance, by China's restrictions on the websites that are returned when one searches on google.cn (Thompson, 2006). However, his indignation makes sense only if one assumes that some essential or pure domain of global civil society is being violated by a similarly essential or rigid institution of sovereignty. In fact, however, claims of state sovereignty have always been based upon the manipulation of signifiers that, at best, apply to only some of the aspects of the sovereign state that are implied when one envisions a transcendental entity that unifies nation, government, and territory. Hence, the partial incorporation of state signifiers and state authority into the Internet should be seen not as a violation of a formerly pure medium or as a parody of the state ideal, but rather as another phase in the ongoing process by which states constitute themselves through uneven integration and signification in the multifaceted social environment within which they construct and exercise their power.

To sum up this chapter so far, we have argued that, although the Internet domain structure supports the system of sovereign states and its underlying power differentials. it also, simultaneously, is in opposition to the idealized nation-government-territory nexus that lies at the root of this system. Country signifiers exist, but the administrators of these signifiers (the ccTLD managers) have unusual latitude to construct new significations of countries, liberated from the signifieds of nation, territory, and (at least until recently) government that normally are pointed to by country-name signifiers. In the next sections of this chapter, we examine how the administrators of two ccTLDs—.PN and .NU—have gone about this signification, and we follow this with a consideration of how these new forms of state signification may be reflecting (or perhaps precipitating) changes in the system within which states interact and within which state legitimacy is constructed.

Pitcairn Island

Pitcairn Island is located 3,300 miles from New Zealand and 4,000 miles from Chile. A two-square-mile volcanic rock with a population of about fifty, the nearest inhabited land is the French Polynesian island of Mangareva (pop. 600), 300 miles away. Pitcairn's steep cliffs and its location at the intersection of two major wind fronts make the construction of an airstrip there impossible and the landing of ships treacherous. The island is an overseas territory of the United Kingdom, administered by an appointed governor serving out of the British Consulate in New Zealand, with the cooperation of a locally elected Island Council. Its ISO country-code is .PN.

Pitcairn was uninhabited until 1790, when it was settled by nine mutineers from the *HMS Bounty*, together with six abducted Tahitian men and twelve Tahitian women. Ten years later, all of the fifteen male settlers were dead save one (twelve had been murdered by other members of the group, one had committed suicide, and one had died of natural causes). In 1808, Mayhew Folger, an American seal ship captain, stumbled upon the island. Captain Folger found the sole male survivor, John Adams, leading a makeshift civilization with ten surviving women and twenty-three children. Adams, no doubt fearing execution in England, told Folger how he had played a moderating role in the mutiny and, after the ruffians on the island had killed each other off, how he had "civilized" the Tahitians and their mixed-race children through Bible study and the teaching of Christian morals. Although probably only partially true, Adams's story earned him a pardon from the British government, and his redemptive journey from sinner to civilizer of savages became a staple of nineteenth-century Anglican sermons. Following the publication of the semifactual *Mutiny on the Bounty* trilogy in 1932, and the subsequent production of "almost 3,000 articles, hundreds of books, dozens of documentaries, and five feature films," the Pitcairn mutineers have become the object of many Westerners' romantic dreams, and it is likely that "Pitcairners have had more ink spilled on their behalf, per capita, than any other people in the world" (Benton, 1999).

Many of the stories about Pitcairn have been at least partially fictional (beginning, perhaps, with Adams's story to Captain Folger) and, considering the sparse number of outsiders who actually encounter the island, the material land that lies beneath a reference to Pitcairn (i.e., the physical Pitcairn Island with its fifty inhabitants) is overshadowed by the signifieds emanating from all the other works that claim to represent the island. Although Pitcairn does exist as a real place, for most outsiders it exists solely as an image of romantic isolation, escape, or a resilient and moral community surviving in the face of all odds and despite the unsavory character of its charter members.

In this context, Pitcairners seized upon the .PN registry as a way to obtain revenue from selling romantic web users an escape from reality. In its early years, the registry's website focused on the marketing of what can best be called "Pitcairn Kitsch." Until 2003, the homepage for the .PN registry (www.government.pn/PnRegistry/PnRegistry.htm) reminded the reader that Pitcairn was the "home of the Bounty Mutineers," and the page featured an image of the island together with a reprint of a Pitcairn postage stamp portraying the *HMS Bounty*. A second page, with the heading "The Mutineers chose well!" (www.government.pn/PnRegistry/Plans.htm) highlighted the problems of communications on Pitcairn, buttressed by an old-fashioned map of the island, surrounded by water. A third page (www.government.pn/PnRegistry/auction.htm) featured images of the *HMS Bounty* and mutiny leader Fletcher Christian, with the heading,

"Oo-arr me hearties, The Greatest Domain Names on the PlaNet be up for auction!"

The designers of these web pages took great pains to connect the signifier .PN with the signified Pitcairn Island that existed in the minds of all who visited the site and were familiar with the Pitcairn story. Indeed, the registry site does not tell visitors anything about the island except that it was the home of the *Bounty* mutineers and that it is isolated. Rather than introducing web surfers to Pitcairn Island, the British territory in the Pacific populated by a dwindling number of Anglo-Tahitians, the website reproduced the Pitcairn Island portrayed in the *Bounty* films, a rugged land of perseverance and escape. The .PN signifier thus was manipulated to point to a signified which, on the one hand, *was* that of a country called Pitcairn Island but which, on the other hand, was *not* the nation-government-territory nexus that normally is signified in the sign of a country's name. This partial signification is consistent with some of the tourist marketing strategies discussed in Chapter 4.

These references to Pitcairn's past were coupled with references to Pitcairn's future. The second webpage (www.government.pn/PnRegistry/Plans.htm) made its appeal for domain-name registrants by informing the viewer that proceeds would go toward bringing the Internet to this island, "one of the most remote spots on Earth." Like John Adams 200 years earlier, the website implored Western readers to support the settlers' efforts to bring civilization to the savages, so that "the schoolchildren on Pitcairn can 'surf the Net' just like kids from schools in the big city." This message lacked conviction, though, in part because the website failed to refer to the present-day Pitcairn Island as a middle ground between its idealized representation of Pitcairn's past and its equally idealized representation of Pitcairn's future. The website, for instance, failed to note that, while it was proposing to bring the Internet to Pitcairn, the island did not even have 24-hour telephone access. Nor did it note that there were only three school-age children on Pitcairn who could be given the opportunity to "'surf the Net' just like kids from schools in the big city."

In 2000, administration of the .PN registry was transferred from Pitcairn resident Tom Christian (great-great-great grandson of mutiny leader Fletcher Christian) and Channel Islands entrepreneur Nigel Roberts to the Pitcairn Island Administration in New Zealand, at the request of the Pitcairn Island Council and in response to a petition signed by every adult Pitcairn resident other than Christian and his wife (IANA, 2000a). Since then, the website has undergone a number of transformations. In 2003, all direct references to mutineers and *The Bounty* were removed, as were all claims that purchasing a .PN domain name would help bring Internet service to Pitcairn residents. Nonetheless, visitors to the website still were informed that by clicking on the link to the registration form they could "acquire a piece of virtual real estate in this remote Pacific Paradise" and there were still several "hidden-treasure"-style maps of the island. A link on the registry's homepage referred to the Pitcairn government website (www.government.pn/homepage.htm), from which one could access pages offering information for tourists, an official history of the island, and the Pitcairn Island Philatelic Bureau. In 2005, the website became even more distanced from both the material and the historical-imaginary constructions of Pitcairn Island. The registry homepage (still at www.government.pn/PnRegistry/PnRegistry.htm) now makes no mention whatsoever of Pitcairn Island, and there are no longer links to any island-associated web pages.

There probably are several reasons for the progressive disassociation of .PN from Pitcairn Island. The website's turn away from campiness is symbolic (and symptomatic) of a more general "professionalization" of the Internet that occurred during the first years of the twenty-first century. In addition, the disassociation of .PN from the image of Pitcairn (even as its administration became integrated with the Pitcairn government) coincided with revelations of an island-wide child molestation scandal that dominated coverage of Pitcairn in the global media for several years. In the early twenty-first century, a virtual citizen of an imagined Pitcairn would, instead of being an honorary mutineer, be an honorary child molester, hardly an attractive pitch for would-be registrants. Indeed, the failure of .PN to attract registrants to its virtual shores is striking: As of July 2006, there were only eight hosts worldwide registered with the .PN ccTLD (ISC, 2006).

Niue

Niue, with a population of just under 2,000, is the world's smallest self-governed territory, although it maintains a relationship of free association with New Zealand, 1,500 miles to the southwest. The .NU ccTLD is managed by the Internet Users Society-Niue (IUS-N), a not-for-profit corporation based in Massachusetts. Whereas .PN was originally marketed through references to a place (or, at least, to an imaginary place that the .PN signifier was idealized as approximating), the .NU signifier, in its early years, pointed to an entirely placeless signified. Indeed, in their initial promotion of the domain name to potential investors and customers, administrators stressed that the value of the .NU "brand-name" lay precisely in its placelessness. IUS-N's 1997 press release introducing the registry stated:

> Other Country Code Domains include .UK in Great Britain, .SE in Sweden and .JP in Japan. Because Niue is a little-known country, unlike Japan or the United Kingdom, for example, its Country Code domain name carries little national identity outside its borders. It is therefore expected it will become popular not only because of its affiliation with a Polynesian island paradise, but also because of its "newness." Examples of .NU Domain names registered for the new meaning include www.really.nu, www.its.nu, www.Internet.nu and www.so.nu.
>
> In addition, the word "nu" means "now" in Scandinavian languages (Swedish, Danish, Norwegian, and Dutch [sic]) and several hundred Scandinavian users have already rushed to register names like www.peace.nu, www.surfa.nu, and www.musik.nu (IUS-N, 1997).

During its initial years, the homepage for the .NU registry (www.whats.nu) contained no clue that .NU was intended to represent a country, let alone the country of Niue. Prior to 2003, one could easily have followed the .NU registration links and registered for a .NU domain name while having no idea that one was signing up for a domain name that was associated with Niue (much as one can now register for a .PN domain name without being aware of the connection to Pitcairn).

There was an "About .NU" page that explained the ccTLD's history and purpose (www.whats.nu/about/about.cfm), but even this page was intriguing for its omissions The original "About .NU" page noted that IUS-N's "primary mission is to fund the development of the Internet infrastructure in Niue, provide free or low-cost Internet connectivity for the people of Niue, provide for technology transfer and education in the Internet and computer use, and other related activities in Niue," but nothing on this page informed the reader (who likely had never heard of Niue) that Niue was a country, let alone a tiny island in the Pacific Ocean with fewer than 2,000 residents. Nowhere on the site were there links to information on the country of Niue. Although the company's first news releases after its November 1997 launching mentioned its association with the country of Niue, these references disappeared from the boilerplate corporate profile after April 1998.

Instead of associating .NU with a country, the marketers of the ccTLD associated it with the hipness of "new" or "now" (depending on one's language), markers of supermodernity, a term that Augé (1995) applies to the world's "non-places" that exist solely in the realm of present-day information flows but that make no reference to histories or futures. Simultaneously, the ccTLD was marketed simply as two letters that meant nothing but that provided an alternative for a company whose desired .COM address was already occupied (hence the slogan: ".NU: The un.COMmon domain"). By any measure, the administrators of the ccTLD have been successful. As of July 2006, .NU was the forty-third most popular ccTLD, with over 277,000 hosts registered to the domain (ISC, 2006). Several other countries have also transformed their ccTLDs into what Mueller (2002, p. 127) calls "quasi-generic country codes," where the two-letter ccTLD is made to stand for some other word or abbreviation. Examples include American Samoa (.AS), Cocos Islands (.CC), Laos (.LA), Mauritius (.MU), Moldova (.MD), Tonga (.TO), Turkmenistan (.TM), Tuvalu (.TV), and Western Samoa (.WS) (Hodgson, 2000; Lloyd, 1999; Murphy and Smith, 1998; Sullivan, 1998; "What's Nu?" 1997; Wilson, 2001). None of these ccTLDs, however, has been as successful as .NU.

In 2003, the administrators of .NU took the ccTLD in a radically new direction, as they began highlighting the domain name's connection with Niue. In addition to adding direct references to Niue on the registry homepage, the "About .NU" webpage (still at www.whats.nu/about/about.cfm) now consists entirely of links to five documents, four of which are "white papers" about IUS-N's activities on Niue. The fifth document on this page, the .NU Domain Newsletter, is primarily about services that IUS-N provides to registrants, but it also contains an information box about Niue.

.NU thus has shifted in a very different direction than .PN. Whereas .PN moved from being a signifier embedded in the historic image of the island to being a floating signifier, .NU has shifted from being a signifier that pointed to a supermodern ideal of poststate (and post-place) "newness" (or "nowness") to one that is embedded in a very real place, with an idealized history of primitive backwardness and an idealized future of progress and development. The .NU registry website now celebrates the ccTLD's connection with the territory and people of Niue. Niue is portrayed as a romantically archaic island, much as Pitcairn was portrayed on the original .PN website, and potential registrants are presented with an opportunity to assist in the island's modernization. In an image highly reminiscent of the original .PN website, the box about Niue in the online .NU Domain Newsletter is dominated by a sepia "hidden-treasure"-style map of the Pacific in which a notably isolated Niue is accompanied by the text "Every Registration Funds Niue's Internet" (IUS-N, 2003).

In contrast with the original .PN website, however, this connection is made not with historical Niueans but with the island's contemporary residents. Material on the .NU website boasts that Niue is now the only nation in the world where every resident has free dial-up Internet access via IUS-N's satellite link, where the capital city of Alofi is one WiFi zone thanks to IUS-N's donated infrastructure, and where free broadband connectivity is provided to all Niueans without PCs in IUS-N's Internet café. The WiFi zone extends into the adjacent harbor as well, assisting Niue's attempts to market itself as an attractive anchorage for visiting yachts. Press releases, newspaper clippings, and special reports on the .NU website tell of the efforts made by IUS-N to restore Niue's Internet and WiFi service after the island was devastated by a Category 5 cyclone in January 2004 (IUS-N, 2004). Despite IUS-N being headquartered in Massachusetts, the connection between .NU and Niueans appears to be genuine, as evidenced, for instance, by the presence of a community website (www.niueisland.nu) spawned by the introduction of Internet service.

Relations between IUS-N and the government of Niue, in contrast, have been tense. As early as 1999, there were signs that this relationship was strained (Vivian, 1999), and, by 2003, relations had deteriorated to the point that Telecom Niue, the government-owned telecommunications company, disconnected the DSL line that ran from IUS-N's satellite dish to its Internet café in Alofi. This line was critical because the Internet café not only provided on-site users access to the Internet, but it also served as the hub through which Alofi residents outside the café and yachters in the harbor accessed the IUS-N WiFi network. According to IUS-N President J. William Semich, IUS-N faced "hostile opposition" from the government-owned telecommunications provider because it "wanted no free services of any sort to be available to Niue's Internet users" (IUS-N, 2004). The government of Niue has kept its distance from IUS-N and the .NU ccTLD in other ways as well. Despite a number of institutions and organizations on Niue that use .NU addresses, the government of Niue maintains its website at www.niuegov.com (although the address www.gov.nu forwards to this address). Although the administrators of .NU appear to have made great strides in linking their ccTLD with the nation and territory of Niue, they still seem far from linking the .NU signifier with the third element of the Niuean state: the government.

State Reterritorialization on the Internet

At first glance, ccTLDs like .NU and .PN appear to challenge the essence of modern statehood. Their very existence suggests a threat to the idealized nation-government-territory nexus that underlies sovereignty in the global political system of states and grounds notions of citizenship. .PN, which originally had little tie to nation, government, or territory, has developed a link with Pitcairn's government but remains disconnected from the contemporary people or territory of Pitcairn Island. .NU, after years of de-emphasizing its links with the territory and nation of Niue has begun to celebrate these links, but still its ties with the Niuean government appear far from complete.

On closer examination, however, the impact of these abrogations of the nation-government-territory ideal in the infosphere may not be so radical, because the nation-government-territory ideal is just that: an *ideal*. The history of telecommunications presents a long history of country signifiers that have "floated away" from the countries to which they purport to refer, as material relations of distance and connection interfere with the ideal of sovereignty. For instance, in the North American telephone system, Canada and the Caribbean have U.S.-style area codes whereas, conversely, Alaska and Hawaii were long treated by U.S. Federal Communications Commission regulations as "international." Indeed, the very history of the ISO 3166-1 list, whereby isolated territories were assigned distinct "country" codes regardless of their sovereign status, reveals that, for some purposes (in this case, the provision of global postal services), recognition of material distance takes precedence over the symbolic reproduction of the nation-territory-government ideal. Similarly, the weak association between corporate identities and country signifiers on the Internet exemplified when, for instance, a Japanese corporation maintains a .DE domain website hosted on a server located in France, has antecedents in corporations that establish foreign subsidiaries and then market their products as "local."

The case studies presented here have more direct antecedents as well. .NU, especially prior to 2003, but to a large extent today as well, could be called a "TLD of convenience." IUS-N adopted a strategy akin to a "flag of convenience," the term used in international shipping when a country's government disassociates its country signifier from the corresponding nation or territory and establishes a regime of minimal governmental regulation so as to create a "business-friendly" national identity for international shippers. Likewise, Pitcairn's strategy resembles that of a "postage stamp republic," the term used for countries that seemingly exist as independent entities solely in the domain of stamp collectors, and for which the selling of stamps generates a substantial portion of government revenues. Under both of these strategies of disassociation there emerge cycles of image production and image consumption that are alien to the territory or people of the countries being represented. Territory and national identity, as well as notions of national citizenship, become irrelevant as affiliation with a country signifier is reconstituted as a legal mechanism available to any entity willing to pay the price.

Given these historical antecedents, it seems to us that the import of ccTLDs like .PN and .NU does not lie in any challenge that they, in and of themselves, pose to the nation-government-territory ideal. Neither do we believe that these signifiers reflect a diminution in the sovereign state as the basic unit of civic identity and territorial governance. Baudrillard's (1988) suggestion that we are entering a new era in which we experience the world as a series of floating signifiers offers a somewhat more plausible explanation, but our analysis suggests that this explanation too is partial at best. The fact that there is a history of floating country signifiers suggests that any change represented by the Internet domain system is at most an incremental and continual transformation rather than a revolution in how we experience reality in the postmodern era.

As an alternative, we suggest that the import of ccTLDs like .NU and .PN lies as much in how they reproduce the state system as in how they either reflect or engender its transformation. For us, the most startling aspect of these country signifiers is that they exist at all, given that they frequently lack material association with nation, government, or territory, and that they occupy an arena of communications that was created with pretensions of transcending the division of the world into sovereign states. To interpret the persistence of these floating state signifiers, we turn away from attempts at identifying acts (whether symbolic or material) that reproduce or challenge state authority. Instead, we focus on the continual process of *re*territorialization by which state institutions (and their signifiers) continually are reconfigured in a manner that navigates between contradictory imperatives (Deleuze and Guatarri, 1988). Thus we continue the line of argument presented in the first chapter of this book: The significance of crises in infosphere management lies not in any new destabilization that the infosphere brings to an otherwise stable social system; rather their significance lies in the location of the infosphere (and its key institutions, such as the Internet) within ongoing dialectical conflicts, and these conflicts occur across the three domains of management (governance, technology, and culture). With reference to Internet domain names, this contradiction is most explicitly seen between the imperative to maintain mobility across an undifferentiated space without state boundaries and the imperative to symbolically reproduce the state as a fundamental organizing unit of society (and thus legitimize and empower it as a guarantor of investments and protector of intellectual property rights). The initial attempt to construct the Internet as an arena of communication that would transcend state borders as well as more recent attempts to institutionalize the role of governments in ccTLD administration represent instances in this ongoing and uneven process of state reterritorialization.

To conclude, the Internet has a political geography that ranges from the inconsistent to the seemingly absurd: gTLDs like .COM and .ORG exist side-by-side with ccTLDs like .JP and .UK; U.S.-based institutions almost never identify their country of affiliation, whereas national signifiers are the norm in most of the rest of the world; some ccTLDs are closely controlled by and affiliated with recognized territorial nation-states, whereas others refer to imaginary places, and still others go to great lengths to obscure that the code ever was intended to signify a country.

Although the inconsistencies and absurdities of this naming system undermine the ideological basis of the modern state (i.e., the idealized nexus of government, nation, and territory), the naming system also reinforces that system (including its uneven power relations). Thus, by furthering its dialectical conflicts, it serves both to maintain the system and preserve its flexibility.

Claims that the Internet and its governing organizations represent a new space of global civil society therefore should be viewed with skepticism. The Internet has emerged as an agent and arena of reterritorialization, neither simply reproducing the state as an abstract ideal nor transcending its divisions. Rather, the Internet and its naming system serve as an arena in which we renegotiate our understandings of the concept of statehood while, simultaneously, we reaffirm the broad contours of the global political system that for centuries has defined the fundamental parameters of civic identity and governmental authority.

6 Fixity, Mobility, and the Governance of Internet Names

One of the striking features in international communication in the 1990s was the emerging and widespread acceptance of proposals advocating for nonstate forms of governance, especially with respect to Internet media. In 1998, rather than situating the formal governance of Internet technologies, protocols, and name assignments in an international organization as a way to recognize the globalization of these media, the United States created the Internet Corporation for Assigned Names and Numbers (ICANN). Thus, by the fiat of one state, a nonstate body effectively took over the national and international management of the naming function for this rapidly growing communications and information network. Although this new governing model originated from the U.S. government, ICANN has emerged as a transnational governing body. Economic and technical elites, the most powerful groups associated with the development and use of Internet-based technologies and services in the United States, contributed to the formation of a new governance arrangement. Self-governance was presented as a model to escape the supposed problems of governance by states and international organizations, in which state involvement might slow technical change and adoption and the open flow and use of information and web-based resources. This claim of a form of governance escaping state power has been questioned from several quarters (Goldsmith and Wu, 2006; Mueller, 2002).

An alterative call for nonstate governance of the Internet has also emerged from voluntary groups and nonprofit organizations across the world, together forming transnational civil society organizations. The technical expertise possessed by citizens of different countries who make their services available to these groups sometimes rivals that of governments, as do their claims to speak for citizens' rights, broadened participation, and speech and civil rights in an era during which concerns are voiced about the democratic legitimacy gap of many governments. Activists and scholarly researchers have pointed to the use of information and communication technologies as tools that can be used to support new forms of social movements on a national, transnational, and global basis, whether to advance human rights, gender equality, environmental concerns, or opposition to elements or impacts of globalization. As the claims, activities, and effectiveness of civil society groups have expanded in many sectors, so too have arguments that the Internet, a unique global resource, should not be governed by states or formal international organizations alone, but that the governance of the Internet should be typified by meaningful participation of civil society groups from all parts of the world. Thierer and Crews (2003) compare perspectives on infosphere governance: "Is it most appropriate to think of the Internet as a public resource and vast information commons, collectively owned or at least controlled by collective decision-making? Or, to look at the opposite choice, is it best to remain open to proprietary avenues, private ownership and control models, and self-selection?" (p. xvi). These debates were central to the civil society conferences that were set up as a part the World Summit on the Information Society (WSIS) meetings in Geneva in 2003 (see Drake, 2005; Raboy and Landry, 2005; Servaes and Carpentier, 2006) and in Tunis in 2006. The governance debates in the formation of ICANN and in the WSIS meetings also evidence the playing out of the four tensions at core of the book's analysis and connect with ongoing questions about the role of states, private industry stakeholders, and civil society groups in governance of the infosphere.

This chapter argues that the move to self-governance is premised upon the assumption, whether explicitly stated or not, that a transnational civil society of nonstate actors, the "Internet community," existed that was sufficiently developed, balanced, and resilient to take over this important allocation and management role. However, the structures and practices adopted by ICANN were criticized for continuing to reflect the interests of industry groups and the dominant government, the United States. As the discussion of "technical code" in Chapter 2 highlighted, decisions that appear to be merely technical, such as the design of a naming system and the allocation of names, may both reflect certain political assumptions and have significant implications for governance. This chapter explores a number of the debates and justifications used to support and advance nonstate governance of the Internet in the United States. The chapter reviews public reports released leading up to the formation of ICANN. These documents, we will attempt to show, demonstrate the development of a political bargain and an ideology of management around several points, including the weakness of state governance of new technology and the ability of nonstate groups' communication, consultation, and decision making to more effectively make choices about allocating a key resource—the names or numbers that position users on the Internet. Without a strong assumption about the formation, interactions, and cooperation of these different interest groups in a civil society-like network structure, we argue, it would be difficult to justify the transfer of such a significant governance activity away from state or interstate bodies. However, the actual role and participation of civil society groups was not specified clearly. Indeed, as was noted in the previous chapter and as shown at the end of this chapter, governments are beginning to reassert their role in global Internet governance, and private sector organizations are calling for more law-based resolution of concerns about Internet names. Nonetheless, the predominance of nonstate entities in the Internet's early years is likely to have a lasting impact on the management of the Internet and, more broadly, the entire universe of the infosphere.

This chapter focuses on developments and debates about the governance of one part of the infosphere; the allocation and management of Internet names and addresses. However, the interaction of governance, technology, and cultural practice becomes evident as proposals for governance are fleshed out. The initial proposals for ICANN were primarily presented as a functional response to manage the supposedly inherent demands arising from a rapidly changing group of technologies. Similarly, the questions of appropriate forms of governance were also presented as arising from the characteristics of the technology and the infosphere space it created, as well as from the depictions of the groups of users or stakeholders who would organize governance mechanisms and responses as needed. This is an agenda with specific political and cultural assumptions and values, as the discussion of "technical code" in Chapter 2 shows. As the account in this chapter outlines, this specific relationship of governance, technology, and cultural practice was not seen as appropriately accountable to broader citizens groups. Nongovernmental organizations and governments outside the United States also sought to ensure more responsiveness to their concerns and interests in broadening the forms of participation of both civil society organizations and governments.

The concluding discussion follows up on themes and examples raised in Chapter 1, as well as issues explored in Chapter 5. Of primary importance are the claims about the Internet and the infosphere—as an uncontrollable space enhancing the natural mobility of information, commerce, and capital, and a space typified by rapid and uncontrollable technology change—that justified the need to explore and to develop a new and unconventional form of self-regulatory governance in ICANN. Whereas governance of the infosphere was first conceived of in the United States as a resource to enhance national *production* (the National Information Infrastructure initiative), the foundational approach to infosphere governance was set as a *trade* agenda in the 1996 "Framework for Global Electronic Commerce" (United States, 1996b). The claims made by many advocates about the importance of the Internet and national infrastructure and information highways as a basic strategic resource for production in the information economy and the basis for national competitive advantage were accepted alongside seemingly contradictory claims about the need for an open and unconstrained space for exchange. The *fixity*-versus-*mobility* tension swung toward the acceptance of the mobility of these resources to encourage new forms of access to the flow of information in the late 1990s, but in the early 2000s swung more toward the consideration of fixity with investments in networks to offer paid services to consumers, to protect against online fraud and deception, and to enhance property rights in the infosphere. In the debates over the management of Internet names and numbers, the mobility of information was emphasized over the fixed infrastructure investments in states that were the physical and technical basis for this mobility. At the same time, the support for protection of intellectual property propped up a form of abstract property rights, both within existing state *territory* and in the newly depicted *nonterritory* of the infosphere. The *politics*-versus-*economics* tension was highlighted in the claims that the political feasibility of promoting a new form of governance was justified on the basis of idealized notions of the mobility of information alongside the emergence of a new type of political community, a transnational civil society of online users that would identify and organize their needs for collective governance as they arose. Later, the politics of state power and efforts to promote competitiveness in a global context were reasserted, as were efforts of some states to assert new forms of national control, or the United States to support certain forms of openness.

Governance, Stakeholders, and Civil Society

Proposals for and practices of nonstate governance of specific activities in democratic societies arise from at least two competing traditions, which are sometimes supportive and sometimes contradictory. An efficiency argument is made that in professional service sectors, where some control over providers and the terms and conditions of service are seen to be in the public interest, certifying the credentials of providers and self-policing by the profession may both allow for flexibility and protect the health and safety of the public while ensuring high quality services. This is less costly than direct regulation by a state agency. Similarly, a political argument can be made for non-state group involvement in specific governance activities. Elections are not enough to ensure democratic governance. Extensive and open consultation and participation by citizen groups and interest groups in civil society are essential for high quality and responsible public decision making, and because most decisions respond to a sectoral problem or issue, the state should involve civil society groups with concerns and expertise in that question in governance.

Efficiency arguments are usually dealt with under the term of "self-regulation." This is often seen as a way to avoid public sector intervention, or to allow for the insertion of market mechanisms. Christoph Engel (2006) notes that law as a mode of governing relations and behavior on the Internet has "powerful competitors, be it technical code, social norms, or private governance" (p. 201). Common forms of self-regulation in market economy countries have included professional self-regulation by doctors, lawyers, engineers, or architects, in which professional membership and standards of professional certification and practice to protect the public interest are determined by the group itself. Stephane Astier (2005) distinguishes between self-regulation, which "consists in the players working out and complying with rules which they themselves have formulated and of which they ensure the application" (p. 135), and "multiregulation, . . . a combination of state regulation with self-regulation of the players in a context of international cooperation" (p. 135). Self-regulation is often explicitly or implicitly overseen by public sector authorities; if the professional group is perceived to be ineffective in policing its members or in protecting the public interest, then more direct and formal public intervention may be required. In the United States, for instance, the practices of self-governance by physicians and lawyers (who may require only minimal formal licensing and professional regulation by states in addition to membership in a professional organization) may be compared with the legal environment and more direct regulation faced by food and drug companies (which may be regulated primarily by state and federal public agencies). In the mass media sector, self-regulation has a long tradition, including predominant examples such as industry film boards in the 1930s in the United States, age-based ratings for films, standards offices in television networks, or ratings labels on sound recordings. Technology standard-setting bodies are also often cited as examples of effective nonstate governance (Kahin and Abbate, 1995). After 1996 in the United States, the television program content labeling system associated with the V-Chip was introduced by the industry under some public and governmental pressure, and there have also been calls for self-regulation of the content of World Wide Web sites and the voluntary use of filtering software (Campbell, 1999; McDowell and Maitland, 1998). A number of legislative attempts have been made in the United States to require content control or filtering software in public libraries.

In contrast, a rich stream of analysis making use of and developing the concept of civil society has been developed in political theory and international studies (Held, 1995; Janoski, 1998; Mapel and Nardin,

1998; Seligman, 1992). Civil society is most often made evident by the actions of private voluntary associations, or even defined as some form of associational activity or linkage. It is these groups and the networks of these groups that have been the focus of much discussion and debate on international or global civil society. This debate includes studies of international organizations in the 1970s, which noted the growing participation of nongovernmental groups in international bodies (Jacobson, 1984), as well as subsequent studies of networks of groups engaged in international humanitarian and environmental activism.

As Laura Macdonald (1997) has noted, the notion of civil society and efforts to "support" civil society through strengthening nongovernmental organizations has received assent from a number of opposing political perspectives. Macdonald argues that state-civil society relations vary widely from country to country, as does the meaning of civil society for different nongovernmental organizations. Michael Walzer (1995) also compares differing perspectives on the concept of civil society: "The words 'civil society' name the space of uncoerced human association and also the set of relational networks—formed for the sake of family, faith, interest, and ideology—that fill this space" (p. 27). Ronnie D. Lipschutz and Judith Mayer (1996) use the term "global civil society" as a fundamental building block in examining environmental governance because, in part, "it underlines the grounding of this sector in societal process as opposed to state-centered, institutionalized political ones" (p. 1). Annabelle Sreberny-Mohammadi (1991, p. 11) notes that even while there are questions about the existence of and actual participation in a public sphere in domestic politics, there is also "a significant call to rethink civil society at the transnational level." She continues, "[Yoshikazu] Sakamoto (1991), in the context of an argument about the need to deepen democracy into the heart of civil society, argues that as issues such as peace, development, the environment, and human rights assume a global character, only the globalization of democracy can provide a solution. This means 'the creation of a global perspective and values in the depths of people's hearts and minds, establishing the idea of a global civil society. . . . In a word, democracy can be deepened only if it is globalized; and it can be globalized only if it is deepened'" (p. 122).

The explorations of the possibilities of forming civil society groupings both nationally and transnationally have animated much research on the infosphere and the Internet. Steve Jones and others examine a variety of instances of cyber-societies (Jones, 1995, 1998). Peter Levine (2000, 2001) considers issues arising with the use of the Internet and implications for civil society organizations. Christopher Weare (2002) notes that, whereas claims have been made about enhanced opportunities for participation using infosphere technologies, broad claims about the Internet and democracy must be tempered by avoiding, "... either a strong technological determinism or an overriding emphasis on the social shaping of technology. Theory must engage the difficult middle ground in which causation is multidirectional and conditional" (p. 662). Sandra Braman connects the Internet with the liberation of the public sphere from state or geographic boundaries:

> The Net in fact may offer the opportunity for creation of a public sphere or public spheres genuinely outside the bounds of any single nation-state or organizational entity.... Because the public sphere is where civil society congregates, it is the place in which civil society recognizes itself as such, drawing system bounds. Because this is no longer "naturally" defined by genetics, geography, culture, or social organization, it must be decided on other grounds (Braman, 1996, p. 36).

This brief survey has highlighted a number of attempts to define more clearly what is meant by the terms self-governance and civil society, and the importance of these concepts for understanding debates on infosphere governance. Although the terms self-governance and civil society have been used most extensively in research on economic and social development, this chapter argues that a strong conception of the role of and possibilities for civil society groups and organizations underlies efforts to introduce nonstate governance in the communications sector. The efforts to shift this responsibility to transnational civil society groups outside the United States is even more striking, considering that, along with ceding authority to a nongovernmental group like ICANN, the U.S. government also ceded governance of country-code top-level domains (ccTLDs) to nongovernmental groups in foreign countries (see Chapter 5).

As will be shown, the devolution of authority to nongovernmental institutions neither necessarily empowers "the people" to participate in governance nor does it necessarily remove state authority from ongoing regulatory conflicts. To further investigate ongoing issues in Internet governance, we return to some of the themes introduced in Chapter 1, including the conflict between establishing the Internet as a space of mobility versus governing it as a space for fixed investments, and the contradictions inherent in establishing it as a space that is both within and beyond state territory. In the remainder of this chapter, we examine how continual shifts in ICANN's structure and policies reflect these contradictions.

The Development of ICANN: Documents and Debates

In this section we discuss the policy justifications advanced to support the Internet naming system that was introduced in Chapter 5. This process resulted in reassigning this important governance function to a new nonstate organization. These justifications build an image of open trade and commercial opportunities, encouraging the mobility of information through unbounded spaces, reducing sovereign territorially based authority, and escaping formal political accountability through a neoliberal ideology of stakeholder self-regulation, recast as participatory civil society.

An important part of the organization and architecture of any communications or service network (transportation, postal, telecommunications) that requires point to point contacts rather than simple broadcast or mass distribution is a common addressing system. One of the most basic tasks of modern governance was for states to establish standard time—both calendar time and clock time—and an authoritative mapping of space, such as longitude and latitude (Carey, 1988). These systems were established in particular states, and spread by the dominant power of the United Kingdom throughout the world political economy. Other naming systems for specific purposes have been either developed or encouraged by states or private groups or, in some instances, by the private and public sectors working in concert with each other. In the United States, for instance, although the ZIP code system was developed by the U.S. Postal Service, this addressing system is also used by couriers, delivery services, utilities in geographic information systems, and municipal property managers, as well as for purposes such as electoral enumeration, census counting, and social policy and planning (Zacher and Sutton, 1996).

The operation of interconnected electronic communications networks also requires tremendous coordination. A common telephone-numbering system allows interactivity of different systems and the connection of any two stations connected to the network. Common technical interfaces allow the interconnection of different types of technologies, whether wireline, cellular, or orbital satellite transmission systems. For instance, the upgraded telegraph system developed and used a system of teletype numbers (which may still appear on the letterhead of some international organizations). As any single user cannot know or have access to an individual store of all numbers, directory services are essential to the effective and useful operation of a telephone network. In a wireline network, numbers also serve as a way to relate the network connectivity to a physical or geographic mapping of network resources and access. Mapping and addressing become even more conjoined in geographic information systems that are used to track a variety of infrastructure resources, each with a unique name or node on the network.

Similarly, Internet domain name allocation has been a key issue in the creation and governance of the infosphere. The Internet domain name is actually assigned to a specific number, and there is no logical connection between the name using alphabetic characters and the numerical address. The number or name refers not to a fixed geographic point, but rather an assignment in the root directory that allows message delivery among the interconnected networks making up the Internet. As discussed in Chapter 5, there are actually two major systems for TLDs: the ccTLDs, and the generic TLDs (gTLDs), each using their own logic to organize naming. These systems are coordinated in that each naming system leads to a number or address, and the two systems do not allocate overlapping or duplicate numbers.

Internet addresses in this case are an abstraction. They do not necessarily refer to a user in a specific physical place but, as noted in Chapter 5, may be used to represent places and countries in different ways. Even the server address may be abstract, in that mirror sites may be created in different parts of the world to manage traffic on the Internet and the flow to different servers (Gorman and Malecki, 2002). A single set of addresses—the root server—allows for coordination and connectivity among network users. No two users have the same address, although users may hold multiple addresses.

The name used in the alphabetic address may be related to a trademark, intellectual property, or corporate or organizational title. Hence, the name becomes an important type of property in electronic communications, representing a position, location, and path, as well as an identity. The stability of names may also serve to build trust among users in the security of the transaction or the reliability of the information. By fixing a single, stable address to an entity in space, this system allows for the bounding and claiming of property. In contrast, by using a functional, rather than geographic, grid, this fixing of location in the infosphere simultaneously facilitates mobility.

In the United States, Internet technologies had been developed through extensive and long-term government support of the Advanced Research Projects Agency Network (ARPANET). Initially, addresses were simply listed as they were added, and an informal assignment of responsibility to Dr. Jon Postel to undertake this role grew into a formal role of identifying names and technical parameters (Hafner and Lyon, 1996). According to the U.S. National Telecommunications and Information Administration, "Eventually these functions collectively became known as the Internet Assigned Numbers Authority (IANA)" (U.S. Department of Commerce, 1998b). Management of the Internet moved from ARPA to the National Science Foundation (NSF) during the 1980s, with NSFNET being formed in 1987 to provide a backbone between research and educational computer networks. After assuming full responsibility for managing the nonmilitary portion of the Internet, in 1992 the NSF contracted with a private firm, Network Solutions, Inc. (NSI), to manage "key registration, coordination, and maintenance functions of the Internet domain name system" (U.S. Department of Commerce, 1998b). Also in 1992, the U.S. Congress authorized the NSF to allow commercial activity and transactions on the Internet. There were numerous policy debates over the next five years as this system of governance was assessed and reviewed.

The Clinton-Gore Administration undertook the National Information Infrastructure (NII) initiative almost immediately after coming into office in 1993. The NII began a national consultation process, which addressed questions such as economic development, universal access, investment, and the introduction of competition (Drake, 1995; Information Infrastructure Task Force [IITF], 1993). The provisions of the Telecommunications Act of 1996 were directed mainly toward the existing telecommunications industry, with an eye to promoting competition at the local level and investment in new technologies and services. More directly connected with Internet technologies were the discussions and deliberations that grew out of the NII and the Global Information Infrastructure (GII) discussions, beginning with the "Framework for Global Electronic Commerce" (Organization for Economic Cooperation and Development [OECD], 1997; United States, 1996b). A presidential advisor, Ira Magaziner, was assigned by U.S. President Bill Clinton to take leadership in developing this policy (Broder, 1997; Feery, 1998; Judis, 1998).

Several documents and requests for comments make up the path of public consultation along the way to forming this policy. On July 1, 1997 a discussion paper was released entitled "Request for Comments on the Registration and Administration of Internet Domain Names" (U.S. Department of Commerce, 1997). Following the receipt of comments, at the end of January 1998, a "Green Paper" for discussion entitled "A Proposal to Improve Technical Management of Internet Names and Addresses: Discussion Draft" was circulated for comment (U.S. Department of Commerce, 1998a). A further round of public comments was received, and on June 5, 1998 a statement of policy, the White Paper entitled "Management of Internet Names and Addresses," was published (U.S. Department of Commerce, 1998b). Based on these policies, and seeking to develop specific mechanisms, a number of proposals and processes were initiated. The Boston Working Group (1998) organized a number of civil society meetings to deal with the policies and procedures of Internet numbers and names for different parts of the world. However, Milton Mueller (2002) argues that the process was controlled by the U.S. administration, which consulted most closely with business groups rather than the forums set up by the broader Internet user community.

Jon Postel and others proposed and incorporated ICANN as a not-for-profit public benefit corporation in the State of California (ICANN, 1998; Postel, 1998). Postel had run IANA, which preceded ICANN, and was central to all number allocation operations until his death in

October 1998. After ICANN was created, a Memorandum of Understanding between it and the Department of Commerce was signed in November of 1998 (U.S. Department of Commerce, 1998c), which gave ICANN the initial mandate for joint participation in a Domain Name System (DNS) Project (although more agreements and modifications were added later). This agreement would provide the Department of Commerce with assurances that the new system would work and was the first step in moving the U.S. government aside from this central role of governing the Internet (Clausing, 1998; U.S. Department of Commerce, 1998a).

The initial framing of this question of governance came from the "Framework for Global Electronic Commerce" (United States, 1996b). It cast the question so that the priority for governance presumably was to facilitate the most effective methods to promote commercial or market exchanges. Governments could best assist the promotion of electronic commerce by taking on a minimal role:

> . . . it is critical to ensure that governments adopt a non-regulatory, market-oriented approach to policy development around electronic commerce. There is a clear need to provide a transparent and harmonized legal environment in which business and commerce can occur. However, official decision makers must respect the unique nature of the medium and recognize that widespread competition and increased consumer participation in marketplace choices should be the defining features of the new digital age (United States, 1996b).

As well, the key assumptions or principles of the policy framework were stated in this document. These included the principles that "the private sector should lead" in determining investments, that "[g]overnments should avoid undue restrictions on electronic commerce," that "[w]here government involvement is needed, its aim should be to support and enforce a predictable, minimalist, consistent and simple legal environment for commerce," that governments "should recognize the unique qualities of the Internet," and that, "[e]lectronic commerce over the Internet should be facilitated on an international basis." In elaborating upon the principle of recognizing the unique qualities of the Internet, it also stated, "Governments should also realize that the Internet's unique structure poses significant logistical and technological challenges to current regulatory models, and should tailor their policies accordingly. Governments also should encourage the evolving industry self-regulation and support efforts of private sector organizations to develop mechanisms to facilitate the successful operation of the Internet." It was these statements—seemingly directed at other governments outside the United States—that were also used as the rationale for the subsequent actions of the U.S. government in pursuing the nonstate and self-regulatory governance model.

These designs for global electronic commerce mirrored the U.S. government's GII initiative. This initiative grew from the 1993 National Information Infrastructure initiative in the United States and soon became global in scale (Drake, 1995; Wilson, 2004). GII-Global Information Society (GIS) advocates placed the construction of advanced communication infrastructures and services at the forefront of governments' priorities, beginning with the industrialized market economies. The initiative, which was endorsed by the Group of Seven in 1995, also led to significant research programs by the OECD and other international organizations (Kahin and Wilson, 1996; OECD, 1997; Smith, 1997).

According to the OECD,

> [GII-GIS] encompasses the development and integration of high speed communication networks, and a set of core services and applications in digital format, into global integrated networks capable of seamless delivery. Such networks provide fully interactive access, to network-based services within countries and across national borders (OECD, 1997, p. 7).

GII-GIS rhetoric clearly presented an ideal of the infosphere as a space of flows that exists (or should exist) beyond national boundaries, state territories, or government regulations. The U.S. Government's IITF, a key promoter of the GII-GIS, identified five principles for the initiative:

> Encouraging private sector investment; promoting competition; providing open access to the network for all information providers and users; creating a flexible regulatory environment that can keep

pace with rapid technological and market changes; and ensuring universal service (IITF, 1995, p. 1).

These principles were reaffirmed by the European Union in 1997:

> Minimise government regulation, and emphasise industry self-regulation instead; Appreciate that the Internet has grown so fast precisely because it has been so unfettered; Set global standards, even if it's not clear yet what is the appropriate forum for setting those standards; Recognise that winning consumers' trust and increasing their comfort level will be important to growth in electronic commerce (Walker, 1997, p. 6; see also, Goodenow, 1996).

The role of states and interstate organizations was limited to setting general ground rules, while a focus on commercial and economic uses of the new technology was paramount. As the OECD report on the GII-GIS stated, "Emphasis in this report is placed on elaborating a set of recommendations of OECD economies aimed at facilitating the transition from closed markets with no, or limited competition, such as in telecommunication and broadcasting areas, to open and dynamic markets (OECD, 1997, pp. 6–7)." There was a contradiction, however, between GII-GIS rhetoric, which focused on deregulation and unfettered mobility, and its more specific policy objectives, which stressed the need for infrastructure and networks. These infrastructural policy objectives implied support for fixed investments and communication between fixed points (that presumably lay within state territory). However, the GII-GIS concept, although making use of these territorially situated and state-bound networks that interconnect, avoided referencing the unevenness, nodes, and unique dynamics of infrastructure in the networked economy or network society. GII-GIS rhetoric assumed that, by loosening market forces from the restrictions of regulation, investment in new technologies would emerge to meet market demands, and this investment would be distributed and deployed to address broader social and developmental needs.

As the GII-GIS initiative proceeded, the U.S. Department of Commerce continued its efforts to construct a formal Internet governance body. On July 1, 1997, the Department of Commerce released a "Request for Comments" that solicited suggestions about the appropriate principles to guide policies on Internet naming and numbers, as well as more specific organizational issues related to current and proposed practices for domain name allocation (U.S. Department of Commerce, 1997). Among the principles that it proposed were four related to governance; these include:

1. The private sector, with input from governments, should develop stable, consensus-based self-governing mechanisms for domain name registration and management that adequately define responsibilities and maintains accountability.
2. These self-governance mechanisms should recognize the inherently global nature of the Internet and be able to evolve as necessary over time.
3. The overall framework for accommodating competition should be open, robust, efficient, and fair.
4. The overall policy framework as well as name allocation and management mechanisms should promote prompt, fair, and efficient resolution of conflicts, including conflicts over proprietary rights (U.S. Department of Commerce, 1997).

Again, the promotion of market competition is the primary goal. The document is more direct, not just in limiting the scope of public governance and encouraging governments to recognize "the evolving industry self-regulation" of the "Framework" but also in promoting private sector "consensus-based, self-governing mechanisms" for domain name registration. The civil society upon which this self-governance will be based is the market-based private sector, seemingly setting aside other voluntary and civil society organizations. The process by which decisions will be made is through consensus formation, reflecting a strong assumption that common interests in making decisions will outweigh the individual or competitive interests of the private sector actors. This framework should also "recognize the inherently global nature of the Internet" (and presumably include participants from other countries). Conflict resolutions, even those over proprietary rights associated with domain names, should be "prompt, fair, and efficient." In these different objectives or principles, a picture is painted of a resilient nonstate community of users and service providers that can develop self-governing mechanisms that are global and flexible and that contribute to rapid conflict resolution. In these visions, the open exchange of information among private-sector groups is emphasized, privileging mobility over fixity. Self-governance seems to suggest governance by a global community of users that transcends state boundaries as it diminishes governmental capacity.

Following the reception of comments, a Green Paper was issued on January 30, 1998. This document took a stronger position on the types of critical and immediate governance problems that were being faced on the Internet and proposed that good global governance was needed to avoid continuous conflict. "Without changes, a proliferation of lawsuits could lead to chaos as tribunals around the world apply the antitrust law and intellectual property law of their jurisdictions to the Internet" (U.S. Department of Commerce, 1998a). Given the "substantial differences among Internet stakeholders" regarding the development of the DNS, and given that "the Internet is changing so rapidly, [so that] no one entity or individual can claim to know what is best for the Internet," the Green Paper suggested a very pointed and limited role for domain name governance. Specifically, the Green Paper proposed that domain name governance be guided by four principles: stability; competition; private, bottom-up coordination; and representation. The explanations of the need for the four principles were stated as:

1. Stability.
   The U.S. government should end its role in the Internet number and name address systems in a responsible manner. This means, above all else, ensuring the stability of the Internet. The Internet functions well today, but its current technical management is probably not viable over the long term. We should not wait for it to break down before acting. Yet, we should not move so quickly, or depart so radically from the existing structures, that we disrupt the functioning of the Internet. The introduction of a new system should not disrupt current operations or create competing root systems.
2. Competition.
   The Internet succeeds in great measure because it is a decentralized system that encourages innovation and maximizes individual freedom. Where possible, market mechanisms that support competition and consumer choice should drive the

technical management of the Internet because they will promote innovation, preserve diversity, and enhance user choice and satisfaction.

3. Private, Bottom-Up Coordination.
   Certain technical management functions require coordination. In these cases, responsible, private-sector action is preferable to government control. A private coordinating process is likely to be more flexible than government and to move rapidly enough to meet the changing needs of the Internet and of Internet users. The private process should, as far as possible, reflect the bottom-up governance that has characterized development of the Internet to date.

4. Representation.
   Technical management of the Internet should reflect the diversity of its users and their needs. Mechanisms should be established to ensure international input in decision making (U.S. Department of Commerce, 1998a).

The deliberations over foundational principles to guide infosphere governance display the working out of a number of tensions we have discussed. Notwithstanding the elevation of "bottom-up coordination" and "representation" as core principles, which suggest the empowerment of civil society, the document's emphasis on stakeholder responsibility and private-sector coordination resonates more strongly with historical calls for industry self-regulation. Rather than democratic and accountable public decision-making being seen as the route most appropriate to expand the range of human choices, market mechanisms were to fulfill both economic and noneconomic functions. They will "promote innovation, preserve diversity, and enhance user choice and satisfaction." Governance is depicted as coordination among actors, not as a way in which those actors can be constituted as citizens. The difficult task would be to divide name and number allocation functions that can be completed in competitive or market settings from those that require conscious coordination of stakeholders. This coordination should "reflect the bottom-up governance that has characterized development of the Internet to date." This statement seems to revise the history of the Internet, both in its minimal depiction of the role of public sector agencies in governing the Internet and in providing the conditions (not evident in information technology sectors dominated by private organizations and proprietary standards) in which more diversified governance could take place. Nevertheless, as statements, these principles still emphasized *mobility* over *fixity* as an approach to governance of this rapidly changing technology, and privileged *nonterritory* over *territory* in their depictions of the scope of the infosphere and its users.

In order to achieve these objectives, several characteristics of the proposed "private, not-for-profit corporation" are outlined. The board would include representatives from a number of interested parties, including "IP number registries, domain name registries, domain name registrars, the technical community, and Internet users (commercial, not-for-profit, and individuals)." However, "[o]fficials of governments or intergovernmental organizations should not serve on the board of the new corporation." The Green Paper also laid out a number of criteria for discussion and decision-making processes for the "new corporation":

> The new corporation's processes should be fair, open and pro-competitive, protecting against capture by a narrow group of stakeholders. Its decision-making processes should be sound and transparent; the bases for its decisions should be recorded and made publicly available. Super-majority or even consensus requirements may be useful to protect against capture by a self-interested faction. The new corporation's charter should provide a mechanism whereby its governing body will evolve to reflect changes in the constituency of Internet stakeholders. The new corporation should establish an open process for the presentation of petitions to expand board representation.
>
> In performing the functions listed above, the new corporation will act much like a standard-setting body. To the extent that the new corporation operates in an open and pro-competitive manner, its actions will withstand antitrust scrutiny. Its standards should be reasonably based on, and no broader than necessary to promote its legitimate coordinating objectives. Under U.S. law, a standard-setting body can face antitrust liability if it is dominated by an economically interested entity, or if standards are set in secret by a few leading competitors. But appropriate processes and

structure will minimize the possibility that the body's actions will be, or will appear to a court to be, anticompetitive (U.S. Department of Commerce, 1998a).

The "White Paper" of June 5, 1998 integrated some of the comments received and consultation since January of 1998 and provided "the U.S. Government's policy regarding the privatization of the domain name system in a manner that allows for the development of robust competition and that facilitates global participation in the management of Internet names and addresses" (U.S. Department of Commerce, 1998b). The document stated that Internet stakeholders "are invited to work together to form a new, private, not-for-profit corporation to manage DNS functions," and went on to describe the general characteristics of that entity. Although the guiding principles remain similar to those stated in the "Green Paper" of January 1998, the explanation and justification of those principles had changed somewhat in the "White Paper," in many instances tempering the preceding draft's pro-market bias.

For instance, in the discussion of the "representation" principle, the White Paper notes that whereas "[m]anagement structures should reflect the functional and geographic diversity of the Internet and its users" (and not "the diversity of its users and their needs" as stated in the first draft), the primary purpose of the new corporation's management should be to "operate as a private entity for the benefit of the Internet community as a whole." The new language mentions the "community" twice, playing off the "broad" and "whole" community against the "diversity of the Internet and its users." It could be argued that this language reflects efforts to point to a sense of common purpose while at the same time supporting the difference and diversity expressed by individuals and firms. Firms, corporations, interests, and markets are not mentioned.

During the design of this new organization, there was much debate about the process of consultation and decision making. There were also concerns about the decision-making processes that were set up within the organization as it emerged, and how open they were to all stakeholders. Rather than using these critiques and weaknesses to move toward a global democratic organization to manage a common technical resource, increasingly ICANN's weaknesses have been used to justify stronger central administration and the assignment of property rights. The literature and public record exploring ICANN's performance and participation is extensive and detailed, as is that calling for various reforms (Auerbach, 2003; Centre for Global Studies, University of Victoria, 2002; Kleiman, n.d.; Mueller, 2002; Palfrey, 2004a, 2004b; Paré, 2003; Thierer and Crews, 2003).

ICANN has also begun to make use of existing international organizations in order to resolve disputes over the allocation of domain names. The World Intellectual Property Organization (WIPO) designed the Uniform Dispute Resolution Policy, and this was used to deal with competing claims for the use of domain names (ICANN, 2001; WIPO, 2004a, 2004b). Rather than adhere to a first-come, first-served policy, as had been the practice for IANA, WIPO looked at the trademarks that were already protected and assumed that these property rights should be extended into cyberspace. As part of the formation of ICANN, in 1999 a Uniform Dispute Resolution Policy was put into operation. WIPO noted in January 2004 that, from 1999 through 2003, around 6,000 disputes were handled involving 10,000 domain names, and that "over 80 percent of the WIPO expert decisions went in favor of the trademark holder, be it a large multinational corporation or a small and medium sized business" (WIPO, 2004a).

WIPO's efforts to protect trademarks on the Internet involved a direct confrontation with "cybersquatters," individuals who registered Internet domain names that were connected with a trademark held by an established business or organization. WIPO calls this "the abusive registration of trademarks as domain names" (WIPO, 2004a). The cybersquatter might use the name for fun, or might register the name with an Internet names registrar and then attempt to sell the name to another party for whom the name might have great value. This is especially important for commercial users in the .COM TLD. The Deputy Director of WIPO has stated that the outcomes of dispute resolution "underlined the bad faith inherent in the practice of cybersquatting," and that "reducing the practice of cybersquatting is an important element in enabling the Internet to develop as a secure and reliable environment which inspires confidence on the part of the ever-growing number of Internet users" (WIPO, 2004b). In contrast, critics of this process argue that the protection of trademarks on the web by WIPO, and the wide range of uses of any supposed trademark that WIPO has viewed as cybersquatting, have actually expanded the range of claims for the protection of intellectual property rights in brands more than in offline settings or applications of trademark law. WIPO's actions have included blocking fair comment and critique that makes use of material that would be allowed in other media (such as the title of a book, motion picture, or magazine article) (Mueller, 2002).

Just as ICANN made efforts to reproduce the boundaries and spaces of the offline world through instituting intellectual property protections, similarly it increasingly relied on contract law to reproduce offline commercial norms, including those of competition and user accountability. For instance, ICANN's efforts to foster competition on the Internet were opposed by NSI, a private corporation that initially was contracted to oversee the gTLD registration system. In 1999, an initial dispute arose with the National Telecommunications and Information Administration (NTIA) and NSI when NSI refused to recognize ICANN's authority to grant registry certification under the DNS Project joint agreement, even after an amendment was made to the registry contract that NSI held with the U.S. Government. Further agreements followed, including the NSI-ICANN Registry Agreement of November 1999 and a contract between ICANN and the NTIA of February 2000. NSI, which since has become VeriSign, continued to have a tendentious relationship with ICANN over a number of issues (Salkever, 2003).

VeriSign also set up a "Site Finder" service which directed users who mistyped website addresses (entering names that did not exist in the root server) to a VeriSign website on which it sold advertising. Technical experts argued that mistyped names, under Internet protocols, should return an error message, whereas other portal providers argued that VeriSign was using its monopoly position as the registrar for .COM and .NET as a way to take advertising business from other portals. In 2003, VeriSign agreed to ICANN's order to take down the "Site Finder" service while the matter was being considered, but then launched a lawsuit over the issue in 2004 (McGuire, 2003; Standeford, 2003b; "VeriSign files suit . . . ," 2004).

Along with its concerns for fostering competition and the protection of intellectual property rights on the Internet, ICANN also directed its energies toward enhancing the security of online transactions by establishing a reliable and accurate system for identifying domain name registrants. With increasing concerns about numerous forms of illegal behavior, network security threats, and losses in the ability to exploit intellectual property rights, many government officials and large users of the Internet called for ways to assist in enforcement through the identification of specific users and website managers. Targeted activities included sending spam (mass mailing of advertising or junk e-mails), disseminating computer viruses, hacking into others' systems, violating copyright, and stealing identifying information, as well as indecent speech and child pornography. Investigations of these activities revealed that many of the registrants holding domain names were fictitious persons. Efforts were made in the United States to pressure ICANN into requiring more accurate information from persons registering domain names and to manage this data more effectively through more frequent updates of the WHOIS system (Bohannon, 2004; Metalitz, 2003; Standeford, 2003a).

In addition to increasingly supporting a managerial-corporate agenda, ICANN itself took on the structure of a management organization, rather than a participatory users' group. In 2003, ICANN was reformed with the creation and implementation of more detailed bylaws that revised participation and decision-making procedures (ICANN, 2003b) and with the hiring of a new executive director, Dr. Paul Twomey. What had been a loose coalition of technical personnel and high tech thinkers has become more like an operating management organization (Twomey, 2003).

The creation of a nongovernmental body composed of various private sector stakeholders was claimed by the U.S. government to be more appropriate for the rapidly changing new technology than traditional intergovernmental organizations such as the International Telecommunication Union (ITU). Others saw this as an effort to freeze out governmental participants from other parts of the world, while the U.S. government still retained control through the contract with ICANN. Similarly, the lack of formal public participation in the formation of ICANN led critics to argue that the goals of the organization had shifted away from providing full public access and exploiting the maximum benefit of web technology and toward limiting the use of top-level domains and thus creating a false scarcity in domain names that provides stability for industrial players and the protection of intellectual property rights (Mueller, 2002).

As the above discussion demonstrates, policymakers who were defining the principles and constructing the institutions that were to govern names and numbers on the Internet vacillated between at least two visions. On the one hand, they were initially driven by a civil society-inspired vision, which emphasized *mobility* of technology, free flow of information across a global community of users, and that the infosphere was outside states (a *nonterritory*). On the other hand, they increasingly turned to a vision based on the ideal of industry-stakeholder self-regulation, which empowered actors to establish boundaries and develop state-connected "territories" and fixed "property" within these boundaries. As was noted in Chapter 1, however, neither the policing of boundaries nor their destruction accurately describes the complexity of the reterritorialization processes that characterizes the global political economy. Indeed, since the creation of the ICANN in 1998, another set of entities, with their own interests in both erecting and transgressing boundaries has become increasingly vocal in the Internet governance debate: states.

States and the World Summit on the Information Society

Even though the Internet name and number assignment function was initially directed by the U.S. government (in coordination with users, via ICANN), other national governments soon pressed for a role in the process, and many questioned the role of ICANN (King, 2004). In response to this call, ICANN has developed a Government Advisory Council, which aims to bring governments and international organizations into the consultation loop. ICANN has also given governments a more formal role in managing the allocation of country-code top-level domain names (as discussed in Chapter 5).

However, most efforts by non-U.S. governments to influence Internet governance have been through the ITU. Whereas ICANN's charge is specifically directed to Internet names and numbers, the ITU has long been concerned with a much larger body of communications issues, including technical standards, interconnection agreements, and many other communication policies that pertain directly to the Internet. In recent years, the focal point of the ITU's efforts in Internet governance has been its sponsorship of the World Summit on the Information

Society (WSIS), which first met in Geneva in December 2003 and which held a second meeting in Tunis in November 2005. The goal of WSIS was to "build a people-centered, inclusive and development-oriented Information Society, where everyone can create, access, utilize and share information and knowledge, enabling individuals, communities and peoples to achieve their full potential in promoting their sustainable development and improving their quality of life" (ITU, 2003, para. 1).

Although the WSIS process has been seen by some as bringing more broadly accountable governance to this sector, others in the Internet governance community have been more guarded about the involvement of an intergovernmental organization. On the one hand, Third World countries who had been concerned about their lack of voice in consultations and decisions about the Internet promoted the WSIS process for the benefits that it would bring in providing access to information and communication technologies. As a Report of the Secretary General of the United Nations noted in 2000:

> Information and communication technologies (ICT) are central to the creation of a global knowledge-based economy and society. ICT can play an especially important part in accelerating growth, eradicating poverty and promoting sustainable development in developing and transition economy countries and in facilitating their beneficial integration into the global economy. At the same time, the experience of developed countries shows that indiscriminate investment in ICT can lead to large-scale waste. For developing and transition economy countries to benefit from the lessons of this experience and to avoid misinvestment and capture benefits, appropriate institutional arrangements need to be made. These opportunities and risks call for urgent and concerted action at the national and international levels (United Nations, 2000, Executive Summary).

Critics, however, have argued that the WSIS process reflects an attempt by some states operating through international organizations to assert government control over the Internet. They expressed concern that this could lead to censorship of content, limitations on online behavior, stifling innovations, and, more generally, a reduction of the Internet's character as a free space of civil society, beyond social and geographic boundaries. Civil society groups became very active, and asserted their right to be actively consulted and included in the WSIS process (Raboy, 2004; Raboy and Landry, 2005; Selian, 2004). At the first 2003 summit in Geneva, 481 civil society organizations were in attendance (Selian, 2004).

Following the WSIS I in Geneva in 2003, a Working Group on Internet Governance (WGIG) was established by the Secretary-General of the United Nations to help implement the plans and goals of WSIS, specifically to:

- Develop a working definition of Internet governance;
- Identify the public policy issues that are relevant to Internet governance;
- Develop a common understanding of the respective roles and responsibilities of Governments, existing international organizations and other forums, as well as the private sector and civil society in both developing and developed countries (WGIG, 2005).

Whereas WGIG's overall charge resembled that of ICANN—the governance of the Internet—WGIG's roots in governments that represented the global community of users led it to broaden the specific topics of its concern. For instance, among the topics about which WGIG requested comments were those also considered by ICANN, such as the administration of Internet names, Internet Protocol (IP) addresses, root server systems, but also other issues such as multilingualization of the Internet naming system, spam, affordable and universal access, cultural and linguistic diversity, and consumer and user protection and privacy.

Even as the WSIS process was gaining momentum, WGIG's recommendations were accepted by WSIS, and the world Internet community was preparing for the 2005 Tunis meeting, in July 2005 the U.S. Department of Commerce issued a Memorandum of Understanding to extend ICANN's contract, which had been set to expire in September 2006. With this move, the U.S. government effectively removed large aspects of Internet governance from consideration, on the eve of the second WSIS meeting.

The extension of ICANN's contract was accompanied by a statement of principles as follows, which is notable for the shift in justifications for this form of governance since the policy papers were issued in 1997 and 1998:

Domain Names:
U.S. Principles on the Internet's Domain Name and Addressing System

The United States Government intends to preserve the security and stability of the Internet's Domain Name and Addressing System (DNS). Given the Internet's importance to the world's economy, it is essential that the underlying DNS of the Internet remain stable and secure. As such, the United States is committed to taking no action that would have the potential to adversely impact the effective and efficient operation of the DNS and will therefore maintain its historic role in authorizing changes or modifications to the authoritative root zone file.

Governments have legitimate interest in the management of their country code top level domains (ccTLD). The United States recognizes that governments have legitimate public policy and sovereignty concerns with respect to the management of their ccTLD. As such, the United States is committed to working with the international community to address these concerns, bearing in mind the fundamental need to ensure stability and security of the Internet's DNS.

ICANN is the appropriate technical manager of the Internet DNS. The United States continues to support the ongoing work of ICANN as the technical manager of the DNS and related technical operations and recognizes the progress it has made to date. The United States will continue to provide oversight so that ICANN maintains its focus and meets its core technical mission.

Dialogue related to Internet governance should continue in relevant multiple fora. Given the breadth of topics potentially encompassed under the rubric of Internet governance there is no one venue to appropriately address the subject in its entirety. While the United States recognizes that the current Internet system is working, we encourage an ongoing dialogue with all stakeholders around the world in the various fora as a way to facilitate discussion and to advance our shared interest in the ongoing robustness and dynamism of the Internet. In these fora, the United States will continue to support market-based approaches and private sector leadership in Internet development broadly (NTIA, 2005).

With this statement, the U.S. government emphasizes stability and *fixity* of investments above all other concerns, thereby reflecting ICANN's continual shift from promoting the multiple perspectives of civil society to fostering consistent industry self-regulation. In addition, with this statement, the United States further supports the *territorialization* of the Internet, both by national governments (that previously had not been given sovereign authority over ccTLDs) and by private actors (who are encouraged, in this statement, to take the lead in developing market-based approaches). It is assumed that as various public and private actors interact in a variety of fora (presumably including, but not limited to WSIS), the Internet will retain its character as an unbounded space of *mobility* of information and communication, but civil society is not given the specific responsibility of insuring that the infosphere retains this crucial characteristic.

Perhaps in response to the reauthorization of ICANN and the U.S. government's emphasis on reterritorialization, control, and the empowerment of governments and private-sector interests, the proclamations that emerged from WSIS II in 2005 differed markedly from those that emerged from WSIS I in 2003. The statement of principles and the action plan arising from the WSIS 2003 had been wide ranging, with a focus on communication for development, a broad view of information society issues, and a similarly large list of possible applications of ICTs in enhancing development; however, the 2005 meeting's outcome was much more restrictive. Its final report (ITU, 2005), the "Tunis Agenda for the Information Society," had a much narrower focus, limiting itself to issues on Internet governance, along with a discussion of financial instruments to implement programs promoting ICT applications. It affirmed that "all stakeholders and relevant intergovernmental and international organizations" should be involved in the management of the Internet. Most notably, in an assertion of *territoriality*, "authority for Internet-related public policy issues is the sovereign right of States. They have rights and responsibilities for international Internet-related public policy issues. . . . The private sector has had, and should continue to have, an important role in the development of the Internet, both in the technical and economic fields... Civil society has also played an important role in Internet matters, especially at community level, and should continue to play such a role ..." (ITU, 2005).

As the above quotation suggests, the 2005 summit marked a practical beginning of a "multistakeholder" effort among individual states, intergovernmental agencies, public and private corporations, and national and international nongovernmental or civil society organizations. These stakeholders, however, are not considered as equals in the WSIS vision of Internet governance. Although the Tunis Agenda specifically lauds the past role of civil society in Internet governance, civil society's future role is diminished to the "community level," a far cry from the original ICANN vision wherein informal user groups were to play a central role in global Internet governance. In contrast, the private sector is the appropriate entity for coordinating developments in "technical and economic fields." Sovereign states, meanwhile, are given overall authority over the organization of the Internet, mimicking the sovereign authority that they have over territory. In short, paralleling the transformation of ICANN, WSIS has shifted to a model that emphasizes territorialization over the nonstate nonterritorial space of the infosphere, and fixity over mobility, albeit with a slightly expanded cast of actors.

The reassertion of an emphasis on territorial sovereignty and state authority was evident in a number of resolutions addressing domain name management, cybersecurity, cybercrime, and spam:

38. We call for the reinforcement of specialized regional Internet resource management institutions to guarantee the national interest and rights of countries in that particular region to manage their own Internet resources, while maintaining global coordination in this area.

39. We reaffirm the necessity to further promote, develop and implement in cooperation with all stakeholders a global culture of cybersecurity... [which] requires national action and increased international cooperation to strengthen security while enhancing the protection of personal information, privacy and data.

40. We underline the importance of the prosecution of cybercrime, including cybercrime committed in one jurisdiction, but having

effects in another. . . . We call upon governments in cooperation with other stakeholders to develop necessary legislation for the investigation and prosecution of cybercrime.

41. We call upon all stakeholders to adopt a multi-pronged approach to counter spam that includes, inter alia, consumer and business education; appropriate legislation, law-enforcement authorities and tools; the continued development of technical and self-regulatory measures; best practices; and international cooperation (ITU, 2005).

One of the recommendations of the Tunis Agenda was the creation of an Internet Governance Forum (IGF). Paragraph 72 of the Tunis Agenda called for the Secretary-General, "in an open and inclusive process" to convene a meeting of this group. The mandate of the group includes efforts to:

a. Discuss public policy issues related to key elements of Internet governance in order to foster the sustainability, robustness, security, stability and development of the Internet;

b. Facilitate discourse between bodies dealing with different cross-cutting international public policies regarding the Internet and discuss issues that do not fall within the scope of any existing body;

c. Interface with appropriate inter-governmental organizations and other institutions on matters under their purview;

d. Facilitate the exchange of information and best practices, and in this regard make full use of the expertise of the academic, scientific and technical communities;

e. Advise all stakeholders in proposing ways and means to accelerate the availability and affordability of the Internet in the developing world;

f. Strengthen and enhance the engagement of stakeholders in existing and/or future Internet governance mechanisms, particularly those from developing countries (ITU 2005).

This group has little formal power, but involves many types of groups and consultations. In October 2006, the IGF held its inaugural meeting in Athens, Greece, and the next meeting will take place in Rio de Janeiro in November 2007. The main themes at the Athens meeting included openness, security, diversity, and access, and panels were planned and submitted by parties that included governmental, nongovernmental, and private sector participants.

In looking at this overall process, Cammaerts and Carpentier (2006), using a Foucauldian framework considering "generative, restricting and resisting power mechanisms" (p. 39), analyze civil society participation in preparatory meetings for the 2003 Geneva WSIS summit. They conclude that increased formal participation has not materialized, but that "the real outcome for civil society was not so much in the formal process . . . but in the informal process of networking and mediation within civil society (p. 40). Raboy and Landry (2005), in assessing the role of civil society actors in the 2003 meeting argue, "the non-governmental actors clearly expressed their determination to be present at the centre of deliberations and to be considered as full partners. In this sense, the WSIS marked a shift from civil society's unrelenting challenges to the supranational decision-making process from the outside to its formal integration into just such a process on the inside. While civil society held firmly to its positions of principle on substantive issues of concern, it continued to be highly critical of the way the process has unfolded and its outcomes" (p. xvii). McLaughlin and Pickard (2005) argue that the price of inclusion in the IGF for civil society organizations has been incorporation into a narrower policy agenda, a "neo-corporatist policy concertation that is oriented toward satisfying neoliberal economic imperative."

The developments in international organizations have also led to new attention to these issues in the United States. In February 2006, the U.S. Secretary of State established a Global Internet Freedom Task Force. Its announcement noted that:

> The Internet is a potent force for freedom around the world, but challenges to its independence by repressive regimes threaten its transformational power. . . . The task force will consider foreign policy aspects of Internet freedom, including the use of technology to restrict access to political content and the impact of such censorship efforts on U.S. companies, the use of technology to track and repress dissidents, and efforts to modify Internet governance

structures in order to restrict the free flow of information (United States, Department of State, 2006b).

The task force held a public presentation in December 2006, and announced a larger public conference to be held in January 2007 (United States, Department of State, 2006a).

As Hans Klein (2005) argues, after Tunis the ICANN was almost untouched. It kept its core functions, and the argument that it provided stability won out over calls for reform and broader participation. In May 2006, the NTIA issued a notice of inquiry asking for public comments on a review of the "continuation of the transition of the technical coordination and management of the Internet domain name and addressing system (Internet DNS) to the private sector" (NTIA, 2006a). Among the questions to which it sought comment were:

- The DNS White Paper articulated principles (i.e., stability; competition; private, bottom-up coordination; and representation) necessary for guiding the transition to private sector management of the Internet DNS. Are these principles still relevant?
- What methods, processes, or both should be considered to encourage greater efficiency and responsiveness to governments and ccTLD managers in processing root management requests to address public policy and sovereignty concerns? Please keep in mind the need to preserve the security and stability of the Internet DNS and the goal of decision-making at the local level. Are there new technology tools available that could improve this process, such as automation of request processing?
- Many public and private organizations have various roles and responsibilities related to the Internet DNS, and more broadly, to Internet governance. How can information exchange, collaboration, and enhanced cooperation among these organizations be achieved as called for by the WSIS?

Numerous comments from within the United States, and from around the world, were received prior to the July 26, 2006 NTIA public meeting on this issue (NTIA, 2006b). A small sampling of these illustrates the range of views expressed. An individual commentator and CEO of Kidsearch Network argued in response to the first question that "[t]he principles are still relevant. ICANN has yet to implement them and they have had sufficient time to do so. There is no bottom-up coordination and no representation for individual users or small business owners and domain holders yet" (McElroy, 2006). Many individual submissions were similar form letters that stated: "The Internet's value is created by the participation and cooperation of people all over the world. The Internet is global, not national. Therefore no single Government should have a pre-eminent role in Internet governance. As the United States reviews its contract with ICANN, it should work cooperatively with all stakeholders to complete the transition to a DNS independent of U.S. governmental control." Some U.S. letter writers also tied this inquiry to debates underway in summer 2006 over "net neutrality": whether broadband service providers should be able to require differential pricing for service providers and residential subscribers who were high bandwidth users. The Internet Governance Project submission argued that, with regard to the four principles of governance articulated in 1998, "[t]he most serious problems and contradictions, however, have arisen around the principle of *private, bottom-up coordination*. That principle was valid when first formulated and is still important. But it has not been implemented properly and is threatened by various developments since 1998" (Mueller, 2006).

Canada (2006) argued that "going forward, ICANN and its stakeholders should be scrupulous in taking a very narrow view of ICANN's policy functions, ensuring that any policy issues considered arise directly from and/or are inextricably linked to the organization's core technical functions. Any other policy issues should be referred to other more appropriate bodies." JFC Morfin (2006) of the network firm INTLNET in France argued that, to allow for the most openness in developing technologies and multilingual platforms, the "role of ICANN should primarily be to manage the NTIA root file and ensure that its TLDs can be accessed worldwide." In its response, the government of India (2006) highlighted sovereignty concerns, noting, "One way to address sovereignty concerns would be to give the GAC representative/s an affirmative vote in the ICANN Board on ccTLD delegation or redelegation matters. Contracts between and among ICANN and all stakeholders formalize relationships and therefore, these must be so drafted that the

terms and conditions subserve global principles of Internet management and at the same time, comply with local laws applicable within
a sovereign territory." As illustrations of perspectives on infosphere
governance, the debates within the United States are now more fully
connected with those around the world. At the same time, the expanded
scope of infosphere governance beyond the technical realm, the increased participation of other states (Drissel, 2006), and their assertion
of sovereignty in national domain space and for state participation in
governance have led to more direct efforts, such as the Internet Freedom Task force, to assert political values and cultural practice more
directly in infosphere governance.

Constraining Mobility and the Reassertion of State Power

Of particular importance in these developments are the ways in which
the initial justifications, goals, and promises of ICANN were revised
and retracted along a number of fronts. The early, relatively weak the-
orization of private property rights in favor of claims about online civil
society and the enlightened self-interest of its members leading to a demand for spontaneous and flexible collective governance was not seen
to protect business and government interests. Mueller (2002) argues
that what actually resulted was an entrenchment of an extremely strong
variant of intellectual property rights that some argue exceeds the allocation of those rights in offline spheres. Claims were also made early
on about the ability of processes of communication, consultation, and
decision-making among private sector groups to make choices about
allocating names and numbers on the Internet more effectively than
would public sector decision-making. Strong assumptions, evident from
the beginning, about the possibility of forming and building a working
organization from these different interest groups or "stakeholders" in a
civil society-like structure were used to justify the transfer of this important governance activity away from state or interstate bodies. However,
concerns have been raised that claims about the efficacy of broad communities of stakeholders were met in actual practice by closed consultation of U.S. government officials with a small group of large private
sector firms. The attempt to form a narrow, targeted nonstate body
for name and number allocation resulted in an extremely strong role

for a conventional intergovernmental organization, WIPO, in the Uniform Dispute Resolution process. The attempt to limit the role of national governments has actually led to the continued dominance of the U.S. Department of Commerce as the sole authority, outsourcing these governance activities to ICANN. A lack of clarity has also led to ongoing disputes with the former private sector monopoly registrar, Network Solutions and then VeriSign. Meanwhile, WSIS, the intergovernmental organization that was established in part to counter the power of ICANN, ended up reproducing many of ICANN's ideological shifts, albeit while increasing the power of governments. The movement between these initial claims and how Internet governance has developed provides numerous illustrations of ongoing and new tensions in the spatial and social construction of the infosphere, and how they are being worked out over time. As was noted in Chapter 1, the infosphere—Manuel Castells' "hyperspace of pure circulation"—is anything but "pure." It is a space that is continually reformed and reterritorialized as actors struggle amid a host of tensions, as outlined conceptually in Table 1.1 and further developed with reference to infosphere management in Table 1.2.

This account shows the presentation of different possible relationships between technology, governance, and cultural practice in the proposals for management modalities for the infosphere. The early efforts to reduce the formal role of states and the debates over political values and cultural practices were met with calls for greater participation by civil society groups and by governments. The agenda of the IGF now includes a range of issues, including many of the same issues that are discussed in national debates in the United States. Other governments are taking a greater interest in ccTLDs, seeing them as national spaces. With new institutional arrangements for Internet governance being implemented, and the role of the ICANN being reviewed once again, the specific arrangements for infosphere management at the international level continues to exhibit the tensions described in Chapter 1.

In debates about what ICANN should be and why, the dialectic between *production* and *trade* (illustrated in the first row of Tables 1.1 and 1.2) was initially managed by emphasizing the importance of the Internet and national information highways as a basic strategic resource for efficient production in the information economy and the basis for national competitive advantage. These types of claims were made at the national level, emphasizing the Internet's importance in production. At the same time, seemingly contradictory claims about the need for an open and unconstrained nonstate space for trade were made. The efforts to promote national information highway strategies were matched by efforts to accentuate e-commerce service activities that crossed borders. It is also notable that the basic terms for ICANN's mandate were set in the "Framework for Global Electronic Commerce" (United States, 1996b), a document that emphasized international trade and investment in open markets and limiting the role of regulation and government.

The balance between *fixity* and *mobility* was first presented as an opportunity to advance the mobility agenda. The Internet was portrayed as an uncontrollable space for mobility of information, commerce, and capital, and a space typified by rapid, unpredictable, and inevitable technology change. The need for a mobile and flexible institution to match technical change and the borderless world of the Internet were accepted by many people inside and outside of government. The new form of governance, by being more flexible and responsive to stakeholders and civil society groups around the world, would allow for the benefits of technological change to emerge more easily and with less friction. The institutions for management of Internet name space that were necessary as a fixed terrain for communication, investment, and trade would emerge spontaneously as stakeholders identified their needs. This discourse that supported the emergence of ICANN has been challenged on a number of fronts, whether by those concerned about property rights protection or by those aiming to control various forms of cybercrime or promote network security (ITU, 2006b). A new emphasis on fixed institutions and the fixed nature of perpetrators of online malfeasance, which is evident in the 2005 WSIS declaration as well as in recent ICANN documents and policies, seems to reflect a reworked approach to resolving this tension in the early twenty-first century.

At the same time, the ongoing tension between constructing the infosphere as a space within state *territories* and its idealization as an arena beyond territorial power (*nonterritory*) has been provisionally resolved through an expansion of state power and authority, both within existing state territories and in the new intergovernmental territory of the infosphere. What was striking about many of these debates from 2003 through 2006 is the extent to which the final authority and accountability came back to traditional governmental and intergovernmental arrangements and bodies. The U.S. Department of Commerce determined whether ICANN was meeting the terms of the Memorandum of Understanding that had been developed and renewed over the years. Those parties with complaints in the United States could go to a committee in Congress and ask for a hearing. These committees could use their oversight responsibilities vis-à-vis the Department of Commerce to raise issues and to ask for a satisfactory resolution from the administration (Victory, 2003). For instance, it was the General Counsel of the Department of Commerce who testified to the House Subcommittee on Courts, the Internet, and Intellectual Property in September 2003, promising to set and review benchmarks on the management of WHOIS data and other DNS management goals as a condition of renewing the Memorandum of Understanding with ICANN (Kassinger, 2003). Just as the protection of intellectual property rights came back to traditional mechanisms of criminal law and civil law, calls for accountability and responsible government likewise were adjudicated through traditional routes. Likewise, in the international arena, the ideal of a governance structure rooted in nonterritorial civil society gave way to one characterized by intergovernmental negotiations with expanded participation by private stakeholder groups.

The tension between *politics* and *economics* was also played out in interesting tangents. Whereas the economic drive to promote e-commerce was seen as paramount, the political feasibility of promoting a new form of governance was initially justified on the basis of the existence of a new type of political community, a transnational civil society of online users that would identify and organize their needs for collective governance as they emerged. In the end, however, as Palfrey notes (2004a), what emerged could be called half a democracy, in which there were neither clear procedures nor clear accountability to stakeholders.

7   The Infosphere: A World of Places, an Ocean of Information, or a Special Administrative Region?

Throughout this book, we have sought to illustrate and investigate the three metaphors presented in the introduction that may be used to describe the infosphere: distinct places of interaction composed of bounded corridors, as in the Mountain City and Appalachia examples; an ocean of information, as related to the world-ocean example; and a special administrative region, similar to Hong Kong. Likewise, we have attempted to outline the complexity of issues that arise when the four tensions—fixity/mobility, production/trade, territory/nonterritory, politics/economics—are taken into consideration within these three metaphoric models. Depending on the context in which and the scale at which we view the infosphere, it can take on the characteristics of any of these three metaphors, either individually or simultaneously. The malleable nature of the infosphere's character makes it a subject of study that is both fascinating and frustrating, so what can we say definitively at this point in time about such an unpredictable technology? We can say this: The crucial element at the heart of the infosphere is *motion* (and the management of that motion by various players ranging in scale from nations to individuals). The management of mobility, whether in terms of data, products, people, boundaries, policies, or some combination is a defining element of the infosphere. Management of mobility takes place through governance actions that set parameters on the deployment and use of infosphere technologies at various formal levels of government (municipal, national, international). Mobility management is also enacted through technology-related decisions that emphasize priorities for research and development (social shaping), design and technical protocols (technical code), processes of adoption and use (diffusion), or the individual and group practices, understandings, and expressions that make up cultural life (social construction). Cultural practices, although undertaken and understood by individuals and groups, and while set within the parameters of governance and systems shaping technology, may emerge in patterns that challenge existing parameters and structures (reinvention). Whereas the tensions in management of mobility may be most evident in the formal processes of governance, we argue that these tensions are also worked out in technology uses and change as well as in cultural understandings and practices.

In the following discussion, we draw out a number of implications that arise when we explore more closely the management of mobility in the infosphere. First, this management is undertaken by a wide variety of actors and institutions, but management of the infosphere also insinuates itself into the daily lives and cultural practices of people perhaps more directly than do trade and investment policy. Second, investigating the management of mobility prompts a rethinking of certain core concepts in the field of new communication technology, including the space of flows, identity, and the characteristics of management. We conclude by identifying a few of the challenges that many of us will face in conducting future research, building theory, and formulating responsible management choices related to the infosphere.

Turning first to the governance of the infosphere, we have stressed throughout this book that the infosphere is simultaneously the creation of one state (the United States), under the management of the international system, and cooperatively governed by a variety of nonstate actors. Although the technical parameters of the Internet were initially established by developments in the United States, individuals and groups in other countries have made significant contributions to Internet applications, including the development of Internet protocols. Other countries have also adopted the policies that support the world space of mobility by allowing a special administrative region in the infosphere to operate in their countries; for example, online gambling and pharmaceutical purchases in the United States generally enjoy more freedom in the infosphere than offline. Characteristics such as open technical interfaces, open movement of information, and nonproprietary standards can and are being redesigned to be more restrictive in nature. States, such as China, use firewalls in their international network access points to control or direct traffic, whereas others employ software, such as Carnivore in the United States, to monitor vast amounts of traffic. Private firms assert intellectual property rights in software, domain name space, and web-based content. The balance between the conditions necessary to support a space of open movement for social and political communication versus those more closed conditions essential for e-commerce applications (e.g., payment systems, security applications, copyright protection) remains a central struggle in infosphere management.

What does the conception of the infosphere as an example of ocean-space mean for international political economy? This is where the parallel metaphor of ocean-space is useful in thinking about the construction of the infosphere, and how it connects to international institutions and organizations. The creation and maintenance of a space of mobility in the infosphere is premised, as in international institutions, on the participation and support of many nation-states as well as nonstate actors. Like diplomatic relations, the laws of war, or the regimes of movement that govern the postal, communication, aviation, and shipping systems, there may be many different formal governing organizations that shape these special zones and the appropriate practices in these zones. Susan Strange (1988), for instance, noted that bilateral treaties in telecommunications have been more important than multilateral treaties in the International Telecommunication Union in governing this sector, in that they are more numerous and seem to bind behavior more tightly and directly. Some states may support this mode of activity and interaction in order to participate more fully in world political economy. Others may recognize the limits and costs of state control, whereas other states may respond to citizens' calls for a zone of liberty and privacy. Freedom and movement in the infosphere, however, do not reflect merely the absence of state power and authority. Rather, state power may support certain liberties of expression and movement, whether by not applying state authority or by deliberately and directly acting to support certain activities.

Perhaps more than other international institutions, infosphere institutions and the practices they guide and reflect have entered directly into the daily lives of many people in the industrialized world. Rules concerning intellectual property, spam, privacy protection, the security of transactions, and access to media potentially shape how we adopt, reinvent, and use infosphere communication. Trade and investment impact people's lives through the social organization of production (e.g., jobs, productivity, income, health and safety, environmental regulation) as well as through the social and cultural patterns associated with consumption (e.g., the availability, prices, and quality of goods and services, and modes of use). It is debatable whether the infosphere, and the multitude of information services and cultural practices made directly available through this technology, presents a more substantial change and challenge to daily life than do transnational trade and investment. There is, however, a case to be made for exploring this claim carefully.

One important implication arising from this analysis concerns the space of flows. Manuel Castells (1996) has presented the concept of the space of flows as an even and friction-free space of movement of information, money, investment, technology, people, and things among the geographic centers of production and commerce in the global network society. We do not dispute that this type of space of mobility seems to be the goal or ideal of some corporations and states in the global political economy. Nor do we dispute that depictions of and efforts to build a space of flows, which collapse time and space for certain types of movement, are part of this effort. However, the motivations of states, firms, groups, and individuals are mixed, as are the outcomes of these occasionally disparate and vying efforts to manage the infosphere.

States, civil society groups, and individuals are often depicted as having the greatest incentives to create places with unique characteristics and features in the infosphere (or special administrative regions) because they are frequently territorially based. By contrast, transnational firms are most often viewed as the champions of creating and maintaining an unfettered space of flows. They seek for their competitive advantage greater mobility of information, technology, capital, goods, services, and people, locating various activities in the chain of value creation to minimize costs to maximize strategic positioning in markets, and to manage the core assets the firm possesses. Locations are chosen for fixed investment by calculations that balance the mobility of some factors of production (capital, goods) with access to other more fixed features (land, labor, skills, business services, and culture). However, these calculations do not always seek to enhance mobility. When a comparative advantage for a firm derives from a fixed asset or place-based feature (location of offices and production facilities, access to skilled workers in regional clusters of high-tech firms, access to national markets, access to government procurement), the firm may also seek to limit mobility to obtain market advantage. Brand management to maximize value can also lead to a mix of transnational and national strategies, using national symbols and web addresses in some contexts, and emphasizing the global nature of the brand or product in other cases. Protection of intellectual property may be tied to enhancing the fixed characteristics of information resources. The marketplace wants to be free, but the freedom to seek higher and predictable rates of return may involve some efforts to stabilize earnings through strategies enhancing the profitability of fixed, national assets.

We are not arguing here that the details of the infosphere are more complex than the broad abstraction of the spaces of flows, and that the details need to be refined through further research. Rather, the point we raise is that conceptualizing motion as occurring in an undifferentiated space of flows as a starting point for thinking about the infosphere may assume too much about core features and capabilities of uses and management of the infosphere, and it may assume, perhaps incorrectly, certain inherent characteristics of the technology or the uses to which it is put. This starting point, which assumes that the infosphere is like the transparent, nebulous cloud frequently represented in network diagrams, can hamper theory-building, research, and analysis of the features and characteristics of mobility; it can also obscure the infosphere's role in shaping mobility. Instead, we argue that the infosphere possesses a geography consisting, in part, of corridors and boundaries of interaction; however, this geography is not solely about the physical areas that are not covered or the regions and populations that have less bandwidth. This geography is also about the terms and conditions of access and use, as well as the multiple forms of, governance, and management of states, firms, groups, and individuals in daily practice as reflected in the social shaping and social construction of the infosphere. In a way, this draws from WJT Mitchell's *City of Bits* (1996), which presents different types of urban spaces and buildings as guides to thinking about interactions on the web (see also Sheller and Urry, 2006b). We suggest that these types of place-based images of the uses and shaping of online space, mobility, and crossing between spaces should be extended to the global level. Mobility may be enhanced by infrastructure and marketing investments or limited by concerns over health by travelers and state authorities (Richter, 2003).

A second point upon which the popular conceptions of mobility in the infosphere should be carefully reconsidered or revised concerns depictions of the mobility of groups and individuals. In the 1990s, a number of authors presented mobility as a radical and fundamental break from place-based identities or affiliations of geographically proximate communities. Identity and membership are considered together here, because they are intertwined and interdependent. Sherry Turkle (1995) explored how early users of the Internet experimented with different online identities, concluding that anonymity and role-playing fostered the ultimate mobility experience by enabling individuals to escape their "real life" identities through the appearance and interaction with others via altered age, gender, race, or other components of the self. Marc Dery (1996) also examined cultural representations of cyberworlds and technology, with a special focus on the body and technologies. These new representations included efforts to transform selves through the use of plastic surgery or to meld bodies and machines into Borg-like designs. Dery argued that many representations of movement and life on the Internet at that time seemed ultimately to lead to efforts to escape the physical body in order to enter an infosphere of pure thought and information.

In contrast to this early work on infosphere identity and community formation, we align ourselves with more recent authors, such as Katie Hafner (2004) and Richard Charbán and Romelia Salinas (2004), who stress the links between the online movement of identities and offline movement of bodies. We propose an understanding of mobility that connects information and media applications in the infosphere in different ways to everyday life and to physical mobility. In Chapter 4, for instance, we demonstrated how tourism involves a mutually reinforcing cycle between the mobility of bodies and the mobility of identities, as travelers move to different national jurisdictions (seeking new experiences and services that may not be available at home, see Pennings, 2002); explore new roles outside of work, family, and community life;

and experience in person the places that have been represented to them in media portrayals and have been coordinated by infosphere applications.

A different notion of management also needs to be incorporated into the examples of management that we have discussed. Management is most often conceived of as authoritative decisions that set norms and behaviors for groups, even if compliance is not total. This is the governance school of management discussed in Chapter 1. Management in the networked infosphere is more democratic, the hierarchy more flattened. This less hierarchical nature of management has led many analysts to conclude that the infosphere is beyond control, both in national contexts and especially internationally. The notion of management that we use suggests that actors can and do have an impact, can and do exert control. A sense that some form of control is possible or impossible is a starting point directing how we react to future introductions of new media, how we respond, and the sense of accountability and responsibility that should be associated with the infosphere. This departs from a central authoritative form of control, or the supposedly revolutionary impacts of new technologies.

The infosphere's being "beyond control" may abrogate responsibility for institutions, relationships, and behaviors that are as not as easily controlled through traditional notions of public policy and regulation, but many people are still inserting and asserting control in the infosphere. Shaping through investments in new technology, coding certain capabilities in the design of information and communication technologies (ICTs), offering certain products and services to organizations and the public, and encouraging the prohibition of certain forms of online communication and behavior are all forms of diffuse control or management in the networked environment. These sites of management may not be easy to pinpoint, and the few sources of policy and regulation have devolved to a larger number of sites of management. Structures of power have not gone away, but the shift from hierarchical to more widely distributed forms of power, with more openness, and new types of actors and institutions makes some of these forms and exercises of power and control more difficult to clearly identify. Because some choices are more widely distributed among members of society it is harder to point to shares of control than in the past. Although single firms may not have the traditional control of end-to-end networks and technology that telephone or broadcast companies possessed, and there are different network layers and hardware, software, and service application sectors, the choices of actors large or small are still constrained. Management in the networked infosphere, even for states and large organizations, must take into account not only formal public policies, but market power, social and political norms, and technological possibilities and change. Although it is difficult to conceptualize the effectiveness and implications of choice and control in the infosphere, the networked notion of power is an important component of the management of mobility.

Looking Ahead

What are the implications of thinking about the infosphere as a space of mobility for theory, policy, and research and for individual cyberlife and group cyberculture? Some choices regarding technology design and infrastructure deployment should take on increased public profile and importance, constructing the social and cultural spaces and contexts in which we live. The infosphere can be seen as institutionally grounded given the malleability of some elements and components. Government, society, and culture become more important rather than less important because the infosphere, we argue, is omnipresent and directly affects us all to greater and lesser extents.

Theoretically, the infosphere should then be seen as socially and culturally grounded. A shift in research has occurred that focuses more on uses, although the celebration of possibilities still predominates the popular understanding. The fantastical visions of the infosphere presented by the mainstream media, in general, and specialized outlets such as *Wired* magazine, in particular, remain focused on the excitement of business strategies and investment, the marketing of new services, and the capabilities and convenience of online services. The investment excitement around the infosphere can be seen as a cultural "happening." The dreams of quick profits for businesses and economic growth for nation-states were seemingly too good to be true. Technology change and the opportunities for leader firms in specific sectors or applications did produce some important winners, but consistent with the experiences of other investment bubbles and gold rushes, some of the excitement has dissipated.

In contrast to the preceding popular emphases, we believe that our analysis contributes to debates on globalization by pointing to the continuities between the spatial organization and governance of the infosphere and the institutions that organize mobility using other communications media and in nonelectronic international trade and investment regimes. The inclusion of intellectual property rights as well as trade and exchange as core institutions in the creation of mobility and the infosphere points directly to the organization of production, exchange, and property in this emerging context or regime of accumulation. The accelerating pace of economic and technical change driven by competitive market dynamics, higher demands on returns from capital, and the global organization of production leads to questions about the characteristics of national and global production patterns.

The roles of state and corporate actors are also central to the analysis. The primary agents of governance are states, whereas the most important agents making choices in the social shaping of technology are states and corporations. Governance and technology establish communication contexts or environments in which cultural practices occur. However, the mythology associated with infosphere activities, of total freedom and total choice online—because of lower costs for individuals to obtain information or adopt alternatives, and because of fewer constraints on actions posed by law, policy, and society—is often contrasted with more grounded choice situations that are faced offline. We do not argue that this is simply a new space unfettered by resource limitations and offering open choices. Rather, we argue that the management choices we face individually and collectively are situated in new ways. Finding that new context, institutionally or in what Charles Taylor (1989) refers to as a horizon of meaning or significance, is very difficult. Although there are governing decisions shaping infosphere deployment and use, there is no single infosphere context or setting. The concept of "the infosphere" needs to be seen as shorthand for multiple but shared experiences, just as "society" and "the market" are experienced in multiple ways. However, this multiplicity does not dissolve all attempts at understanding the infosphere. Nor does it dissolve all attempts at generating significant action to transform the infosphere or one's place within it. Choices and practices are being resituated, with limitations or encouragements for certain possibilities in different settings. Our uses in universities, households, Internet cafés, and workplaces may differ. Similarly, our uses at different times of life, or the uses allowed in different countries, may also differ.

This brings us back to the question of continuity and change. How much have the political, economic, social, and cultural institutions and contexts really changed in the period that we associate with the infosphere? The political system is still a state system. The range of choices made by states has varied among different historical periods, but states still retain the power and authority to wage war, to set rules for production, exchange, and property, and to guide social and cultural life. The infosphere is to a great extent still a nationalized space. Political conflict and cultural divides do not mean that the states are less important; they are important in different ways. People still look to authoritative public processes to deal with issues of consequence to them. Privatization of individual life and the supposed depoliticization of the infosphere mean only that some groups have occupied those spaces to produce and reproduce their visions, not that these visions do not exist. The social shaping of technology, technical code, and diffusion underline the importance of these considerations. New interstate and substate forms of governance mean that collective political decisions are made in different places and in different ways. Yet, authoritative decision-making has not ceased, whether in adoption decisions or in efforts to guide and control uses.

By shifting the focus of inquiry from the governance of the infosphere to its management, we open up several important questions. Management suggests a defined set of responsibilities, and also an "action" agenda. The management stance retains certain goals, but in recognizing that the situational context of decisions shifts and that the nature of options and choices in the infosphere is shifting, management also addresses both elements of motion described in Chapter 1: (1) the geographic motion of bodies, ideas, commodities, and capital, and (2) the historic motion of institutions and technologies. Motion characterizes the changing context in which management decisions and actions take place, and it also is one of the most important (albeit often unstated) goals for decisions made in managing the construction and reconstruction of the infosphere.

The task we have laid out here is to expand the notion of management beyond the centralized control of organizational processes to produce goods and services. The recognition that important governing choices are being made in the design of technologies, in technology adoption, and in the use of services and web applications also means that these processes and choices must be examined closely. The task then includes expanding the range of choices, the information composing those choices, and participation by groups in the types of choices made by infosphere managers. This also includes expanding the number of components of choice models beyond the costs, benefits, and risks associated with certain location-based and technical decisions in production practices. It also means expanding the information available for public choices.

In conclusion, choices in infosphere construction and management are complicated by the nature of governance, continuous technology change, the interaction of collective and individual action, and the transnational connections among networks. Creating and managing an environment or architecture for interaction (Mitchell, 1996) may be more difficult than specifying behavior. With no given set of rules, practices emerge or are created and debated "on the fly." However, choices still need to be made as to whether in nonstate spaces (such as ocean-space or special administrative regions) governing agencies will be accountable, or whether the public will allow them to abdicate their responsibility and authority. Finding this balance in democratic accountability remains one of the central challenges in the management of the infosphere as a space of mobility.

 Notes

Chapter 1

1. If local residents were refusing to use the ATM during banking hours in a conscious effort to maintain local social relations and employment structures, this would be consistent with the analysis suggested by Gaventa (1980) in his study of indirect acts of resistance in rural Appalachia. This interpretation is debatable, however. Given the enthusiasm with which rural Americans have abandoned small, independent, downtown stores for chain superstores located on bypass highways, one must question the level of sacrifice that individual rural Americans are willing to make to maintain local social structures. Although refusal to use an ATM and refusal to shop at Wal-Mart are not strictly comparable, the existence of this counterexample further suggests that there is a complex sociology behind decisions to adopt or reject technological innovations and social transformation.

2. In pointing to the heterotopic aspects of the infosphere, we follow the definition of heterotopia offered by Hetherington (1997), who stresses the ambiguous political position of these in-between spaces, rather than that of Foucault (1986), who is considerably more enamored of their transformative potential.

3. See Steinberg (2001), in which the discussion of the ocean presented here is developed in much greater detail.

4. Friction refers to any obstacle to movement, whether a physical obstacle or an intangible one, established by political divisions, property rights, or bureaucratic regulations.

5. The iceberg model was originally developed by Samuelson (1952), but most new economic geographers use the revised version developed by Krugman (1991a, 1991b). For a comparison of the versions of this model, see McCann (2005).

6. Although we focus on spaces of movement, rather than spaces of production and consumption, this critique of the new economic geographers closely parallels that made by economic geographers from within the discipline of geography who note that economists practicing new economic geography tend to treat space as a homogeneous field of points that exist prior to the social (or economic) activities that, in fact, reflect and construct space's social character and institutional texture (e.g., Martin, 1999a, 1999b; Sheppard, 2000; Thrift, 2000). At a broader theoretical level, our critique also echoes Massey's (2005) criticism of social theories that fail to view space and time as mutually constitutive.

7. Here, we utilize Cox's (1987) distinction between logical and historical precedence.

8. In linking Innis' work in institutional economics with Harvey's in economic geography, we draw upon recent studies by Barnes (1999).

Chapter 2

1. This pattern of greater initial customer access to and participation in the formation of a communication technology during its formative years is also evident, for example, with early telephone and early radio. As time passes, however, and corporations invest more heavily in the developing technology, individual freedoms generally erode, but do not necessarily disappear, in favor of corporate interests (Fidler, 1997) that take on a retroactive social shaping role.

2. In their prologue, Hafner and Lyon (1996), write:

> They came to Boston from as far away as London and Los Angeles, several dozen middle-aged men, reuniting for a fall weekend in 1994 to celebrate what they had done twenty-five years earlier . . . Bob Taylor, the director of a corporate research facility in Silicon Valley [and coordinator of the ARPANET experiment], had come to the party for old times sake, but he was also on a personal mission to correct an inaccuracy of long standing. Rumors had persisted for years that the ARPANET had been built to protect national security in the face of a nuclear attack. It was a myth that had gone unchallenged long enough to become widely accepted as fact. . . The project had embodied the most peaceful intentions—to link computers at scientific laboratories across the country so that researchers might share computer resources (pp. 9–10).

Granted, Paul Baran of the United States–based Rand Corporation (and unwitting co-inventor of packet-switching with Donald Davies of the U.K.) was concerned about the network's survival in the event of a catastrophic event, such as a nuclear explosion, but he was not an original member of the ARPANET group (Hafner and Lyon, 1996; Waldrop, 2001). Additionally, nothing in Licklider's *Man-computer Symbiosis* (1960) explicitly states that military or defense uses of the network factored into his original vision, even though the project was originally funded by the U.S. Defense Department and Licklider himself had a long history of working on U.S. military-based projects (Waldrop, 2001).

Chapter 3

1. It should be noted that infosphere management is mediated through the particularities of place. Hence, although the examples in this chapter, which are almost all U.S.-based, are illustrative of these dynamics, they may or may not apply in different patterns of governance and social contexts outside the United States.

Chapter 5

1. There are a few exceptions to this rule. For instance, the United Kingdom's ccTLD is .UK whereas its ISO 3166-1 listing is .GB. The assignment of .UK was made before IANA adopted the ISO 3166-1 list (IANA, 2000b).

2. Over time, the administration of the Internet has become somewhat more internationalized. There has been a progressive distancing from the U.S. government as Internet coordination has devolved from the Department of Defense, to the National Science Foundation, to IANA, to ICANN. ICANN has somewhat expanded the role of its Government Advisory Council, which has given non-U.S. governmental entities a formal role in Internet governance. Also, the abolition of Network Solutions, Inc.'s monopoly as registrar for all .COM, .NET, and .ORG domains has allowed non-U.S. entrants into this sector of Internet governance. Nonetheless, these devolutions have been limited (Hodgson, 2001b; Shaw R., 1997). In Chapter 6 we discuss further the continuing, albeit reshaped, role of the U.S. government in Internet governance.

References

Abbate, Janet. 1999. *Inventing the internet*. Cambridge, MA: MIT Press.

Abler, Ronald, John S. Adams, and John R. Borchert. 1976. *The twin cities of St. Paul and Minneapolis*. Cambridge, MA: Ballinger Publishing Company.

Agnew, John. 2005. Sovereignty regimes: Territoriality and state authority in contemporary world politics. *Annals of the Association of American Geographers* 95:437–461.

Agnew, John, and Stuart Corbridge. 1995. *Mastering space: Hegemony, territory and international political economy*. London: Routledge.

Albert, Mathias. 1999. On boundaries, territory and postmodernity: An international relations perspective. In *Boundaries, territory and postmodernity*, ed. D. Newman, 53–68. London: Frank Cass.

Amin, Ash. 1994. *Post-Fordism: A reader*. Oxford, U.K.: Basil Blackwell.

Amirahmadi, Hooshang, and C. Wallace. 1995. Information technology, the organization of production, and regional development. *Environment and Planning* 10:1745–75.

Anderson, Benedict. 1991. *Imagined communities: Reflections on the origin and spread of nationalism*. London: Verso.

Anderson, Christopher. 1994. Disneyland. In *Television: The critical view*, 5th ed., ed. H. Newcomb, 70–86. New York: Oxford University Press.

Anonymous. 1998. Tax-free cyberspace. *State Government News* 41(9):6.

Appadurai, Arjun. 1996. *Modernity at large: Cultural dimensions of globalization*. Minneapolis: University of Minnesota Press.

Arends, Brett. 2007. Good call, city hall, in reviving hub's wi-fi [Op-ed]. *Boston Herald*, January 17, O21.

Armstrong, Peter, Pat Miles, and John W. Pestle. 1997. Memorandum regarding FCC City of Troy decision. Grand Rapids, MI: Varnum, Riddering, Schmidt & Howlett. October 13.

Astier, Stéphane. 2005. Ethical regulation of the internet: The challenges of global governance. *International Review of Administrative Sciences* 71:133–50.

Attallah, Paul. 1996. Canadian television exports: Into the mainstream. In *New patterns in global television: Peripheral vision*, ed. J. Sinclair, E. Jacka, and S. Cunningham, 161–91. New York: Oxford University Press.

Auerbach, Karl. 2003. Statement to the Communication Subcommittee, United States Senate Committee on Commerce, Science, and Transportation. July 31.

Augé, Marc. 1995. *Non-places: Introduction to an anthropology of supermodernity*. London: Verso.

Azarya, Victor. 2004. Globalization and international tourism in developing countries: Marginality as a commercial commodity. *Current Sociology* 52:949–67.

Baldwin, Thomas, D. Stevens McVoy, and Charles Steinfield. 1996. *Convergence: Integrating media, information, and communication*. Newbury Park, CA: Sage.

Barnes, Trevor J. 1999. Industrial geography, institutional economics and Innis. In *The new industrial geography: Regions, regulation and institutions*, eds. T. J. Barnes and M. S. Gertler, 1–20. London: Routledge.

Barnes, William, and Larry C. Ledebur. 1994. Local economies: The U. S. common market of regional economies. *National League of Cities, Research Reports on America's Cities*. Washington DC: National League of Cities.

Barnett, Michael, and Raymond Duvall, eds. 2005. *Power in global governance*. Cambridge: Cambridge University Press.

Baudrillard, Jean. 1988. *Selected writings*, ed. M. Poster. Stanford: Stanford University Press.

Beauprez, Jennifer. 1998. Cities unite the build cable council, communication networks. *Crain's Cleveland Business*, January 19, 2.

Beirman, David. 2003. Review of *Tourism and the media*. *Journal of Vacation Marketing* 9:101–3.

BelAir Networks. 2006. *Municipal wireless networks: Solution overview*. http://www.belairnetworks.com/resources (accessed February 10, 2007).

Beniger, James. 1986. *The control revolution: Technological and economic origins of the information society*. Cambridge, MA: Harvard University Press.

Benton, Joshua. 1999. The dwindling days of "A heaven on Earth," *Toledo Blade*. July 22. http://www.clipfile.org/1999/08/22/357 (accessed June 2007).

Bernt, Phyllis, Hans Kruse, and David Landsbergen. 1993. Impact of alternative technologies on universal service and competition in the local loop. *Telematics and Informatics* 10:359–77.

Bertot, John C. 2006. E-government [Special issue]. *Government Information Quarterly* 23(2).

Bhabha, Homi. 1994. *The location of culture*. London: Routledge.

Biersteker, Thomas J., and Cynthia Weber, eds. 1996. *State sovereignty as social construct*. Cambridge: Cambridge University Press.

Bird, Jon, Barry Curtis, Tim Putnam, George Robertson, and Lisa Tickner, eds. 1993. *Mapping the futures: Local cultures, global change*. London: Routledge.

Bohannon, Mark. 2004. Statement of Mark Bohannon, General Counsel and Senior Vice President Public Policy, Copyright Coalition on Domain Names, to the Subcommittee on Courts, the Internet and Intellectual Property, House Judiciary Committee. February 4.

Bonnet, Thomas. 1998. Is the new global economy leaving state/local tax structures behind? *Public Management* 80:4–9.

Borins, Sanford. 1998. *Innovating with integrity: How local heroes are transforming American government*. Washington, DC: Georgetown University Press.

Boston Working Group. 1998. *Re: United States Department of Commerce, National Telecommunications and Information Administration, Management of Internet names and addresses*. September 28. Docket Number: 980212036-8146-02.

Braman, Sandra. 1996. Interpenetrated globalization: Scaling, power, and the public sphere. In *Globalization, communication and transnational civil society*, eds. S. Braman and A. Sreberny-Mohannadi, 36. Cresskill, NJ: Hampton Press.

Braudel, Fernaud. 1982. *On history*. Chicago: University of Chicago Press.

———. 1984. *The perspective of the world. Civilization and capitalism 15th–18th century*, vol. 3. New York: Harper and Row.

Brietbart, Joshua. 2006. Wireless Philadelphia: An interview with helmsman Greg Goldman. *Digital Communities* (December):6–11. http://media. govtech.net/Digital_Communities/DC12_06_single.pdf (accessed February 10, 2007).

Briffault, Richard. 1990a. Our localism. Part 1, Localism and legal theory. *Columbia Law Review* 90:1–115.

———. 1990b. Our localism. Part 2, Localism and legal theory. *Columbia Law Review* 90:346–454.

———. 2000. Localism and regionalism. *Buffalo Law Review* 48:1–30.

Britton, Nadia J., Peter Halfpenny, Fiona Devine, and Rosemary Mellor. 2004. The future of regional cities in the information age: The impact of information technology on Manchester's financial and business services sector. *Sociology* 38:795–814.

Broder, John M. 1997. Man behind doomed health plan wants minimal regulation of net. *New York Times Cybertimes*. June 30. http://www.nytimes.com/ library/cyber/week/063097magaziner.html (accessed June 14, 2007).

Brook, James, and Iain Boal, eds. 1995. *Resisting the virtual life: The culture and politics of information.* San Francisco: City Lights.

Brown, David. 2005. Electronic government and public administration. *International Review of Administrative Sciences* 71:241–54.

Brunn, Stanley D., and Charles D. Cottle. 1997. Small states and cyberboosterism. *Geographical Review* 87(2):240–58.

Brunn, Stanley D., and Thomas R. Leinbach, eds. 1991. *Collapsing space and time: Geographic aspects of communication and information.* London: HarperCollins Academic.

Burch, Kurt. 1994. The "properties" of the state system and global capitalism. In *The global economy as political space*, eds. S. J. Rosow and N. Inayatullah, 37–59. Boulder, CO: Lynne Rienner.

Butterfield, Katherine, and Stephen D. McDowell. 1998. FCC spectrum auctions: Evaluating a public policy experiment. Paper presented at the annual meeting of the International Communication Association, San Francisco, CA.

Buzinde, Christine N., Carla A. Santos, and Stephen L. J. Smith. 2006. Ethnic representations: Destination imagery. *Annals of Tourism Research* 33:707–28.

Cammaerts, Bart, and Nico Carpentier. 2006. The unbearable lightness of full participation in a global context: WSIS and civil society participation. In *Towards a sustainable information society: Deconstructing WSIS*, eds. J. Servaes and N. Carpentier, 17–49. Bristol, U.K.: Intellect Books.

Campbell, Angella J. 1999. Self-regulation and the media. *Federal Communications Law Journal* 51:711–71.

Canada. 2006. *Comments by the government of Canada on the continued transition of the technical coordination and management of the internet domain name and addressing system.* Department of Commerce, National Telecommunications and Information Administration, Docket No. 060519136-6136-01. http://www.ntia.doc.gov/ntiahome/domainname/dnstransition/comments/dnstrans_comment0675.htm (accessed February 10, 2007).

Carey, James W. 1988. *Communication as culture: Essays on media and society.* Boston: Unwin Hyman.

Castells, Manuel. 1996. *The rise of the network society.* Malden, MA: Blackwell.

———. 1997. *The power of identity.* Oxford: Blackwell.

———. 1998. *End of millennium.* Oxford: Blackwell.

Celeste, Richard F. 1996. Making technology count for America's communities. *Forum for Applied Research and Public Policy* 11:45–8.

Centre for Global Studies, University of Victoria. 2002. *Enhancing legitimacy in the Internet Corporation for Assigned Names and Numbers: Accountable and transparent governance structures.* Final Report to the Markle Foundation.

Chabrán, Richard, and Romelia Salinas. 2004. Place matters: Journeys through global and local spaces. In *Technological visions: The hopes and fears that shape new technologies*, eds. M. Sturken,D. Thomas, and S. J. Ball-Rokeach, 305–338. Philadelphia: Temple University Press.

Christensen, Sandra L. 1997. The new federalism: Implications for the legitimacy of corporate political activity. *Business Ethics Quarterly* (July):81–91.

Ciccantell, Paul S., and Stephen G. Bunker, eds. 1998. *Space and transport in the world-system*. Westport, CT: Greenwood Press.

Civille, Richard, and Kathleen Gygi. 1995. *Developing Four Corners regional telecommunications: Community and economy*. Conference Report. San Juan Forum, Durango, CO.

Clausing, Jeri. 1988. U.S. and domain registry reach accord. *New York Times Cybertimes*. October 6. http://www.nytimes.com/library/tech/98/10/cyber/articles/07domain.html (accessed June 14, 2007).

Clifford, James. 1997. *Routes: Travel and translation in the late twentieth century*. Cambridge, MA: Harvard University Press.

Clift, Steven. 2004. *E-government and democracy: Representation and citizen engagement in the information age*. http://www.publicus.net (accessed September 2, 2006).

Coburn, Christopher, Dan Berglund, and Robert Usher. 1996. Collaboration key to competitiveness. *Forum for Applied Research and Public Policy* 11:7–74.

Cohen, Erik. 1995. Contemporary tourism—trends and challenges: Sustainable authenticity or contrived post-modernity. In *Change in tourism: People, places, processes*, eds. R. Butler and D. Pearce, 12–29. London: Routledge.

Comor, Edward. 1998. *Communication, commerce, and power: The political economy of America and the direct broadcast satellite, 1960–2000*. New York: St. Martin's Press.

Competitors suffering from limited access to buildings, rights-of-way, *Communications Today*, November 5, 1997.

Cooper, Ann, and Jon Postel. 1993. *RFC 1480: The U.S. domain*. Marina Del Rey, CA: Network Working Group, Internet Assigned Numbers Authority (IANA), June. http://www.ietf.org/rfc/rfc1480.txt (accessed July 2001).

Cox, Kevin R., ed. 1997. *Spaces of globalization: Reasserting the power of the local*. New York: Guilford Press.

Cox, Robert W. 1987. *Production, power and world order: Social forces in the making of history*. New York: Columbia University Press.

Crothers, Lane. 2007. *Globalization and American popular culture*. Lanham, MD: Rowman & Littlefield.

Czitrom, Daniel J. 1982. *Media and the American mind: From Morse to McLuhan*. Chapel Hill, NC : University of North Carolina Press.

de Saussure, Ferdinand. 1916/1986. *Course in general linguistics*. Trans. R. Harris. La Salle, IL: Open Court.

de Souza e Silva, Adriana. 2006. From cyber to hybrid: Mobile technologies as interfaces of hybrid spaces. *Space and Culture* 9:261–78.

Deleuze, Gilles, and Felix Guattari. 1988. *A thousand plateaus: Capitalism and schizophrenia*. Trans. B. Massumi. London: Athlone.

Dell, Kristina. 2007. Welcome to Wi-Fi-Ville. *Time* January 5. http://www.time.com/time/magazine/article/0,9171,1574164,00.html (accessed February 10, 2007).

Dening, Greg. 1980. *Islands and beaches: Discourse on a silent land, Marquesas, 1774–1880*. Honolulu: University of Hawaii Press.

Der Derian, James, and Michael J. Shapiro, eds. 1989. *International/intertextual relations: Postmodern readings of world politics*. Lexington, MA: Lexington Books.

Dery, Mark. 1996. *Escape velocity: Cyberculture at the end of the century*. New York: Grove Press.

Digital Communities. 2007. *Government technology's digital communities: Building twenty-first century communities*. http://www.govtech.net/digitalcommunities/highlights.php (accessed February 10, 2007).

Dinan, John. 1997. State government influence in the national policy process: Lessons from the 104th Congress. *Publius* Spring:129–42.

Dodge, Martin, and Rob Kitchin. 2001. *Mapping cyberspace*. London: Routledge.

Doheny-Farina, Stephen, and Mark A. Herwick. 1997. Review of *The wired neighborhood*. *Journal of Urban Affairs* 19.

Dorsey, Elizabeth R., H. Leslie Steeves, and Luz Estella Porras. 2004. Advertising ecotourism on the internet: Commodifying environment and culture. *New Media & Society* 6:753–79.

Doty, Roxanne L. 1999. Racism, desire, and the politics of immigration. *Millennium: Journal of International Studies* 28:585–606.

Drache, Daniel, and Meric S. Gertler, eds. 1991. *The new era of global competition: State policy and market power*. Kingston, Ontario: McGill-Queen's University Press.

Drake, William J., ed. 1995. *The new information infrastructure: Strategies for U. S. policy*. New York: Twentieth Century Fund.

———. 2005. *Reforming internet governance: Perspectives from the Working Group on Internet Governance (WGIG)*. New York: United Nations ICT Task Force.

Drissel, David. 2006. Internet governance in a multipolar world: Challenging American hegemony. *Cambridge Review of International Affairs* 19:105–20.

Dupagne, Michel, and P. B. Seel. 1997. *High-definition television: A global perspective*. Ames, IA: Iowa State Press.

Eadington, William R. 1995. The emergence of casino gaming as a major factor in tourism markets: Policy issues and considerations. In *Change in tourism: People, places, processes*, eds. R. Butler and D. Pearce, 159–86. London: Routledge.

Edge, David. 1995. The social shaping of technology. In *Information technology and society*, eds. N. Heap,R. Thomas,G. Einon,R. Mason, and H. Mackey, 4–32. London: Sage.

Elmer, Greg. 2004. *Profiling machines: Mapping the personal information economy*. Cambridge, MA: MIT Press.

Elmer, Greg, and Mike Gasher, eds. 2005. *Contracting out Hollywood: Runaway productions and foreign location shooting*. Lanham, MD: Rowman & Littlefield.

Engel, Christoph. 2006. The role of law in the governance of the internet. *International Review of Law, Computers and Technology* 20: 201–16.

Enloe, Cynthia. 1989. *Bananas, beaches and bases: Making feminist sense of international relations*. London: Pandora.

Esbin, Barbara S. 1998. Panel discussion: *Telecommunications deregulation— A threat to state and local land use and zoning policies?* Paper presented at the meeting of the National Conference of State Legislatures, Commerce and Communications.

Estabrooks, Maurice, and Rudolph Lamarche, eds. 1987. *Telecommunications: A strategic perspective on regional economic and business development*. Moncton, New Brunswick: The Canadian Institute for Research on Regional Development.

Estrella, Joe. 1997. Denver preps 'test case' on telecom fees. *Multichannel News*. September 22,10. http://www.multichannel.com.

Flanagin, Andrew J., Maynard W. Farinola, and Miriam J. Metzer. 2000. The technical code of the Internet/World Wide Web. *Critical Studies in Media Communication* 17:409–28.

Fayol, Henri. 1916/1949. *General and industrial management*. London: Pitman.

Federal Communications Commission. 1997a. *FCC state and local advisory committee met today: Discussed impact of Telecom Act on state and local communities*. Press release, April 18.

———. 1997b. California Payphone Association Petition for Preemption of CCB Pol 96-26 Ordinance No. 576 NS of the City of Huntington Park, California Pursuant to Section 253 (d) of the Communications Act of 1996, FCC 97-251, Memorandum Opinion and Order, July 17.

———. 1997c. In the matter of TCI Cablevision of Oakland County, Inc. CSR-4790, Petition for Declaratory Ruling, Pre-emption and Other Relief Pursuant to 47 U.S.C. 541, 544 (e), and 253, Memorandum Opinion and Order, FCC 97-331, Released September 19.

———. 2003. Chairman Powell names members of FCC's Intergovernmental Advisory Committee. Press release, December 18.

———. 2006. Eleventh annual report to Congress on the state of competition in the commercial mobile radio services (CMRS) industry. Report (FCC 06-142). http://hraunfoss.fcc.gov/edocs_public/attachmatch/FCC-06-142A1.pdf (accessed February 10, 2007).

———. 2007. High-Speed Services for Internet Access: Status as of June 30,

2006. Industry Analysis and Technology Division, Wireline Competition Bureau. http://hraunfoss.fcc.gov/edocs_public/attachmatch/DOC-270128A1.pdf (accessed February 10, 2007).

Feenberg, Andrew. 1995. *Alternative modernity*. Berkeley: University of California Press.

Feery, Tom. 1998. Govt. regs. Message posted to NTIA in response to January 30, 1998 Green Paper. (February 12). http://www.ntia.doc.gov/ntiahome/domainname/130dftmail/02_12_98.htm

Ferré, Frederick. 1995. *Philosophy of technology*. Athens: University of Georgia Press.

Fidelman, Miles. 1997. *Telecommunications strategies for local government: A practical guide*. Washington DC: Government Technology Press.

Fidler, Roger. 1997. *Mediamorphosis: Understanding new media*. Thousand Oaks, CA: Pine Forge Press.

Fischer, Claude S. 1992. *America calling: A social history of the telephone to 1940*. Berkeley: University of California Press.

Fischer, Howard. 2000. "Qwest loses appeal on tax appeals court sides with Tucson." *Arizona Business Gazette* (November 2):5.

Fiscus, Chris. 1997. "Phone, cable fee to buy desert: Telecommunications firms say phoenix is imposing tax." *Arizona Republic* (December 16):A1.

Florida, House of Representatives. 1997. Telecommunications Rights-of-Way Act, HB 3291.

Florida, House of Representatives, Committee on Utilities and Communications. 1997. Bill Research and Economic Impact Statement, HB 3291, Telecommunications Rights-of Way. December 17.

Fornäs, Johan, Kajsa Klein, Martina Ladendorf, Jenny Sunden, and Malin Sveningsson, eds. 2002. *Digital borderlands: Cultural studies of identity and interactivity on the Internet*. New York: Peter Lang.

Foucault, Michel. 1986. Of other spaces. *Diacritics* 16:22–7.

Fox, Sharon E. 1996. The influence of political conditions on foreign firm location decisions in the American states (1974–1989). *Political Research Quarterly* (March):51–75.

Frangialli, Francesco. 2004. *Inaugural address*. http://www.world-tourism.org/newsroom/speeches/2004/sg_tourcom_eng.pdf (accessed June 12, 2007).

Frost, Warick. 2006. Braveheart-ed Ned Kelly: Historic films, heritage tourism and destination image. *Tourism Management* 27:247–54.

Frost, Warwick, Glen Croy, and Sue Beeton, eds. 2004. *International Tourism and Media Conference Proceedings*. Tourism Research Unit. Monash University, Narre Warren, Australia.

Fuentes-Bautista, Martha, and Nobuya Inagaki. 2006. Reconfiguring public internet access in Austin, TX: Wi-Fi's promise and broadband divides. *Government Information Quarterly* 23:404–34.

Fujita, Masahisa, Paul Krugman, and Anthony J. Venables. 1999. *The spatial economy: Cities, regions, and international trade*. Cambridge, MA: MIT Press.

Fursich, Elfriede. 2002. Packaging culture: The potential and limitations of travel programs on global television. *Communication Quarterly* 50:204–26.

Fursich, Elfriede, and Melinda B. Robins. 2004. Visiting Africa: Constructions of nation and identity on travel websites. *Journal of Asian and African Studies* 39:133–52.

Galperin, Hernan. 2004. *New television, old politics: The transition to digital TV in the United States and Britain*. Cambridge: Cambridge University Press.

Gammack, John. 2005. Tourism and media. *Annals of Tourism Research* 32: 1148–9.

Gaventa, John. 1980. *Power and powerlessness: Quiescence and rebellion in an Appalachian valley*. Urbana: University of Illinois Press.

General Agreement on Tariffs and Trade (GATT). 1994. Final act embodying the results of the Uruguay round of multilateral trade negotiations. Geneva, Switzerland: GATT. May 3.

Gillett, Sharon E., William H. Lehr, and Carlos Osorio. 2003. *Local government broadband initiatives*. Massachusetts Institute of Technology, Program on Internet and Telecoms Convergence, December 3. http://itc.mit.edu/itel/docs/2003/localgovbrbd.pdf. (accessed June 12, 2007).

Gilroy, Paul. 1993. *The black Atlantic: Modernity and double-consciousness*. Cambridge, MA: Harvard University Press.

Goldsmith, Jack, and Tim Wu. 2006. *Who controls the internet? Illusions of a borderless world*. New York: Oxford University Press.

Goodenow, Ronald. 1996. The cyberspace challenge: Modernity, post-modernity and reflections on international networking policy. *Comparative Education* 32:197–216.

Gorman, Sean P., and Edward J. Malecki. 2002. Fixed and fluid: Stability and change in the geography of the Internet. *Telecommunications Policy* 26:389–413.

Gottdiener, Mark. 1995. *Postmodern semiotics: Material culture and the forms of postmodern life*. Oxford: Blackwell.

Gould, Peter. 1991. Dynamic structures of geographic space. In *Collapsing space and time: Geographic aspects of communication and information*, eds., S. D. Brunn and T. R. Leinbach, 3–30. London: Harper Collins.

Graham, Gordon. 1999. *The Internet: A philosophical inquiry*. New York: Routledge.

Graham, Stephen, and Simon Marvin. 1996. *Telecommunications and the city: Electronic spaces, urban places*. London: Routledge.

Grant, Alexis. 2007. San Francisco picks EarthLink for citywide wireless network: Atlanta-based internet provider is one of 2 finalists for Houston job. *Houston Chronicle* (Texas). January 9.

Gray, Irwin. 1984. Introduction. In *General and industrial management: Revised by Irwin Gray*, ed. H. Fayol, 1–7. New York: Institute of Electrical and Electronics Engineers Press.

Grubesic, Tony H., and Alan T. Murray. 2005. Geographies of imperfection in telecommunication analysis. *Telecommunications Policy* 29:69–94.

Gunkel, David J. 2003. Second thoughts: Toward a critique of the digital divide. *New Media & Society* 5:499–522.

Hadden, Susan E., and Edward Lenert. 1995. Telecommunications networks are not VCRs: The public nature of new information technologies for universal service. *Media, Culture and Society* 17:121–40.

Hafner, Katie. 2004. When the virtual isn't enough. In *Technological visions: The hopes and fears that shape new technologies*, eds. M. Sturken, D. Thomas, and S. J. Ball-Rokeach, 293–304. Philadelphia: Temple University Press.

Hafner, Katie, and Matthew Lyon. 1996. *Where wizards stay up late: The origins of the Internet*. New York: Simon & Schuster.

Halavais, Alexander. 2000. National borders on the World Wide Web. *New Media & Society* 2:7–28.

Hall, Jennifer. 2003. Eighteen Utah cities collaborate to build high-speed fiver-optic network. *Knight Ridder Tribune Business News*, November 18.

Harasim, Linda M., ed. 1993. *Global networks: Computers and international communication*. Cambridge, MA: MIT Press.

Harvey, David. 1982. *The limits to capital*. Chicago: University of Chicago Press.

———. 1985. The geopolitics of capitalism. In *Social Relations and Spatial Structures*, eds. D. Gregory and J. Urry, 128–63. London: Macmillan.

———. 1989. *The condition of postmodernity: An enquiry into the origins of cultural change*. Cambridge, MA: Basil Blackwell.

Hassan, Robert. 2003. *The chronoscopic society: Globalization, time and knowledge in the network economy*. New York: Peter Lang.

Haynes, Cynthia, and Jan R. Holmevik, eds. 2001. *High wired: On the design, use, and theory of educational MOOs*, 2nd ed. Ann Arbor: University of Michigan Press.

Headrick, Daniel R. 1991. *The invisible weapon: Telecommunications and international politics, 1851–1945*. New York: Oxford University Press.

Heeks, Richard, ed. 2001. *Reinventing government in the Information Age: International practice in IT-enabled public sector reform*. London: Routledge.

Held, David. 1995. *Democracy and the global order*. Stanford: Stanford University Press.

Held, David, and Anthony G. McGrew, eds. 2002. *Governing globalization: Power, authority and global governance*. Cambridge, U.K.: Polity.

Helft, Miguel. 2007. San Francisco to go wireless. *New York Times*, January 6, C9.

Hepworth, Mark. 1990. *Geography of the information economy*. New York: Guilford Press.

Hershberg, Theodore. 1996. Regional cooperation: Strategies and incentives for global competitiveness and urban reform. *National Civic Review* 85(Spring/Summer):25–30.

Herz, John H. 1959. *International politics in the atomic age*. New York: Columbia University Press.

Hetherington, Kevin. 1997. *The badlands of modernity: Heterotopia and social ordering*. London: Routledge.

Hodge, Robert, and Gunther Kress. 1988. *Social semiotics*. Cambridge, U.K.: Polity.

Hodgson, Lee. 2000. Eight domain name predictions for 2001. *DEMC E-Magazine*. http://www.demc.com/Writers/Hodgson/article4/article4.html (accessed July 2001).

———. 2001a. International domains: Think globally, act locally to capture local markets. *DEMC E-Magazine*. http://www.demc.com/Writers/Hodgson/article7/article7.html (accessed July 2001).

———. 2001b. VeriSign retains control of domain name world. *DEMC E-Magazine*. http://www.demc.com/Writers/Hodgson/article6/article6.html (accessed July 2001).

Honeck, Dale B. 2001. *Overview of GATS disciplines and commitments*. Presentation for Symposium on Tourism Services. World Trade Organization, Geneva. http://www.wto.org/English/tratop_e/serv_e/ symp_outldbh_e.doc (accessed February 3, 2007).

Horrigan, John B., Chandler Stolp, and Robert H. Wilson. 2006. Broadband utilization in space: Effects of population and economic structure. *Information Society* 22:341–54.

Horwitz, Robert B. 1989. *The irony of regulatory reform: The deregulation of American telecommunications*. New York: Oxford University Press.

Hudson, Simon, and J. R. Brent Ritchie. 2006. Promoting destinations via film tourism: An empirical identification of supporting marketing initiatives. *Journal of Travel Research* 44:387–96.

Hugill, Peter J. 1993. *World trade since 1431: Geography, technology, and capitalism*. Baltimore: Johns Hopkins University Press.

———. 1999. *Global communications since 1844: Geopolitics and technology*. Baltimore: Johns Hopkins University Press.

Ilka, Douglas. 1997. In Oakland County: Troy, TCI applaud split decision on cable. *Detroit News*, September 25, C5.

Inayatullah, Naeem, and Mark Rupert. 1994. Hobbes, Smith and the problem of mixed ontologies in neorealist IPE. *The global economy as political space*, eds. S. Roscow,N. Inayatullah, and M. Rupert. Boulder, CO: Lynne Rienner.

India, Government of. 2006. *Government of India's response to the Notice of Inquiry on the Continued Transition of the Technical Coordination and Management of the Internet Domain Name and Addressing System*.

http://www.ntia.doc.gov/ntiahome/domainname/dnstransition/comments/dnstrans_comment0581.htm (accessed February 10, 2007).

Indiana. 1998. IN 1376 (Indiana code 8-1-1-1). Cited by Michael Chui on telecomreg listserv. http://www.in.gov/legislative/ic/code/title8/ar1/ch2.html (accessed June 14, 2007).

Information Infrastructure Task Force. 1993. *Global information infrastructure: Agenda for action.* Washington, DC: U.S. Government Printing Office.

Innis, Harold. 1951. *The bias of communication.* Toronto: University of Toronto Press.

———. 1972. *Empire and communications.* Toronto: University of Toronto Press.

———. 1995a. *Global information infrastructure: Agenda for action.* Washington, DC: Government Printing Office.

———. 1995b. *Staples, markets, and cultural change*, ed. D. Drache. Montreal and Kingston: McGill-Queen's University Press.

Intel Corporation. 2007. *Digital community deployments.* http://download.intel.com/business/bss/industry/government/digital-community-deployments.pdf (accessed February 10, 2007).

International Standards Organization. 2004. *ISO 3166-1: English country names and code elements.* Geneva: International Standards Organization. http://www.iso.org/iso/en/prods-services/iso3166ma/02iso-3166-code-lists/list-en1.html (accessed April 2004).

International Telecommunication Union. 2003. *Declaration of principles. Building the information society: A global challenge in the new millennium.* World Summit on the Information Society. Document WSIS-03/GENEVA/DOC/4-E. December 12, 2003. http://www.itu.int/wsis/docs/geneva/official/dop.html (accessed September 2, 2006).

———. 2005. *Tunis agenda for the information society.* WSIS-05/TUNIS/DOC/6 (rev. 1). http://www.itu.int/wsis/docs2/tunis/off/6rev1.html (accessed September 2, 2006).

———. 2006a. *Internet indicators 2004: Hosts, users and number of PCs.* http://www.itu.int/ITU-D/ict/statistics/at_glance/Internet04.pdf (accessed September 2, 2006).

———. 2006b. *Research on legislation in data privacy, security, and the prevention of cybercrime.* Geneva: ITU. http://www.itu.int/ITU-D/e-strategy/publications-articles/pdf/ Guide_cybercrime_fin.pdf (accessed September 2, 2006).

Internet Assigned Numbers Authority. 2000a. *IANA report on request for redelegation of the .pn top-level domain.* Marina del Rey, CA: IANA, February 11. http://www.iana.org/reports/pn-report-11feb00.htm (accessed April 2004).

———. 2000b. *IANA report on request for delegation of the .ps top-level domain*. Marina del Rey, CA: IANA, March 22. http://www.iana.org/reports/ps-report-22mar00.htm (accessed April 2004).

———. 2003. *Procedures for establishing ccTLDs*. Marina del Rey, CA: IANA, March 19. http://www.iana.org/cctld/cctld-establishment-procedures-19mar03.htm (accessed April 2004).

Internet Corporation for Assigned Names and Numbers. 1998. *Bylaws for Internet Corporation for Assigned Names and Numbers, a California nonprofit public benefit corporation*. http://www.ntia.doc.gov/ntiahome/domainname/proposals.icann/bylaws.htm

———. 2000. *Principles for delegation and administration of ccTLDs presented by governmental advisory committee*. Marina del Rey, CA: ICANN, February 23. http://www.icann.org/committees/gac/gac-cctldprinciples-23feb00.htm (accessed April 2004).

———. 2001. *Uniform Domain-Name Dispute-Resolution Policy*. http://www.icann.org/udrp/udrp.htm

———. 2002. *Model ccTLD sponsorship agreement—Triangular situation, third version*. Marina del Rey, CA: ICANN, January 31. http://www.icann.org/cctlds/model-tscsa-31jan02.htm (accessed February 2002).

———. 2003a. *Administering the root: Delegations and redelegations – Every country is unique* (ccTLD Doc 26 Rev. 1, March 3–4, 2003). Geneva: ITU. http://www.icann.org/cctlds/administering-the-root-25feb03.pdf (accessed May 2006).

———. 2003b. *Bylaws for Internet Corporation for Assigned Names and Numbers, a California Nonprofit Public-Benefit Corporation, as amended effective 26 June 2003*. http://www.icann.org/general/archive-bylaws/bylaws-26jun03.htm

———. 2004. *Frequently asked questions (FAQs)*. Marina Del Rey, CA: ICANN, January 16. http://www.icann.org/faq (accessed April 2004).

Internet Corporation for Assigned Names and Numbers / Internet Assigned Numbers Authority. 1999. *ICP-1: Internet domain name system structure and delegation (ccTLD administration and delegation)*. Marina del Rey, CA: ICANN/IANA, August 16 update. http://www.icann.org/icp/icp-1.htm (accessed April 2004).

Internet oversight board's leader proposes larger government role. 2002. *Wall Street Journal, Online Edition*. February 24. http://online.wsj.com/article_email/0,,SB1014605787304403400,00.html (accessed March 2002).

Internet Systems Consortium (ISC). 2006. *Distribution of top-level domain names by host count: July 2006*, Redwood City, CA: ISC. http://www.isc.org/ops/ds/reports/2006-07/dist-bynum.php (accessed October 2006).

Internet Users Society-Niue (IUS-N). 1997. *New Internet domain name, ".NU," now available for everyone worldwide*. Alofi, Niue: IUS-N. News release, November 10. http://www.whats.nu/Press/NUAnncfinal.cfm (accessed April 2004).

————. 2003. *.NU domain customer newsletter*. Alofi, Niue: IUS-N, April. http://www.whats.nu/about/about1.pdf (accessed April 2004).

————. 2004. *First hand report: Niue's .NU rebuilds after a super cyclone destroys the WiFi nation*. Alofi, Niue: IUS-N. http://www.whats.nu/about/cyclone_US.PDF (accessed April 2004).

Jacobson, Harold K. 1984. *Networks of interdependence*. 2nd ed. New York: Knopf.

James, Beverly. 1995. Learning to consume: An ethnographic study of cultural change in Hungary. *Critical Studies in Mass Communication* 12:287–305.

Jameson, Justin. 1996. New media: The likely development path and future regulatory requirements. *Telecommunications Policy* 20:399–413.

Janoski, Thomas. 1998. *Citizenship and civil society: A framework of rights and obligations in liberal, traditional, and social democratic regimes*. Cambridge: Cambridge University Press.

Jansson, Andre. 2002. Spatial phantasmagoria: The mediatization of tourism experience. *European Journal of Communication* 17:429–43.

————. 2005. *Specialized spaces. Touristic communication in the age of hyperspace-biased media*. Working Paper 137-06, Centre for Cultural Research, University of Aarhus. http://www.hum.au.dk/cfk/pages/publications/aj/specialized_spaces.pdf (accessed February 10, 2007).

Johnson, J. David, Omar S. Oliveira, and George A. Barnett. 1989. Communication factors related to closer international ties: An extension of a model in Belize. *International Journal of Intercultural Relations* 13:1–18.

Johnson, Kirk. 2000. *Television and social change in rural India*. London: Sage Publications.

Jones, Martin. 1997. Spatial selectivity of the state? The regulationist enigma and local struggles over economic governance. *Environment and Planning* 29:831–64.

Jones, Stephen G., ed. 1995. *CyberSociety: Computer-mediated communication and community*. Thousand Oaks, CA: Sage Publications.

————. 1998. *CyberSociety 2.0: Revisiting computer-mediated communication and community*. Thousand Oaks, CA: Sage Publications.

Judis, John B. 1998. Online Magaziner. *New Republic* 219(26):22.

Kahin, Brian, and Janet Abbate, eds. 1995. *Standards for information infrastructure*. Cambridge, MA: MIT Press.

Kahin, Brian, and Charles Nesson. 1997. *Borders in cyberspace: Information policy and the global information infrastructure*. Cambridge, MA: MIT Press.

Kahin, Brian, and Ernest J. Wilson, III., eds. 1996. *National Information Infrastructure initiatives: Vision and policy design*. Cambridge, MA: MIT Press.

Kakabadsiie, Mario A. 1995. The World Trade Organization and the commodification of cultural products. *Media Asia* 22:71–7.

Kalathil, Shanthi, and Taylor C. Boas. 2003. *Open networks, closed regimes: The impact of the Internet on authoritarian rule*. Washington DC: Carnegie Endowment for International Peace.

Kasarda, John D., and Dennis A. Rondinelli. 1998. Innovative infrastructure for agile manufacturers. *Sloan Management Review* 39:73–83.

Kassinger, Theodore W. 2003. Statement of Theodore W. Kassinger, General Counsel, U.S. Department of Commerce, Subcommittee on Courts, the Internet and Intellectual Property, House Judiciary Committee. September 4.

Kellerman, Aharon. 1993. *Telecommunications and geography*. London: Belhaven.

Kennard, William. 1997. Speech of FCC Chairman William E. Kennard to the Annual Convention of the National Association of Regulatory Utility Commissioners. November 10.

Keohane, Robert O., and Joseph S. Nye. 1998. *Power and interdependence*. 2nd ed. Glenview, IL: Scott Foresman.

Kern, Stephen. 1983. *The culture of time and space 1880–1918*. Cambridge, MA: Harvard University Press.

King, Ian. 2004. Internationalizing internet governance: Does ICANN have a role to play? *Information and Communications Technology Law* 13:243–58.

Kirby, Jack T. 1986. *Media-made Dixie: The South in the American imagination*. Athens: University of Georgia Press.

Kleiman, Kathryn. *Internet governance: A view from the trenches. Participation needed for successful advocacy in the ICANN arena*. Report for the Association for Computing Machinery's Internet Governance Project. Washington DC.

Klein, Hans. 2005. Understanding WSIS: An institutional analysis of the UN World Summit on the Information Society. *Information Technology and International Development, [Special Issue on WSIS]* 1(3–4):3–13.

Kling, Rob., ed. 1996. *Computerization and controversy: Value conflicts and social choices*, 2nd ed. San Diego: Academic Press.

Kotval, Zenia. 1999. Telecommunications: A realistic strategy for the revitalization of American cities. *Cities* 16:33–41.

Kowalski, Robert. 1998. "Railroad deal questioned: Lawmakers quiz Sheffield on fiber-optic cable easement." *Anchorage Daily News*, February 7,1C.

Kratochwil, Friedrich. 1986. Of systems, boundaries and territoriality: An inquiry into the formation of the state system. *World Politics* 39:27–52.

Kriz, Harry M. 2006. *About ILLiad: ILLiad development*. http://www.ill.vt.edu (accessed August 31, 2006).

Kriz, Harry M., M. Jason Glover, and Kevin C. Ford. 1998. ILLiad: Customer-focused interlibrary loan automation. *Journal of Interlibrary Loan, Document Delivery & Information Supply* 8(4):31–47.

Krugman, Paul. 1991a. *Geography and trade*. Cambridge, MA: MIT Press.

————. 1991b. Increasing returns and economic geography. *Journal of Political Economy* 99:483–99.

————. 1998. What's new about the new economic geography? *Oxford Review of Economic Policy* 14:7–17.

Kunstler, James H. 1993. *The geography of nowhere: The rise and decline of America's man-made landscape.* New York: Simon & Schuster.

Lai, Bruce, and Gale A. Brewer. 2006. New York City's broadband problem and the role of municipal government in promoting a private-sector solution. *Technology in Society* 28:245–59.

Lakamp, Patrick. 1998. Town board rejects increase in cable TV franchise fee. *Buffalo News,* February 24, 4B.

Lassman, Kent, and Randolph J. May. 2003. A survey of government-provided telecommunications: Disturbing growth trend continues. *Progress on Point, October. Progress and Freedom Foundation Report.* Washington DC. http://www.pff.org/issues-pubs/pops/pop10.17municipaltelecom.pdf (accessed June 13, 2007).

Leahy, Kimberly A. 2006. Circumscribing the public interest in the VoIP policy debate. Unpublished doctoral dissertation. Florida State University, Tallahassee.

Lefebvre, Henri. 1974/1991. *Production of space.* Oxford: Basil Blackwell.

Lehr, William, Marvin Sirbu, and Sharon Gillett. 2004. *Municipal wireless broadband: Policy and business implications of emerging access technologies.* Massachusetts Institute of Technology, Program on Internet and Telecoms Convergence, May 7. http://itc.mit.edu/itel/docs/2004/wlehr_munibb_doc.pdf (accessed June 13, 2007).

————. 2006. Wireless is changing the policy calculus for municipal broadband. *Government Information Quarterly* 23:435–53.

Leibowitz & Associates. 1998. Background documents for Sixth Annual Telecommunications Seminar, Orlando, Florida.

Lenard, Thomas M. 2004. Government entry into the telecom business: Are the benefits commensurate with the costs? *Progress on Point, February.* Progress and Freedom Foundation Report. Washington DC. http://www.pff.org/issues-pubs/pops/pop11.3govtownership.pdf (accessed June 13, 2007).

Lessig, Lawrence. 1999. *Code and other laws of cyberspace.* New York: Basic-Books.

Levine, Peter. 2000. The Internet and civil society. *Report from the Institute for Philosophy and Public Policy* 20(4):108. School of Public Affairs, University of Maryland.

————. 2001. Civic renewal and the commons of cyberspace. *National Civic Review* 90:205–12.

Levinson, Paul. 2003. *Realspace: The fate of physical presence in the digital age, on and off planet.* New York: Routledge.

Leyshon, Andrew, and Nigel Thrift. 1997. *Money/space: Geographies of monetary transformation*. London: Routledge.

Libicki, Martin. 1996. The emerging primacy of information. *Orbis* 40:261–74.

Licklider, Joseph C. R. 1960. Man-computer symbiosis. *IRE Transactions on Human Factors in Electronics, HFE-1*, 4–11.

Lievrouw, Leah, and Sonia Livingstone, eds. 2002. *The handbook of new media: Social shaping and consequences of ICTs*. Thousand Oaks, CA: Sage.

Lipshutz, Ronnie D., and Judith Mayer. 1996. *Global civil society and global environmental governance: The politics of nature from place to planet*. Albany: State University of New York Press.

Lloyd, Robin. 1999. Country domain names not yet downtown. *CNN.com*, October 13. http://www.cnn.com/TECH/computing/9910/13/domain.names (accessed July 21).

Macdonald, Laura. 1997. *Supporting civil society: The political role of nongovernmental organizations in Central America*. London and New York: Macmillan and St. Martin's Press.

Mackenzie, Adrian. 2005. Untangling the unwired: Wi-fi and the cultural inversion of infrastructure. *Space and Culture* 8:269–85.

Maerowitz, Marlene P. 1997. Hello Gilbert! Pass proposed telecom rules. *Arizona Republic*, December 13, EV10.

Malecki, Edward J. 2004. Fibre tracks: Explaining investment in fibre optic backbones. *Entrepreneurship & Regional Development* 16:21–39.

Mandaville, Peter G. 1999. Territory and translocality: Discrepant idioms of political identity. *Millennium: Journal of International Studies* 28: 653–73.

Mann, Michael. 1984. The autonomous powers of the state: Its origins, mechanisms and results. *Archives Européenes de Sociologie* 25:185–213.

Mansell, Robin. 1993. *The new telecommunications: A political economy of network evolution*. London: Sage Publications.

Mansell, Robin, and W. Edward Steinmueller. 2000. *Mobilizing the information society: Strategies for growth and opportunity*. New York: Oxford University Press.

Mansell, Robin, and Uta Wehn, eds. 1998. *Knowledge societies: Information technology for sustainable development* (published for the United Nations Commission on Science and Technology for Development). Oxford: Oxford University Press.

Mapel, David R., and Terry Nardin, eds. 1998. *International society: Diverse ethical perspectives*. Princeton, NJ: Princeton University Press.

Martin, Ron. 1999a. The new "geographical turn" in economics: Some critical reflections. *Cambridge Journal of Economics* 23:65–91.

———. 1999b. Editorial: The 'new economic geography': Challenge or irrelevance? *Transactions of the Institute of British Geographers* 24:387–91.

Marvin, Carolyn. 1988. *When old technologies were new: Thinking about electric communication in the late nineteenth century.* New York: Oxford University Press.

Massey, Doreen. 2005. *For space.* London: Sage.

Matsumoto, Hidenobu. 2007. International air network structures and air traffic density of world cities. *Transportation Research Part E: Logistics and Transportation Review* 43:269–88.

Mazierska, Ewa, and John K. Walton. 2006. Tourism and the moving image. *Tourist Studies* 6:5–11.

McCann, Philip. 2005. Transport costs and new economic geography. *Journal of Economic Geography* 5:305–18.

McCaughey, Marthe, and Michael D. Ayers, eds. 2003. *Cyberactivism: Online activism in theory and practice.* London: Routledge.

McChesney, Robert W. 1993. *Telecommunications, mass media, and democracy: The battle for the control of U. S. broadcasting, 1928–1935.* New York: Oxford University Press.

McChesney, Robert, and J. Podesta. 2006. Let there be wi-fi. *Washington Monthly,* January-February. http://washingtonmonthly.com/features/2006/0601.podesta.html (accessed February 10, 2007).

McClelland, Stephen. 1998. California dreaming? The crowds are gathering in gigabit valley, the new label for the Californian hive of thousands of high-tech companies. *Telecommunications* 32:94–96.

McDowell, Stephen D. 1994. Policy research institutes and liberalized international services exchange. In *The political influence of ideas: Policy communities and the social sciences,* eds. S. Brooks and A. G. Gagnon, 107–133. Westport, CT: Praeger Publishers.

McDowell, Stephen D., and Carleen Maitland. 1998. Developing television ratings in Canada and the United States: The perils and promises of self-regulation. In *The V-chip debate: Content filtering from television to the internet,* ed. M. E. Price, 23–46. Mahwah, NJ: Lawrence Erlbaum.

McDowell, Stephen D., and Philip Steinberg. 2001. Non-state governance and the Internet: Civil society and the ICANN. *Info: The Journal of Policy, Regulation and Strategy for Telecommunications Information and Media* 3:279–98.

McElroy, Chris. 2006. *Comments on the Continued Transition of the Technical Coordination and Management of the Internet Domain Name and Addressing System by ICANN.* Department of Commerce, National Telecommunications and Information Administration, Docket No. 060519136-6136-01. http://www.ntia.doc.gov/ntiahome/domainname/dnstransition/comments/dnstrans_comment0001.htm (accessed February 10, 2007).

McGuire, David. 2003. VeriSign freezes search service. *WashingtonPost.com,* October 3.

McLaughlin, Lisa, and Victor Pickards. 2005. What is bottom-up about global internet governance? *Global Media and Communication* 1:357–73.

Mercille, Julien. 2005. Media effects on image: The case of Tibet. *Annals of Tourism Research* 32:1039–55.

Metalitz, Steven J. 2003. Statement of Steven J. Metalitz, Counsel, Copyright Coalition on Domain Names, before the Subcommittee on Courts, the Internet, and Intellectual Property, House Judiciary Committee. September 4.

Meyrowitz, Joshua. 1985. *No sense of place: The impact of electronic media on social behavior.* New York: Oxford University Press.

Mitchell, Don, Scott Bradner, and K. C. Claffy. 1997. In whose domain? Name service in adolescence. In *Coordinating the Internet*, eds. B. Kahin and J. H. Keller, 258–70. Cambridge, MA: MIT Press.

Mitchell, Timothy. 1991. The limits of the state: Beyond statist approaches and their critics. *American Political Science Review* 85:77–94.

Mitchell, William J. 1996. *City of bits: Space, place, and the Infobahn.* Cambridge, MA: MIT Press.

Mittelman, James. 2000. *The globalization syndrome: Transformation and resistance.* Princeton, NJ: Princeton University Press.

Monash Tourism Research Unit. 2007. *Conferences and seminars.* http://www. buseco.monash.edu.au/units/tru/conferences.php (accessed February 10, 2007).

Morfin, Jefsey F. C. 2006. *Comments on the Continued Transition of the Technical Coordination and Management of the Internet Domain Name and Addressing System by ICANN.* Department of Commerce, National Telecommunications and Information Administration, Docket No. 060519136-6136-01. http://www.ntia.doc.gov/ntiahome/domainname/ dnstransition/comments/ dnstrans_comment0574.htm (accessed February 10, 2007).

Morley, David, and Kevin Robins. 1995. *Spaces of identity: Global media, electronic landscapes and cultural boundaries.* London: Routledge.

Mosco, Vincent. 1996. *The political economy of communication.* London: Sage Publications.

Moss, Mitchell L., and Anthony M. Townsend. 2000. The internet backbone and the American metropolis. *Information Society* 16:35–47.

MoveOn.org. 2006. *What is MoveOn?* http://www.moveon.org/about.html (accessed August 31, 2006).

Mueller, Milton. 1998. The battle over Internet domain names: Global or national TLDs? *Telecommunication Policy* 22:89–107.

———. 2002. *Ruling the root: Internet governance and the taming of cyberspace.* Cambridge, MA: MIT Press.

———. 2006. *The continued transition of the technical coordination and management of the internet domain name and addressing system.* Department of Commerce, National Telecommunications and Information Administration, Internet Governance Project, Docket No. 060519136-6136-01. http://www.ntia.doc.gov/ntiahome/domainname/

dnstransition/comments/dnstrans_comment0588.htm (accessed February 10, 2007).

Mulgan, Geoff. 1991. *Communication and control*. New York: Guilford Press.

MuniWireless. 2007. *MuniWireless: The voice of public broadband*. http://www.muniwireless.com/ (accessed February 10, 2007).

Murphy, Craig. 1994. *International organization and industrial change: Global governance since 1850*. New York: Oxford University Press.

Murphy, Jamie, and Nicole Smith. 1998. Out-of-the-way nations capitalize on catchy domain names. *CyberTimes: New York Times on the Web*, February 1. http://www.nunames.nu/cybertimes/020198domain.html (accessed July 2001).

Murtha, Thomas P., Stefanie A. Lenway, and Jeffrey A. Hart. 2001. *Managing new industry creation: Global knowledge formation and entrepreneurship in high technology*. Stanford: Stanford University Press.

Nash, Dennison. 1995. An exploration of tourism as superstructure. In *Change in tourism: People, places, process*, eds. R. Butler and D. Pearce, 30–46. London: Routledge.

National Lawyers Guild Committee on Democratic Communications. 1997. *"Court rejects FCC's constitutional catch 22."* Press release, December 25.

National League of Cities. 1997. *Issues background*. Mimeograph.

National Telecommunications and Information Administration. 2004. *A nation online: Entering the broadband age*. Department of Commerce. http://www.ntia.doc.gov/reports/anol/NationOnlineBroadband04.pdf (accessed February 10, 2007).

———. 2005. *Domain names: U.S. principles on the internet's domain name and addressing system*. http://www.ntia.doc.gov/ntiahome/domainname/USDNSprinciples_06302005.htm (accessed September 2, 2006).

———. 2006a. *The Continued Transition of the Technical Coordination and Management of the Internet Domain Name and Addressing System*. Department of Commerce. Notice of Inquiry, Notice of Public Meeting, May 23. Docket No. 060519136-6136-01. http://www.ntia.doc.gov/ntiahome/frnotices/2006/NOI_DNS_Transition_0506.htm (accessed February 10, 2007).

———. 2006b. *DNS transition, comments received*. Department of Commerce. http://www.ntia.doc.gov/ntiahome/domainname/dnstransition.html (accessed February 10, 2007).

Neilson, Christian. 2001. *Tourism and the media*. Melbourne: Hospitality Press.

Nelson, Jeffrey. 1997. Fees OK'd for rights of way; cable, phone firms to pay rent in Peoria. *Arizona Republic*, (December 19):1.

NeuStar, Inc. 2002. *The usTLD nexus requirements*. Sterling, VA: NeuStar. http://www.nic.us/policies/docs/ustld_nexus_requirements.pdf (accessed April 2004).

———. 2004. U. S. online advertisement. Sterling, VA: NeuStar. Pop-up window accessible via NeuStar Press Room. http://www.nic.us/press/index. html (accessed April 2004).

Newman, David, ed. 1999. *Boundaries, territory and postmodernity*. London: Frank Cass.

ÓTuathail, Gearoid. 1996. *Critical geopolitics: The politics of writing global space*. Minneapolis: University of Minnesota Press.

Oberbeck, Steven. 2003a. Tech agency asks Salt Lake city to help with high-speed Nirvana. *Knight Ridder Tribune Business News*, November 18, 1.

———. 2003b. 18 Utah cities pursue dream of "Utopia," a high-speed broadband network. *Knight Ridder Tribune Business News*, December 14, 1.

———. 2003c. Utah fiber-to-home network consortium "Utopia" signs up AT&T services. *Knight Ridder Tribune Business News*, December 24, 1.

———. 2004. Mayors, others lobby Utah governor to support telecommunications agency. *Knight Ridder Tribune Business News*, February 27, 1.

———. 2006. Fed loan expedites building UTOPIA. *Salt Lake Tribune* (Utah), August 15.

Ong, Aihwa. 1999. *Flexible citizenship: The cultural logics of transnationality*. Durham: Duke University Press.

Organization for Economic Cooperation and Development (OECD). 1996. *Tourism policy and international tourism in OECD countries 1993–1994*. Paris: OECD.

———. 1997. *Global information infrastructure—Global information society (GII-GIS) policy requirements*. Paris: OECD. Committee for Information, Computers, and Communications Policy.

———. 2006. *OECD Broadband Statistics, December 2006*. http://www.oecd.org/sti/ict/broadband (accessed September 2, 2006).

Paasi, Anssi. 1996. *Territories, boundaries, and consciousness: The changing geographies of the Finnish-Russian border*. New York: Wiley.

Palan, Ronen. 2003. *The offshore world: Sovereign markets, virtual places, and nomad millionaires*. Ithaca, NY: Cornell University Press.

Palfrey, John G., Jr. 2004a. The end of the experiment: How ICANN's foray into global Internet democracy failed. *Harvard Journal of Law and Technology*, 17:409–474.

———. 2004b. *Submission to the workshop on Internet governance*. Geneva, International Telecommunications Union. February 26–27.

Paré, Daniel J. 2003. *Internet governance in transition: Who is the master of this domain*. Lanham, MD: Rowman & Littlefield.

Park, Chunil, and Stephen D. McDowell. 2005. Direct broadcast satellites and the social shaping of technology: Comparing South Korea and Canada. *Canadian Journal of Communication* 30:111–38.

Parsons, Patrick R. 2003. The evolution of the cable-satellite distribution system. *Journal of Broadcasting and Electronic Media* 47:1–17.

Pavlik, John V. 1998. *New media technology: Cultural and commercial perspectives*. 2nd ed. Boston: Allyn and Bacon.

Peck, Francis W. 1996. Regional development and the production of space: The role of infrastructure in the attraction of new inward investment. *Environment and Planning* 28:327–39.

Peel, Victoria, and Adam Steen. 2006. Victims, hooligans and cash-cows: Media representations of the international backpacker in Australia. *Tourism Management* 28:1057–1067.

Pennings, Guido. 2002. Reproductive tourism as moral pluralism in motion. *Journal of Medical Ethics* 28:337–41.

Perotin, Maria M. 1998. Laying cable may cost companies: Deltona leaders are reviewing an ordinance that would require paying up before digging. *Orlando Sentinel* January 11, K2.

Polanyi, Karl. 1944. *The great transformation: The political and economic origins of our time*. Boston: Beacon Press.

Pons-Novell, Jordi, and Elisabet Viladecans-Marsal. 2006. Cities and the internet: The end of distance? *Journal of Urban Technology* 13:109–32.

Postel, Jon. 1994. *RFC 1591: Domain name system structure and administration*. Marina Del Rey, CA: Network Working Group, Internet Assigned Numbers Authority (IANA), March. http://www.ietf.org/rfc/rfc1591.txt (accessed April 2004).

———. 1998. *Re: Management of internet names and addresses*. Letter to William M. Daley, Secretary of Commerce. http://www.ntia.doc.gov/ntiahome/domainname/proposals/icann/letter.htm

Powell, Alison, and Leslie R. Shade. 2006. Going Wi-Fi in Canada: Municipal and community initiatives. *Government Information Quarterly* 23:381–403.

Pred, Allan R. 1973. *Urban growth and the circulation of information: The United States system of cities, 1790–1840*. Cambridge, MA: Harvard University Press.

———. 1980. *Urban growth and city systems in the United States, 1840–1860*. Cambridge, MA: Harvard University Press.

Pestle, John W., and Patrick Miles. 1997. Memorandum regarding further FCC preemption of local zoning – Cellular and broadcast towers. September 12. Grand Rapids, MI: Varnum, Riddering, Schmidt & Howlett.

Price, Patricia L. 2004. *Dry place: Landscapes of belonging and exclusion*. Minneapolis: University of Minnesota Press.

Quick, Bob. 2004. Ticket to oblivion. *Santa Fe New Mexican (New Mexico)*, February 8, D-1.

Raboy, Marc. 2004. The World Summit on the Information Society and its legacy for global governance. *International Communication Gazette* 66:225–32.

Raboy, Marc, and Normand Landry. 2005. *Civil society, communication, and global governance: Issues from the World Summit on the Information Society*. New York: Peter Lang.

Reich, Robert B. 1991. *The work of nations: Preparing ourselves for 21st century capitalism*. Boston, MA: Addison-Wesley.

Richards, Thomas. 1993. *The imperial archive: Knowledge and the fantasy of empire*. London: Verso.

Richter, Linda K. 1995. Gender and race: neglected variables in tourism research. In *Change in tourism: People, places, process*, eds. R. Butler and D. Pearce, 71–91. London: Routledge.

———. 2003. International tourism and its global public health consequences. *Journal of Travel Research* 41:340–7.

Rodino-Colocino, Michelle. 2006. Laboring under the digital divide. *New Media & Society* 8:487–511.

Rogers, Everett M. 2003. *Diffusion of innovations*. 5th ed. New York: The Free Press.

Rosenau, James N. 1990. *Turbulence in world politics: A theory of change and continuity*. Princeton, NJ: Princeton University Press.

———. 1992. Governance, order, and change in world politics. In *Governance without government: Order and change in world politics*, eds. J. N. Rosenau and E-O Czempiel, 1–29. Cambridge: Cambridge University Press.

Rosenau, James N., and Ernst-Otto Czempiel, eds. 1992. *Governance without government: Order and change in world politics*. Cambridge: Cambridge University Press.

Rosenau, James N., and J. P. Singh, eds. 2002. *Information technologies and global politics: The changing scope of power and governance*. Albany: State University of New York Press.

Rubenstein, Steven. 2001. Colonialism, the Shuar Federation, and the Ecuadorian state. *Environment and Planning D: Society & Space* 19:263–93.

Ruggie, John G. 1993. Territoriality and beyond: Problematizing modernity in international relations. *International Organization* 47:139–74.

Sakamoto, Yoshikazu. 1991. *The global context of democratization*. New York: World Policy Institute.

Salkever, Alex. 2003. "Beyond the VeriSign vs. ICANN battle." *Business Week Online*, October 20.

Salwen, Michael B. 1991. Cultural imperialism: A media effects approach. *Critical Studies in Mass Communication* 8:29–38.

Samuelson, Paul. 1952. The transfer problem and transport costs: The terms of trade when impediments are absent. *Economic Journal* 62:278–304.

Sassen, Saskia. 1991. *The global city: New York, London, Tokyo*. Princeton, NJ: Princeton University Press.

Saxenian, Anna L. 1994. *Regional advantage: Culture and competition in Silicon Valley and Route 128*. Cambridge, MA: Harvard University Press.

———. 2006. *The new argonauts: Regional advantage in a global economy*. Cambridge, MA: Harvard University Press.

Schiller, Dan. 1999. *Digital capitalism: Networking the global market system*. Cambridge, MA: MIT Press.

Schwartz, Shelly. 1998. Local telecom taxes cause uproar in Maryland. *Daily Record* (Baltimore, MD), February 18, 1.

Scott, Ben, and Frannie Wellings. 2005. *Telco lies and the truth about municipal broadband networks*. Free Press. http://freepress.net/docs/mb_telco_lies.pdf (accessed February 10, 2007).

Selian, Audrey. 2004. The World Summit on the Information Society and Civil Society Participation. *Information Society* 20:201–15.

Seligman, Adam B. 1992. *The idea of civil society*. New York: The Free Press.

Selwyn, Neil. 2004. Reconsidering political and popular understandings of the digital divide. *New Media & Society* 6:341–62.

Servaes, Jan and Nico Carpentier, eds. 2006. *Towards a sustainable information society: Deconstructing WSIS*. Bristol, U.K.: Intellect Books.

Shannon, Claude E., and Warren Weaver. 1949. *The mathematical theory of communication*. Urbana: University of Illinois Press.

Shaw, Gwyneth K. 1997a. Deltona clears up cable fees spat. *Orlando Sentinel*, December 17, D3.

Shaw, Robert. 1997b. Internet domain names: Whose domain is this? In *Coordinating the Internet*, eds. B. Kahin and J. H. Keller. 107–34. Cambridge, MA: MIT Press.

Sheller, Mimi S., and John Urry, eds. 2006a. *Mobile technologies of the city*. New York: Routledge.

———. 2006b. The new mobilities paradigm. *Environment and Planning A* 38:207–26.

Sheppard, Eric. 2000. Geography or economics? Conceptions of space, time, interdependence, and agency. In *The Oxford handbook of economic geography*, eds. G. L. Clark, M. P. Feldman, and M. S. Gertler, 99–119. Oxford: Oxford University Press.

Shields, Robert M., ed. 1996. *Cultures of internet: Virtual spaces, real histories, living bodies*. London: Sage Publications.

———. 2000. Cyberspace. In *Unspun: Key concepts for understanding the World Wide Web*, ed. T. Swiss 66–72. New York: New York University Press.

Shiver, Jube. 2004. Tired of slow speeds, some cities build their own net, study finds. *Los Angeles Times*, January 11, C1.

Singhal, Arvind, and Everett M. Rogers. 2001. *India's communication revolution: From bullock carts to cyber marts*. London: Sage Publications.

Smith, Gordon S. 1997. Cyberspace frontier. *Vital speeches of the day* 63:591–595.

Smith, Neil. 1990. *Uneven development: Nature, capital and the production of space*. 2nd ed. Oxford, U.K.: Basil Blackwell.

Snyder, Brady, and Geoffrey Fattah. 2004. S. L. given low-risk option on UTOPIA. *Deseret Morning News (Salt Lake City)*, April 9.

Soja, Edward W. 1980. The socio-spatial dialectic. *Annals of the Association of American Geographers* 70:207–25.

————. 1989. *Postmodern geographies: The reassertion of space in critical social theory*. London: Verso.

————. 1996. *Thirdspace: Journeys to Los Angeles and other real-and-imagined places*. London: Blackwell.

Sparke, Matthew. 2005. *In the space of theory: Postfoundational geographies of the nation-state*. Minneapolis: University of Minnesota Press.

Sreberny-Mohammadi, Annabelle. 1996. Globalization, communication and transnational civil society. In *Globalization, communication and transnational civil society*, eds. S. Braman and A. Sreberny-Mohammadi, 11, 122. Cresskill, NJ: Hampton Press.

Standeford, Dugie. 2003a. Commerce will extend ICANN MOU despite WHOIS-related criticism. *Washington Internet Daily*, September 5.

————. 2003b. VeriSign halts site finder ahead of ICANN panel meeting. *Washington Internet Daily*, October 6.

Steinberg, Philip. 1998. Transportation space: A fourth spatial category for the world-systems perspective? In *Space and transport in the world-system*, eds. P. Ciccantell and S. Bunker, 19–35, Westport, CT: Greenwood Press.

————. 1999. The maritime mystique: Sustainable development, capital mobility, and nostalgia in the world ocean. *Environment and Planning D: Society & Space* 17:403–26.

————. 2001. *The social construction of the ocean*. Cambridge: Cambridge University Press.

Stewart, Concetta M., Gisela Gil-Egui, Yan Tian, and Mairi I. Pileggi. 2006. Framing the digital divide: A comparison of US and EU policy approaches. *New Media & Society* 8:731–51.

Storper, Michael. 1994. The transition to flexible specialization in the U. S. film industry: External economies, the division of labour and the crossing of industrial divides. In *Post-Fordism: A reader*, ed. A. Amin, 195–296. Oxford: Basil Blackwell.

Storper, Michael, and Susan Christopherson. 1987. Flexible specialization and regional industrial agglomerations: The case of the U. S. motion picture industry. *Annals of the American Geographers* 77:104–17.

Strange, Susan. 1988. *States and markets*. London: Blackwell Publishers.

Straubhaar, Joseph. 1991. Beyond media imperialism: Assymetrical interdependence and cultural proximity. *Critical Studies in Mass Communication* 8:39–59.

————. 2006. (Re)asserting national television and national identity against global, regional, and local levels of world television. In *Media and cultural studies: Key works*, Rev. ed., eds. M. G. Durham and D. M. Kellner, 681–702. Malden, MA: Blackwell.

Stross, Randall. 2007. "Digital domain: Wireless internet for all, without the towers." *New York Times*, February 4.

Strover, Sharon. 1995. Recent trends in coproductions: The demise of the national. In *Democracy and communication in the new Europe*, eds. F. Corcoran and P. Preston, 97–123. Creskill, NJ: Hampton Press.

Strover, Sharon, Gary Chapman, and Jody Waters. 2004. Beyond community networking and CTCs: Access, development, and public policy. *Telecommunications Policy* 28:465–85.

Strover, Sharon, and Seung-Hwan Mun. 2006. Wireless broadband, communities, and the shape of things to come. *Government Information Quarterly* 23:348–58.

Sullivan, Jennifer. 1998. The trouble with tiny domains. *Wired*, May 11. http://www.wired.com/news/business/0,1367,12226,00.html (accessed July 2001).

Suzukamo, Leslie B. 2004. Court ruling moot in Minnesota, where municipal phone firms aren't banned. *Knight Ridder Tribune Business News*, March 25, 1.

Swiss, Tom, ed. 2000. *Unspun: Key concepts for understanding the World Wide Web*. New York: New York University Press.

Tabin, Barrie. 1988. Court strikes down Chattanooga's telecom franchise fee. *Nation's Cities Weekly*, January 12, 7.

Tapia, Andrea, Carleen Maitland, and Matt Stone. 2006. Making IT work for municipalities: Building municipal wireless networks. *Government Information Quarterly* 23:359–80.

Taylor, Charles. 1989. *Sources of the self: The making of the modern identity*. Cambridge, MA: Harvard University Press.

Taylor, Peter J. 1994. The state as container. *Progress in Human Geography* 18:151–62.

———. 1995. Beyond containers: Internationality, interstateness, interterritoriality. *Progress in Human Geography* 19:1–15.

———. 1996. *The way the modern world works: World hegemony to world impasse*. Chichester, U.K.: John Wiley.

Teske, Paul, ed. 1995. *American regulatory federalism and telecommunications infrastructure*. Hillsdale, NJ: Lawrence Erlbaum.

Thierer, Adam, and C. Wayne Crews, Jr., eds. 2003. *Who rules the net? Internet governance and jurisdiction*. Washington, DC: Cato Institute.

Thompson, Clive. 2006. Google's China problem (and China's Google problem). *New York Times Magazine*, April 23, National Newspapers (27):64.

Thomson, Janice. 1994. *Mercenaries, pirates and sovereigns: State-building and extraterritorial violence in early modern Europe*. Princeton, NJ: Princeton University Press.

Thrift, Nigel. 2000. Pandora's box? Cultural geographies of economies. In *The Oxford handbook of economic geography*, eds. G. L. Clark, M. P. Feldman, and M. S. Gertler, 689–704. Oxford: Oxford University Press.

To the Point. 2005. *EU domain name registration*. http://www.eu-domain.bz (accessed May 2006).

Tonkiss, Fran. 2006. *Contemporary economic sociology: Globalisation, production, inequality*. New York: Routledge.

Trainor, Brenda J. 1995. The local government perspective: Can the harmonica play in the symphony? Paper presented at the New York Law School Conference "Universal Service in Context: A Multidisciplinary Perspective." http://www.benton.org/publibrary/policy/uniserv/Conference/trainor.html

Trauer, Birgit. 2006. Conceptualizing special interest tourism—Frameworks for analysis. *Tourism Management* 27:183–200.

Tropos Networks. 2007. *Chaska.net and Tropos unwire Chaska, Minnesota, a Tropos Networks case study, January 2007*. http://www.tropos.com/pdf/chaska_casestudy.pdf (accessed February 10, 2007).

Turkle, Sherry. 1995. *Life on the screen: Identity in the age of the Internet*. New York: Simon & Schuster.

Twomey, Paul. 2003. Testimony by Mr. Paul Twomey, President and Chief Executive Officer, Internet Corporation for Assigned Names and Numbers, before the Senate Commerce, Science and Transportation Committee, Communications Subcommittee, Federal Document Clearing House. July 31.

United Nations, Economic and Social Council. 2000. *Development and international cooperation in the twenty-first century: The role of information technology in the context of a knowledge-based global economy*. Report of the Secretary-General, New York, May 18. http://www.un.org/documents/ecosoc/docs/2000/e2000-52.pdf (accessed September 2, 2006).

United Nations World Tourism Organization (UNWTO). 1995a. *Yearbook of tourism statistics*. Madrid: WTO.

———. 1995b. *Compendium of tourism statistics*. Madrid: WTO.

———. 2003. *Tourism highlights*. http://www.world-tourism.org

———. 2004a. *WTO global campaign stresses the importance of tourism*. News release. February 16. Madrid, Spain.

———. 2004b. *Tourism enriches*. http://www.world-tourism.org

United States. 1996a. *Telecommunication Act of 1996* (Public Law 104-104). February 8.

———. 1996b. *A framework for global electronic commerce*. Draft 9. December 11.

United States Department of Commerce. 1997. *Request for comments on the registration and administration of internet domain names* (Docket No. 970613137-7137-01). Washington, DC: Department of Commerce. July 1. http://www.ntia.doc.gov/ntiahome/domainname/dn5notic.htm

———. 1998a. *A proposal to improve technical management of internet names and addresses: Discussion draft*. Washington, DC: Department of Commerce. January 30. http://www.ntia.doc.gov/ntiahome/domainname/dnsdrft.htm

————. 1998b. *Management of internet names and addresses*. Washington, DC: Department of Commerce. June 5. http://www.ntia.doc.gov/ntiahome/domainname/6_5_98dns.htm

————. 1998c. *Memorandum of understanding between the U.S. Department of Commerce and Internet Corporation for Assigned Names and Numbers*. Washington, DC: Department of Commerce. November 25. http://www.ntia.doc.gov/ntiahome/domainname/icann-memorandum.htm

United States Department of State. 2006a. *Global Internet Freedom Task Force Presentation*. Paula Dobriansky, Under Secretary for Democracy and Global Affairs. December 21. http://www.state.gov/g/rls/rm/78142.htm (accessed February 10, 2007).

————. 2006b. *Secretary of State establishes new Global Internet Freedom Task Force* (February 14). http://www.state.gov/r/pa/prs/ps/2006/61156.htm (accessed February 10, 2007).

United States, President's Commission on Critical Infrastructure Protection. 1996. *Executive Order 13010* by President Bill Clinton. July 15.

Urry, John. 2002. *Consuming places*. New York: Routledge.

Van Bergh, Mark, and Barrie Tabin. 1997. "FCC issues ruling in City of Troy case, leaves local telecommunications ordinance in place." *Nation's Cities Weekly*, September 29, 6.

Van Tassel, Joan. 1996. Yakety-yak, do talk back! PEN, the nation's first publicly funded electronic network, makes a difference in Santa Monica. *Computerization and controversy: Value conflicts and social choices*. 2nd ed. Ed. R. Kling. 547–551. San Diego: Academic Press.

Van Winden, Willem, and Paulus Woets. 2004. Urban broadband internet policies in Europe: A critical review. *Urban Studies* 41:2043–59.

Venables, Anthony J., and Andrea Boltho, eds. 1998. Issue on trade and location. *Oxford Review of Economic Policy* 14(2):1–92.

"VeriSign files suit over ICANN authority; Internet form says regulator overstepped its power in blocking new web service." 2004. *Los Angeles Times*, February 29, C12.

Vernon, Raymond. 1972. *Sovereignty at bay: The multinational spread of U.S. enterprises*. New York: Basic Books.

Victory, Nancy J. 2003. Testimony by Nancy J. Victory, Assistant Secretary for Communications and Information, before the Senate Commerce, Science and Transportation Committee, Communications Subcommittee, Federal Document Clearing House. July 31.

Vivian, Young. 1999. Cabinet memo: Government Internet policy. Alofi, Niue: Government of Niue, Office of the Acting Premier, December 16. http://www.gov.nu/news1.htm (accessed July 2001).

Volti, Rudi. 2001. *Society and technological change*. 4th ed. New York: Worth Publishers.

Waldrop, M. Mitchell. 2001. *The dream machine: J.C.R. Licklider and the revolution that made computing personal*. New York: Viking.

Walker, Ruth. 1997. Resisting the urge to regulate cyberspace. *Christian Science Monitor* July 18:6.

Wallerstein, Immanuel. 1979. The rise and future demise of the world capitalist system: Concepts for comparative analysis. In *The capitalist world economy*, ed. I. Wallerstein, 1–36. Cambridge: Cambridge University Press.

Wallis, Allan D. 1996. Regions in action: Crafting regional governance under the challenge of global competitiveness. *National Civic Review* 85(Spring/Summer):15–24.

Walzer, Michael, ed. 1995. *Toward a global civil society*. Providence, RI: Berghahn Books.

Weare, Christopher. 2002. The internet and democracy: The causal links between technology and politics. *International Journal of Public Administration* 25:659–91.

Webster, David. 1984. Direct broadcast satellites: Proximity, sovereignty and national identity. *Foreign Affairs* Summer:1161–74.

Weeks, Linton. 2006. "See me, click me: The publizen's life? It's an open blog. The idea he may be overexposed? LOL!" *Washington Post*, July 23, D01.

Wendt, Alexander. 1999. *Social theory of international politics*. Cambridge: Cambridge University Press.

What's NU? Domain name shortage sparks idea. 1997. *Wall Street Journal, Interactive Edition*. December 8. http://www.nunames.nu/wsj/wsj.htm (accessed July 2001).

Wilkinson, Rorden, and Steve Hughes, eds. 2002. *Global governance: Critical perspectives*. London: Routledge.

Wilson, Ernest J., III. 2004. *The information revolution and developing countries*. Cambridge, MA: MIT Press.

Wilson, Mark I. 2001. Location, location, location: The geography of the dot com problem. *Environment and Planning B: Planning and Design* 28(1):59–71.

Winger, Alan R. 1997. Finally: A withering away of cities? *Futures* 29:251–6.

Wireless Philadelphia. 2007. *Website: Wireless Philadelphia*. http://www.wirelessphiladelphia.org/ (accessed February 10, 2007).

Working Group on Internet Governance. 2005. Report of the working group on internet governance. World Summit on the Information Society. Château de Bossey, June. http://www.wgig.org/docs/WGIGREPORT.pdf (accessed September 2, 2006).

World Intellectual Property Organization. 2004a. *WIPO continues efforts to stamp out cybersquatting*. Press release, January 17.

———. 2004b. WIPO arbitration and mediation center. http://www.wipo.int/amc/en/index.html (accessed June 14, 2007).

World Trade Organization. 1998. *Tourism services: Background note by the secretariat*. September 23. http://www.wto.int/english/tratop_e/serv_e/w51.doc (accessed February 3, 2007).

————. 2001. Services: Symposium on tourism services. February 22–23. http://www.wto.int/english/tratop_e/serv_e/symp_tourism_serv_feb01_e.htm (accessed February 3, 2007).

Wriston, Walter B. 1992. *The twilight of sovereignty: How the information revolution is transforming our world*. New York: Scribner.

WTO calls on media to play responsible role in tourism. 2004. *Global News Wire–Asia Africa Intelligence Service*, February 6.

WTO global campaign stresses tourism importance. 2004. *Global News Wire–Asia Africa Intelligence Service*, February 20.

Zacher, Mark, and Brent Sutton. 1996. *Governing global networks: International regimes for transportation and communication*. Cambridge: Cambridge University Press.

Index

Note: tables indicated with *t* following page number